JAPANESE THEATRE

o
b
d   nd las

FIN   k canno
but   it ha
I   y an

week
k.

d

A PUPPET

Photograph by Isamu Noguchi
By Courtesy of *Harper's Bazaar*

JAPANESE THEATRE

by FAUBION BOWERS

Foreword by JOSHUA LOGAN

PETER OWEN LIMITED
London

PETER OWEN LIMITED

50 OLD BROMPTON ROAD

LONDON S. W. 7

MADE AND PRINTED IN THE U.S.A.

MCMLIV

1954

1122

Foreword

The Kabuki theatre of Japan is one of the few great living arts in the world today. It is a dazzling experience for the Western theatregoer to sit through a series of Kabuki plays at the splendid new Kabukiza Theatre in Tokyo.

All theatrical excitement is there. The great wide proscenium, seventy feet across, is blazingly alight and filled with quantities of three-dimensional scenery—cherry trees, bridges, boats floating on painted waves, houses showing the surrounding gardens and complete with straw-matted floors and sliding paper walls. Most of this is shifted before the eyes of the spectator on a huge revolving stage.

Across the left side of the auditorium sweeps the *hanamichi,* or Flower Walk, a platform that extends from the stage to the rear of the auditorium and is used for spectacular entrances and exits during the performance of the play.

The plays themselves are comedies, melodramas and dance plays which are so visually delightful to the foreigner that he soon forgets the language barrier and is completely captivated by what he sees and hears.

There is always a great assortment of noises to add to

the theatrical effect of a Kabuki play. The clatter of the wooden sticks that announce the opening of the curtain, the shouts of approval from all parts of the audience when one of the Kabuki actors has done an extraordinary bit of acting or pantomime, the sound of the samisens which accompany a great deal of the action, and the strange string-like sound of the falsetto voices used by the actors who play women's parts.

The whole effect of Kabuki is so startling that I felt it would be a great theatrical experience for New York playgoers, and I set about trying to find a method of transporting one of these great troupes from Japan to the United States. The process is a complicated one, and in trying to find the answers to the many questions that arose I have met many people. The most helpful to me has been Faubion Bowers, who is the author of this fascinating book. He is a young American who has made a thorough study of the Japanese theatre, and although his work is a scholarly one it is full of entertainment.

The history of Kabuki and the other great theatres of Japan—the Noh theatre, the early dances, the doll theatre and all of the origins of these dramatic forms are described with ease and authority in Mr. Bowers' book. I find the history of Kabuki to be as full of dramatic incident as one of the Kabuki plays.

There are many walls between the East and the West: our languages, our music, our painting. It would take a great deal of care and study for us to penetrate these walls. Only the specialists have the patience. But the Kabuki theatre is so vivid, spontaneous and dynamic that it throws open a door and gives us a clear view of the Japanese people, customs and art.

The Kabuki theatre is universal and timeless and reaches the core of man. If this great theatre ever arrives in America I believe it will be a great contribution to world understanding. The readers of Mr. Bowers' book will have an insight into the Japanese character that cannot be found in the newspapers.

JOSHUA LOGAN

Preface

This book is a report on the theatre in all its forms in Japan. It is a survey of what theatre arts exist there today and how they arose. Because Kabuki is the dominant type of drama in Japan today, and has been for some three centuries, I have given most attention to it.

This book is intended to be a key to the theatre of Japan. Since the theatre is one of the stronger forces and influences in Japan's civilization, it is hoped that the result of this book will be to help the Westerner to understand better the instincts and impulses of the Japanese people—if only by indirection and inference.

A foreigner's introduction to Japan's theatre is a curious experience. In fact, his first reactions to the country itself are strange.

The Westerner arriving in Japan is at once in a completely foreign world. He is struck by the uniformity of the Mongolian racial type. The colorful kimono, the national costume, has not yet disappeared despite Western and Allied Occupation influences. It smoothly wraps the small and sturdy builds of most Japanese women, and of a good number of men. Sounds heard on the street are dominated by the grating clicks of wooden clogs. Occasionally the nostalgic foreigner hears a shuffle of leather against stone. Architecture is dominated by flimsy structures of bamboo, straw, paper, and breakable tiles. After leaving the business centers of the cities, the foreigner looks in vain for the stability of timber and heavy concrete. Even to the traveled foreigner, there is a discomfort in the unfamiliarity of the signs in Japanese. No lettering; not even a related or derivative alphabet links Japan with the West. The ideographs and symbolic decorations hanging outside of shops offer few hints as to what is contained behind their sliding doors.

In the numerous theatres of Japan's cities and villages ways of life and living still more unfamiliar to the foreigner are daily unfolded. My first experience with Japanese theatre, which was in 1940 in Tokyo, was unexpected and in a way unfortunate. My preparation had been negligible—although in later years I consoled myself by saying that after all I had come to Japan to learn from scratch. I approached the theatre after having been told only two things: 1) That the type of drama I would see was the people's popular theatre called Kabuki; 2) that *Chushingura,* the greatest of the Japanese Kabuki play-cycles, would be performed. This was all.

The place was the large and picturesque theatre house, Kabuki-Za. *Za* means theatre-house, but the ideograph is also the same as for "sit." It is composed of the character for "earth" onto which the lines representing "person" or "people" have been drawn. Over the whole thing is a symbol for roof. The time of the performance was less easy to find than the imposing theatre-house. I appeared at matinee time, around two-thirty in the afternoon. I thought that the play had not yet begun, but it turned out to be merely an intermission. The play had been in progress since eleven that morning, and would continue until perhaps midnight. By two-thirty the actors had reached only the fourth act.

During the entr'acte when I arrived, already twenty-five hundred people were present, milling around the theatre halls and aisles looking for seats, or patiently waiting for the curtain to be pulled to one side. A pitch of excitement was maintained by irregular and intermittent beats of *hyoshigi* (clapper sticks of resonant wood with a peculiarly piercing sound) behind the curtain. The sharp smack of these clappers alerts the audience to the impending opening of the curtain, and informs the actors of the imminence of their required presence on stage. In the audience mothers were quietly nursing their babies; lost children were running up and down the aisles in search of their parents; and many had begun to open their little lunch-boxes of cold rice and pickles.

In the side-boxes which lined the sides of the main floor and balcony, the rich paid the maximum price for a minimum view of the stage and a modicum of comfort. In these boxes one sits on the straw mat flooring in Japanese style with one's legs tucked under the haunches. The sole advantage seemed to be that one could be seen by all the rest of the audience.

Until the performance began, I had thought that the stage could scarcely reveal anything more colorful or interesting than the audience itself. Geishas in their brightest kimonos, *hangyoku* (a sort of adolescent geisha popular in Tokyo) with their decorative bits of tinsel and ornaments stuck into their characteristic "peach-part" hairdo's, actor's wives with large hand-painted *obis* or belts depicting scenes from the very plays to be performed—these spread glamour over the entire audience.

The continuous beat of the clappers suddenly began to get faster and steadier. The audience quieted, and a little man, dressed in black with his face covered by a black veil (to create the illusion of invisibility), began to run across the stage, effortlessly pushing aside the wide Kabuki curtain of alternating stripes of black, terra cotta, and green colors. Even more brilliant than the house lights of the theatre proper (which incidentally are never dimmed throughout the course of most Japanese theatrical performances) were the dazzling lights of the stage reflecting on the clean and polished oak floor-boards.

To me, at that time still a stranger, the most startling aspect of the Japanese theatre of course was the *hanamichi,* an elevated passageway on the left side of the house. It leads from the back of the theatre through the audience at head-level, and directly onto the stage. Full use is made of this passage-way for ceremonial processions, dramatic entrances, and exits of leading characters. It represents garden-paths, rivers, mountain passes, and the like. The only comparable feature to it in Western theatre, although the analogy is misleading, would be the burlesque-show ramp which extends partly into the spectators' seats from the center of the stage.

Even odder than the world represented by the theatre-house and its gay audience, was the world revealed by the stage. As I was unprepared and ignorant, and inexperienced with either Japan or her art-forms, that first afternoon was for me one of entirely bewildering impressions.

Granted that the fourth act of *Chushingura,* the death scene of Enya Hangan and ensuing obsequies, with its specialized atmosphere, is excessively difficult for an outsider to understand, it was nevertheless a humiliating experience to be unable to recognize even the sexes of the various roles. I had heard that Kabuki, like Elizabethan plays, was played with all-male casts. But it seemed impossible to sort out the men and women parts on the stage. Voice, which normally is the quickest way of recognition, was of little guidance. Players of female parts, or *onnagata,* speak in falsetto for stage purposes; but they retain the sonorous heaviness of the male voice in order to project their semi-chanted words throughout the huge auditorium of the Kabuki theatre-house. Further complicating the foreigner's effort to differentiate the actors by voice, players of handsome or dashing young hero roles also speak in a high voice, almost as shrill as the *onnagata's*.

Hair styles, at first, also failed to help. In historical dramas, the wigs of nearly all the players consist of long hair elaborately done up on the head. Men's hair styles generally have a shaven bald spot from the forehead to the middle of the head, and position and placement of the tufts and pigtail-like hair indicate the rank and nature of the characters. But at that time, any long hair, regardless of the style, seemed to me feminine.

During the funeral ceremonies, even the kimono style offered me no clue as to which roles were male or female. Usually Japanese women wear brightly colored and heavily brocaded kimonos, but that afternoon both men and women were in white, the color of mourning, with pale watery blue under-kimonos showing through at the collar. To add to my confusion, the basic style of the kimono in Japan is the same for both men and women. It is the simple wrapper with pendant sleeves (less long for men), generally worn in layers of kimono upon kimono, each secured at the waist by a tied sash. In Japanese fashions, kimonos, for women at least, are all of a single size, and adjustments to the individual figure are made by the cloth belts which control the length and keep the kimono from opening accidentally at the line of overlapping down the center of the body.

The make-ups of the Kabuki characters offered equally little assistance in sorting out the scramble of characters. I was at that time Western enough to think that all Japanese look alike. On the stage this seemed to be literally true. Each actor's face was painted a deathly chalk-white. Each had short black lines of mascara underlining the lower eyelids and punctuated at the bridge of the nose with a thickish red dot. Each had his natural lips obliterated by heavy white paint, and in their stead was painted a perfectly shaped tiny mouth of vermilion which also supplied the only color to the actors' faces.

The reaction of the audience was as far from my previous experience in the Western theatre as was the Kabuki performance itself. In climactic moments on the stage, the audience gave shouts of approval. Particularly from the third balcony and the standing room areas at the back of the second balcony where the poor but genuine fans always sat or stood, the shouts were deafeningly loud.

As the intensely moving story unfolded, telling its tragic tale of the enforced suicide of the innocent Lord Enya Hangan, virtually the entire audience was moved to tears. As part of the last rites, the body of Enya Hangan is placed in a funeral palanquin, and a bowl of burning funeral incense is placed with it. The house became permeated with the mournful fragrance as the palanquin was carried along the *hana-michi* through the audience. A deep hush fell over the audience. From all ranks and rows of the theatre the quiet suppression of tears and the gentle blowing of noses became clearly audible.

The hold of the theatre over the people of Japan impressed me. It seemed to me that there was a deep and important relationship between the people, who were moved to ecstasy and to tears, and their obviously great drama-form. In watching the play and in noting the reaction of the audience, I realized that here was a key to learning about a race of "inscrutable Orientals." What makes a Japanese laugh or cry, what and where are the roots of how he thinks, seemed to have answers in his theatre.

As a stranger and a foreigner, I began to feel that I had found a way in which I too could share in the historical and contemporary cultural background of the Japanese. A sense of the humanity, and an awareness of the sensitivities and culture, of another nation should, I thought, develop inevitably into a sense of the essential oneness of human beings. No matter how one may presume to deplore particular aspects of a national life, such a step must be taken in order to make possible real understanding. Understanding in the last analysis means feeling and knowing how the mind of another works. Certainly in drama, which is generally conceded to represent the innermost aspirations and thoughts of a nation, the basis of how a people's mind works can be found. What amuses, moves, disturbs, and excites a people in their cultural expressions is bound to be reflected in their lives.

Because Kabuki was the most popular of Japan's numerous drama forms, it seemed to be the sensible point at which to start my studies. The beginning fortunately was not as formidable as it had first seemed. My bafflement at Kabuki soon wore off. Long before the play that day was over, I began to notice the subtle differences which clearly mark each character—each detail of his dress—his role—and his nature. The conventions of the Kabuki stage quickly became familiar. Later I came to accept them as scarcely more artificial than our own stage conventions in the West.

Kabuki's sway over the Japanese nation has been unchallenged since the 18th century. Even today it is regarded as the annual entertainment for the average family. During the war it was not until 1943 when the bombing of Japan became intense that for safety reasons large congregations of people were forbidden, and Kabuki, the last of the theatres functioning at that time, reluctantly closed down. It was the first to re-open after the war.

Kabuki, together with the more recently perfected Chinese opera, are perhaps the oldest popularly supported, traditionally performed, classic theatre arts still active in the world. Age alone does not necessarily make for importance but it has considerable significance. And although the Japanese, and Asians in general, lack the Western cult of antiquity as an end in itself, the age of Japan's drama forms is a matter of great interest to the scholar in the 20th century.

Dire predictions have for some time been made about the future of Kabuki. It was said that the pre-war fascistic restrictions and encouragements of Kabuki would mean its death. Actually post-war Allied censorship, which was based on complete ignorance, came as near to producing the death of Kabuki as anything in its past history. At one time in 1946 Occupation authorities persuaded producers of Japan to "ban voluntarily" all Kabuki except dances. This, however, was quickly rescinded. Censorship was soon completely removed from the Japanese classical stage. Kabuki now is once again in peril because of the deaths of some of the oldest and best Kabuki actors. Koshiro VII, Kikugoro VI, Sojuro, and Baigyoku have all died within the past five years, and perhaps a mature and ancient perfection of Kabuki has gone with them. Today Kabuki, with the exception of Nakamura Kichiemon and Bando Mitsugoro, is largely in the hands of younger, impetuous actors who, suddenly released from the disciplinary guidance of their four great elders, are perhaps feeling boisterous at reaching stardom so early in life.

I remember once talking to the aged head of Shochiku Company, the largest theatrical monopoly in Japan, and producer of most Kabuki since the beginning of the 20th century. At that time I was fearful for the future of Kabuki. He looked at me and said, "I grant you every danger you mention. But for half a century I have been hearing the same thing, 'Kabuki cannot live.' You may question my logic, but the fact has remained that Kabuki isn't dead yet. In my opinion it never will disappear."

For this reason perhaps, and because of Kabuki's eminence as yet, I have made it the core of this book. But Kabuki cannot be considered alone and out of context. There is an entire backlog of theatrical history which leads into it, and a number of recent theatre forms which follow and revolt against it. While I am mainly concerned with Kabuki, of necessity I have included a survey of the entire field of Japan's theatre, in so far as it pertains to those theatre forms still living today.

Much of the historical tradition in the theatres of the Western world has vanished. The blood-and-thunder plays of the Elizabethan Era, the Mysteries of Europe performed on the parvis of cathedrals, and revenge plays which were popular until recent times, have all disappeared. Masked plays are now hardly ever performed, and the convention of using only male actors has died out. How the Greek tragedies and comedies were actually staged and with what music is not known definitely. While certain historical records remain, the actual plays with their attendant customs, once lost, can rarely be successfully revived or reconstructed by scholarly study.

Japan, however, has maintained in a living form most of the traditions of her earlier theaters. Some Japanese scholars refer to 2600 years of continuous theatrical tradition. This is of course an exaggeration. The simple truth itself is just as impressive. Known and documented dance-drama forms of Japan cover thirteen centuries of history. These forms, in as close approximation of their originals as any country can show, are still being presented on the stage today.

They can be classed into six types:

1) Early dances both imported and indigenous, dating from the 7th century.
2) Noh, a classical lyric drama beginning with the 14th century.
3) Kyogen, comic interludes in Noh, also beginning with the 14th century.
4) Bunraku, or *ayatsuri shibai,* the puppet theatre, dating from the 16th century.
5) Kabuki, popular classical dance-dramas, dating from the 17th century.
6) Modern theatre, foreign translations and original works, dating from the 19th century.

Japan's isolated geographical position accounts to a large extent for this long theatrical tradition. Internally, the fact that she boasts of the longest line of Imperial rule of any country in the world means that despite shifts in actual power to military rulers or shoguns for part of her history, she has politically never suffered a fundamental structural upheaval which would disrupt the continuity of her theatre. The Emperor served as a stabilizing and steadying force within Japan even before the Occupation.

In addition, the tradition of the theatre was protected by a peculiar national characteristic which enables Japan to assimilate rather than be engulfed by outside cultures, as well as by a deep-rooted respect for hereditary systems. This latter quality expresses itself in various ways—the emperor system, the tightly knit family groups, and the inviolate artistic hierarchies of units of actors and musicians. Also the methods of thought control which arose after the radical changes during the late 19th century and which reached a climax before and during the recent war contributed to this result. They successfully prevented a wholesale incursion of ideas which would, through a desire for the new, cause a sloughing off of the past.

No theatre in the world has had as continuous and unbroken a history. The fact that the Japanese have preserved not only their own indigenous theatre but also importations from India, China, and Korea, already forgotten in the countries of their origin, was used during the Pacific War by nationalistic drama critics as foundation for the thesis that Japan was the "Museum of the Orient" and therefore a rallying station for other Asian nations who had allowed their own classic arts to disappear. Divested of propaganda overtones, the fact is still of interest and importance to the student of culture.

The present state of preservation of Japan's dance-drama forms affords unrivaled material for the study not only of the history of a nation's theatre, but of language, customs, general history, geography, costumes, and social traditions. Among many examples are the court costumes of *Bugaku* dances borrowed from China in the 7th century, the humorous commentary on daily 15th century life in *Kyogen* comic interludes, the social protest of commoner against aristocrat implicit in Kabuki, the nationalistic thought processes revealed by a study of the changes in the theatre made by actors in the 19th century, and the mirror-held-to-life realism of modern drama. All these represent a visual source of study and a living basis for reflection on the nature of the Japanese nation at various periods of its history.

Despite this excellent opportunity, scholarly research into the history of Japan's theatre was not seriously undertaken until the late 19th century. Foreign ideas brought from the West at that time included the concept of research which until then had been only a casual and unscientific process. During this period substantial changes were made in Kabuki's traditions, and the first break-away from the Kabuki dominance was attempted. The movement towards dramatic research started from these two factors. The technical methods for historical research were copied from the West, and the labor was impelled by the fear that perhaps the end of Japan's great traditional arts had begun.

The first history of the theatre was written in 1893 by the pioneer Dr. Tsubouchi Shoyo. The most important document pertaining to Noh, *Kadensho,* Zeami's theories of drama, expertly translated into English by Arthur Waley, was only discovered in 1907, four centuries after it was written. Only since the Pacific War have some of the early dances become available to the public for research. If there are few books in English to guide the prospective student of the Japanese theatre, the reason lies in the fact that the number in Japan was until, very recently, commensurately small.

Japan's defeat in the recent war has increased the urgency of scholarship in the field of classic theatre. The tremendous social and economic changes resulting from the impact of enforced influences and ideologies from abroad have once again perhaps signaled the end of Japan's traditional drama. Before it becomes too far removed from the life of the people, it is important to record it as it is today—the flower of centuries of growth.

The written sources for much of the information in this book are manuscripts and now out-of-print books in Japanese.

In a few cases I have been somewhat arbitrary about dates. There is violent disagreement among scholars today in Japan as to most dates, particularly those regarding Kabuki's beginnings. The original manuscripts are conflicting on almost every score. I have selected middle dates in some instances, somewhere between the extremes of differences in opinion.

I am primarily indebted to three scholars for a large part of my information. First and foremost, I owe much to my warm and devoted friend, Dr. Komiya Horyu who was once Minister of Education, and is now Head of the Ueno Academy of Music in Tokyo; in the opinion of many he is perhaps the finest academic mind in Japan today. Also I am indebted to Dr. Shuzui Kenji whose love of precise scholarly detail made him able to give many of my facts and figures authority. And I also owe a great deal to Dr. Kawatake Shigetoshi, Head of the Drama Department of Waseda University in Tokyo, whose inspired amiability and accessibility have done more for Kabuki in Japan and abroad than perhaps any other single figure.

The actual working out of this book took place in the course of daily visits to the theatre and nightly talks with the actors, over a period of about four years. During this period some of the deepest attachments that I have ever known were made. To begin to thank the numerous actors who have helped and guided me would almost be like thanking one's family for one's sustenance. No question of mine was ever too silly, no repeated request for re-explanation or actual demonstration was ever refused. Their patience and tolerance won my complete amazement and my devotion. I must particularly mention Nakamura Kichiemon, Ichikawa Ebizo, Matsumoto Koshiro, Onoe Shoroku, Onoe Baiko, and Nakamura Shikan—as artists, as friends, as invaluable helpers and advisors.

For help and encouragement, I must also mention the American nisei, Edward Mitsukado, and his Japanese wife, Suda Keiko, Stanley Kaizawa, Haruichi Umeda, and Edward Wakamiya.

The hand-drawn illustrations were all done by Sachio Takahashi. Photographs are by kindness of Shochiku Co., Toho Co., *Screen and Stage Magazine, Yakusha Magazine,* Zenshin Za, the Nohgaku Kai, and the Signal Corps of the US Army.

To this long list of indebtedness I must also add the name of Santha Rama Rau who most kindly corrected the typescript and offered extremely useful suggestions as to how to make an exegesis of a complex subject more readily comprehensible.

I am also grateful to *Theatre Arts Magazine, Dance Magazine,*

Nippon Times (Tokyo) and *Stage and Screen Magazine* (Tokyo) for permission to use material which was originally written for and first appeared in their magazines and papers.

F. B.

New York, N. Y.
August, 1951

Table of Contents

CONTENTS

List of Illustrations

JAPANESE THEATRE

OUTLINE OF JAPAN'S THEATRE ARTS

DANCE FORMS

Uzume's Dance before the Sun-Goddess
(*Mythological Times*)

Kagura Shrine Dances

Imported from Asia

Gigaku Mask Dances
(*7th century*)

Bugaku Court Dances
(*7th century*)

Indigenous to Japan

Dengaku Field Dances
(*12th-14th centuries*)

DRAMA FORMS

Sarugaku Mimes
(*12th-14th centuries*)

COMBINED DANCE-DRAMA
FORMS

Noh Lyric Dramas
(*15th century*)

Kyogen Comic Interludes
(*15th century*)

Musical Story Telling
and Recitations
(*11th-13th centuries*)

Bunraku Puppet Theatre
(*16th century*)

Kabuki Popular Theatre
(*17th century*)

Shimpa New School Theatre
(*19th century*)

Imported from the West

Vaudeville, Takarazuka, etc.
(*20th century*)

Modern Theatre
(*19th century*)

I

Historical Introduction to the Japanese Theatre

1.

Legendary Origin of the Japanese Theatre. The story which is related in the oldest recorded history of Japan, the *Kojiki* or *Record of Ancient Matters,* written in 712 A.D., describes the first theatrical performance known to Japan. Those scholars who believe in the validity of mythological history regard this incident as the physical and spiritual origin of all subsequent Japanese stage of performances.

Among the legends concerning the prehistoric creation and peopling of Japan which are related in that book, there are many stories of the various antics of the gods in the peculiar hierarchy of Japan's mythology. The one we are concerned with here tells of the Sun-Goddess, Amaterasu O-mikami, who had been offended by the playfulness of her brother, and who in a fit of sulking had hidden herself in a cave and had sealed the opening with a great rock. Since the world was in darkness as a result of her concealment, the other gods assembled to persuade her to show her face again. One of the assembly, Amano-Uzume-no-Mikoto, (whom Basil Hall Chamberlain calls "Her Augustness Heavenly-Alarming-Female"), elaborately clad, placed a sounding-board outside the cave and stomped until it resounded, "and doing as if possessed by a deity, and pulling out the

[3]

nipples of her breasts, pushed down the skirt-string *usque ad privatas partes."*

This spectacle caused the gods, (eight myriad of them) to laugh until the Sun-Goddess, piqued by curiosity, looked to see for herself what had caused the uproar. Once she had pushed back the rock from the cave, she became interested.* After she had watched the performance for some time, she felt appeased, and returned to her place in the heavens. Uzume then said to the Sun-Goddess, "We rejoice and are glad because there is a deity more illustrious than Thine Augustness." What Uzume meant by "deity" is not clear. Perhaps she meant a personification of art or even of sexuality. The statement might also have been made out of sheer malicious delight at having lured the Almighty One from her hiding place.

Aside from its importance as the first reference to any type of dramatic performance in Japanese history, the legend has a deeper significance. It embodies three fundamental aspects of all subsequent Japanese theatre arts:

1. The supernatural or religious element primarily associated with Noh.
2. The erotic element, particularly characteristic of Kabuki and certain types of post-war modern theatre.
3. The dance element, an integral part of all Japanese dramatic arts.

These three elements, to a greater or a lesser degree, singly or in harmonious combination, have never been absent throughout Japan's theatrical history. Only since the rise of modern drama in the 19th century has a tendency developed to separate dance from drama, or the supernatural from the normal, realistic dramatic fare. The self-

---

* According to some schools of thought (probably fanciful) the current Japanese word for "interesting," *"omo-shiroi"* (literally "white-face"), derives from this incident. As the Sun-Goddess peered out, her face was white, and Uzume's face, while she was dancing, shone white from the reflected light.

[4]

KABUKI ACTOR IN AN *ARAGOTO* COSTUME AND MAKE-UP

Photograph by Isamu Noguchi
By Courtesy of *Harper's Bazaar*

conscious modern drama in general has also omitted the erotic element. This was to some extent a reaction against the open bawdiness and sometimes brash vulgarity of the classical theatres.

2.

Early Dance No. 1, Kagura. Of present-day dance forms, *Kagura* is most directly connected with Uzume's original dance. *Kagura,* basically, is a symbolic re-enactment of the dance before the Sun-Goddess. The word *"Kagura"* literally denotes "god-music," and has come to mean, by usage, any dance offered to console or placate the gods. It is now an integral part of Shinto religion—that peculiarly Japanese form of worship and theology which combines mythology with the system of Imperial rule. *Kagura* was performed for the Imperial court, the theoretical gods on earth, until the 18th century. The dancers were supposed to be descendants of Uzume, and held a court rank and a special title of *Sarumi-no-Kimi.*

From the 9th to the 12th century (the Heian period), *Kagura* was at a zenith. Even as late as the 16th century, it enjoyed the patronage of such a celebrated temporal ruler of Japan as Toyotomi Hideyoshi. Although all Shinto shrines featured the dance in one form or another, *Kagura* declined and degenerated considerably. It was revived in the 19th century, after the Emperor was re-instated in full glory and the country was unified—the events known as the Meiji Restoration. At that time it was quite removed from its original intent, and *Kagura* was filled with emperor loyalty. Now it is usually performed by *miko* or dancing girls attached to shrines, and this reconstructed type of *Kagura* is still to be seen on festival days in various parts of the country.

3.

Early Dance No. 2, Gigaku. A Korean who adopted Japan as his permanent home and who took the name Mimashi, was responsible for the first foreign importation in the Japanese theatre world. In 612

A.D. he performed *Gigaku,* literally "skill-music," a kind of drama-dance.

Gigaku came from very simple dances performed before the image of Buddha in India. It accompanied the spread of Buddhism from its native country, and was shaped into a broader art form in that part of Southern China then called Go, or in Japanese, Kure. By the time it reached Korea it was again altered. In this modified, final form it eventually reached Japan where it was performed in Buddhist temples as religious entertainment.

Gigaku was encouraged by a Buddhist of great faith, Shotoku, Prince Regent during the Empress Suiko's reign in the early 7th century. Shotoku established a school for this dance in Nara under the tutelage of Mimashi. From there graduates and qualified performers were attached to various temples throughout the country.

Apparently there were ten varieties of *Gigaku* dances. They were accompanied by a three-piece orchestra of a flute, hand-drum and cymbals, the standard instruments of classical dance in India. All *Gigaku* was performed with enormous masks covering the entire head. The finest examples of these masks still in existence are preserved in Nara, and may be seen at the Shoso-in, an Imperial storehouse established in 756 A.D. Although they differ from Noh masks, they are obviously the origin of masks in Japan, as well as the source of what later in Kabuki and the puppet theatre became elaborate and stylized make-ups.

What the dances were actually like can now only be conjectured. If they had any detailed story originally, its complexity has completely disappeared with the passage of time. Although technically not a living form today, *Gigaku's* influence on subsequent types of theatre has, however, been considerable.

Most noteworthy of the known *Gigaku* types of dance was the *shishi-mai,* a dance symbolizing a mythological animal something like a small lion. This lion, which appears wherever Buddhism has spread, generally represents a guardian. In the original *Gigaku* dance, it was probably treated as a part of exorcistic ritual, something remotely akin to the Chinese New Year's lion.

The religious function *per se* of this particular lion's dance is no longer consciously felt in the Japanese theatre; but its actual, bodily mechanics are still a force. A large number of Noh plays and Kabuki dances focus on this lion—an animal unknown in Japan except through these dances. The generic term for lion plays or dances has changed from *shishi-mai* to *shakkyo-mono,* so-called after a famous Noh play which tells the story of a court noble who has renounced the world to become a priest. He goes to China to visit the tomb of Monju Bosatsu (Manjusri), a disciple of Buddha who is usually depicted as either riding or leading the lion-like animal on a leash. At a stone bridge (*shakkyo*), the lion appears and dances. In the Japanese theatre, this lion is invariably associated with the peony flower which attracts him, and butterflies which irritate him. The peony affords the decorative color for a stage property, and the butterflies create movement. In this there is a basic esthetic satisfaction for the spectator in witnessing an expression of the duality of the lion's nature—repose (symbolized by the peonies) and anger (aroused by the butterflies). This frequent and important aspect of Japan's classical theatre is directly traceable to *Gigaku.*

Unfortunately for posterity, *Gigaku* was short-lived. Like most masked plays, with the major exception of Noh, few in the world's history have survived. The natural face seems inevitably to win out over the artifice of wood or plaster. The decline and decay of *Gigaku* was actually premature. Had it not been for the introduction of *Bugaku* into Japan, *Gigaku* might have endured longer.

4.

Early Dance No. 3, Bugaku. In the 7th century when intercourse between Japan and China had reached a high diplomatic and artistic level, the numerous Japanese envoys to the continent, returned with, among other things, *Bugaku* (literally, dance-music). Despite the lack of religious import, Prince Shotoku, the dance lover, patronized *Bugaku* as ardently as he had once encouraged *Gigaku*.

Bugaku is of two main types: the left dances (*sa-mai*) imported from India, China, and Central Asia during the T'ang dynasty (618-907 A.D.), costumed mainly in red; and the right dances (*u-mai*) imported from Korea and Manchuria, costumed predominantly in green. The dancers originally formed a "V" as they approached the elevated, temporarily erected stage in the open, passing through the audience which sat around the four sides of the square stage. Those entering from the left, danced the left dances; those from the right, the right dances. This V-shaped approach to the stage is one of the several remote origins of the famous passage-way, unique to Japan, leading from the back of the theatre through the audience to the stage, now known as the *hanamichi*.

Today there are thirty-seven left dances and twenty-four right dances still remaining. Although they are clearly derivative and not native in origin, as may be seen from the costumes and the musical instruments, in the course of more than a thousand years, considerable Japanese refinement has been added both to the music and the complexity of the dances. By the 11th century, it was the fashion for Japanese courtiers to compose their own original music for *Bugaku*.

Noblemen became so addicted to this pastime that scholars of the 12th century blamed *Bugaku* for rendering the court effete and the courtiers effeminate.

There is a word, *Gagaku* (literally "graceful music"), which is frequently used in connection with *Bugaku*. *Gagaku* actually includes in its concept not only *Bugaku*, the dances and their accompanying music, but also *Kangen*, an orchestral companion art-form to *Bugaku*. *Kangen*, however, consists only of music and is not designed to accompany dances. *Bugaku* programs are generally preceded by a concert of *Kangen* music. Such a combined performance is *Gagaku* in its full sense.

Kangen orchestras comprise voices, strings, wind, and percussion instruments. However, in *Bugaku* dances, an orchestra including strings or voices, with their subtle and wavering melodies, would hamper the precision of the dancers' movements. The *Bugaku* orchestra (as opposed to a *Kangen* orchestra) is composed exclusively of wind and percussion instruments. Most characteristic of *Bugaku* and *Kangen* instruments, and common to both orchestras, is the *sho,* a type of miniature, hand-held pipe-organ blown by mouth. It is still used in parts of Tibet and China. Each orchestra requires about twenty musicians. The music for both forms is harmonious and contrapuntal. It is interesting to note that some five centuries before the West had learned to pit two melodies against each other, *Gagaku* was weaving two and more strands of musical lines. The rhythm of *Gagaku* is, in general, slow and sustained. Its meters best lend themselves to odd numbers, groupings of fives, nines and elevens.

Bugaku dances in standard form are long, with three movements: *Jo,* a slow introduction; *Ha,* a break or movement with a different tempo; and *Kyu,* an extended coda, or what would roughly compare, in Western music, to a concluding, swift movement. During *Jo* the rhythm is not marked precisely, and the dancers proceed casually to the stage to assume their positions. During *Ha* they begin to move slowly. The tempo gradually increases and leads into *Kyu.*

The subject matter of *Bugaku* dances is abstract and of the most fragmentary nature. Their content can, for instance, signify nothing more tangible than a stylized croquet game, or dragons basking in the sun, or a mere dance with a spear, or a war dance showing a god symbolically subduing his enemies. The dancers on rare occasions perform with masks, Indian in origin and borrowed directly from *Gigaku.* Even when they are not masked, at no time do the dancers show expression on their faces.

There are certain characteristics of *Bugaku* dances which distinguish them from other Japanese dances. Usually the *Bugaku* dancers hold a short silver rod in each hand. Sometimes the rod is omitted and the dancers extend their hands stiffly with the second and third fingers stretched out while the thumb is held tightly on the nails of the bent fourth and fifth fingers. This arbitrary position for the hand is related to *Kabuki* where the position of the hand in the dances for women is always with the fingers held closely together. (Such hand formalizations are also familiar in Western classical dance, as for example the ballerina's hand position.) However, in view of the enormous dictionary of hand gestures and finger symbolism in the dances of India, the country of some of *Bugaku's* origins, it appears that such rigidity of the hand position is a restrictive Japanese refinement.

Bugaku is generally four-square. Movements are repeated four times in the four directions by dancers who perform in solos, in two's, four's, or their multiples. Properly performed, these dances last for hours. However, post-war *Bugaku* has lost the protection of the Imperial court because of heavy restrictions on the Emperor's privy purse. It now must resort to public recitals for financial support. As a result, some of the traditional repetitiousness has had to be curtailed to meet the demands of modern, unceremonious audiences. Besides this, in conformity with the nature of the modern stage, movements are now made only in a single direction, toward the audience.

In essence, *Bugaku* is a virile and bold art form. At all times it has a stately and courtly appearance. It requires broad strong steps with changes in posture. *Bugaku's* clarity of movement stands in vivid contrast to much later Japanese dancing, which is often soft and willowy to the point of attenuation. This solidity of form is akin to architecture, and like architecture it does not directly convey human emotions. Nowhere does it strike at the heart or speak of passion. It delights as sheer pattern or form, moving as if in outline only. This same basic sense of moving pattern in space is also found in passages from the dramas of *Kabuki,* but there it is used only to increase the impact of an already established emotional effect.

There is a kind of magic in *Bugaku,* closely related to hypnosis engendered by incantation or stereotyped rite. The magnetic attraction is greatly assisted by the long, sustained, reedy sounds of the *sho* which do not change their quality either when the performer inhales or exhales, as well as by the repetitions of identical dance movements at different points of the compass. *Bugaku* was undoubtedly influenced by Buddhism, and its balance of movement and spiritual calm are also connected with the mandalas of India, Tibet and China —those symmetrical drawings produced out of the subsconscious when purged of temporal (emotional or psychic) disturbances. *Bugaku's* magic also has a parallel in the symbolic, mathematical structures and ground-plans of churches in medieval Europe. *Bugaku,* although years earlier in time, has this same sort of mysticism of form, not in stone, but in human movement through the dance. The effect on the spectator is that he feels attuned to something cosmic and eternal, and welcomes in it the absence of representational content and of the cluttering encumbrances of the emotions.

5.

Early Dances Nos. 4 and 5, Dengaku and Sarugaku. While religious dances and foreign importations patronized by the nobles were crystallizing in form, folk dances of humble origin were also in vogue. Of these *Dengaku* and *Sarugaku* were of greatest importance and influence historically.

Dengaku, as its name "field-music" implies, was closely connected with the earth. Originally it was an elaboration in the dance of rice-planting festivities and harvest ceremonies. In due course, acrobatics, jugglery, and a semblance of story-content were added. Still later, it fell under Buddhist influence and became patronized by the priests. With religious blessing, it finally rose to be a fashionable accomplishment for the nobility. It was practised as a social dance in palaces and in feudal manors with much zeal. Until the time of the Shogun Hojo Takatoki (1303-1333), *Dengaku* was ardently patronized, and even the highest nobles participated in it.

There is a delightful short *Kabuki* dance-play called *Takatoki* in which a kind of modern, reconstructed *Dengaku* is danced. The story of the play concerns Takatoki, the ninth of the Hojo rulers of Japan, and the last of the great patrons of *Dengaku*.

Takatoki, an extremely overbearing and extravagant man, hears one day that his pet dog has been killed. As soon as the culprit is discovered, Takatoki decrees the death sentence, and refuses to listen to an appeal for mercy even when urged by his chief advisor of state. However, when the court priest reminds him that the day is holy because it is the anniversary of the death of one of the Hojo ancestors, Takatoki grudgingly revokes his order.

That night Takatoki holds a moonlight banquet. While attendants fill his cup with wine, he watches a dance of the beautiful Kinugasa, his chief concubine. Suddenly the candles of the palace are all mysteriously blown out by a gust of wind. Kinugasa stops in the middle of her dance and leaves with the entourage to help them bring more lights. Takatoki is alone. One by one, swinging down from the trees near the terrace, appear a large number of long-nosed goblins (*tengu*).* By some strange enchantment, they seem to Takatoki to be masters of his favorite dance, *Dengaku*, and he asks them to give him a lesson.

At first they dance with him, saying, "Right foot forward, left foot forward, now turn around . . ." The tempo increases and Takatoki becomes less and less able to follow the steps. When he is helplessly confused, the goblins begin to torture him in punishment for his tyrannical excesses. They throw him into the air, whirl him around, poke and belabor him. Finally, shrieking with demoniac laughter, they leave the bruised and furious Takatoki to regret his stupidities.

Another form of *Dengaku,* though extremely rudimentary and perhaps as far from the original as the Takatoki dance, may still be seen in certain country-side folk festivals. Characteristic of this dance is the large colorful straw hat peculiar to *Dengaku* dancers. The hats are conical in shape and gaily decorated with flowers—a stylization of the farmer's field hat.

---

* These *tengu* are familiar in many of the fairy tales of Japan. They are covered with reddish hair, and their noses are so long as to be almost beaks. Because of their resemblance to the Westerners, in contrast to the Japanese who are hairless, brownish and small-nosed, the word *tengu* has become a semi-jocular epithet for foreigners in general.

Sarugaku, in contrast to *Dengaku* which was pure dance, was primarily mime. Literally the word means "monkey-music," but it euphemistically allows for a shift in pronunciation to *"sangaku"* which alters the meaning to "scattered music." *Sarugaku* were originally vulgar and comic interludes designed to break the monotony of the austere *Kagura* dances.

The earliest *Sarugaku* performance known is recorded in a contemporary book (untranslated), the *12th Century Annals.* An evening is described when Emperor Horikawa (1087-1107), apparently out of boredom, commanded an "amusing" entertainment to enliven one of the customary performances of sacred music and *Kagura* dances at the inner shrine of the palace. The court awaited in eager anticipation. During the interval, Yukitsuna, a *Saragaku* performer, appeared in shabby clothes, rolled up his skirt, and trembling with affected cold ran ten times round the courtyard fire exclaiming, "The night deepens and I grow cold. I will warm my scrotum at the fire." The spectators were moved to great laughter.*

In a somewhat later work, *The Letters of Fujiwara Akihira,* a historical document of the period which has not been translated into English, another primitive *Sarugaku* is described. By then *Sarugaku* was a standard entertainment in its own right. On this occasion, the players disguised themselves as a married couple. The husband was emaciated, but the wife was healthy and beautiful. After billing and cooing, they copulated. This performance, too, was greeted with much laughter, so the document reads.

These and similar reference to *Sarugaku* emphasize a delight in the erotic which derives from Uzume's dance and directly presages the origin of *Kabuki* some five hundred years later. More important, *Sarugaku* reveals a sense of mimicry and may be considered the first beginning of naturalism on the Japanese stage. This type of mimicry was called *monomane* (imitation of things), a word which, with the

* Arthur Waley refers to this incident as well as other *Sarugaku* matters in his *The Noh Plays of Japan,* London, 1921.

[13]

rise of *Kabuki* was to become virtually synonomous with the theatre and its dramatic elements as we know them today.

Gradually the mimicry of *Sarugaku* and the pure dance element of *Dengaku* started to affect and modify each other. While each drew heavily upon the other, they still retained their individuality and developed along their separate lines. *Dengaku,* with some elements of mime added to its pure dance, became known as *Dengaku-no-Noh,* and *Sarugaku,* incorporating certain dance aspects into its mimetic action, was called *Sarugaku-no-Noh.*

6.

Noh, the classical lyric drama of Japan. Noh is the culmination of several dance-drama forms which preceded it. It amalgamates within itself a variety of techniques and influences. The result is a synthetic and near-perfect art form. It embraces people's folk dance, temple entertainments, a blend of *Dengaku* and *Sarugaku* (i.e., a well-proportioned balance between dance and mime with the emphasis on representation and plot), moral instruction infused by the priests; and, lastly, the refinement resulting from patronage by the nobles.

Two geniuses, Kan'ami Kiyotsugu (1333-1384) and his son, Zeami (also spelled "Seami") Motokiyo (1363-1444), perfected *Noh.* Under the exalted protection of the Ashikaga Shogun, Yoshimitsu, the supreme ruler toward the end of the 14th century, these two men evolved *Noh* art. In the form which they perfected, *Noh* has since become familiar and respected in the Western world, largely through the Pound-Fenellosa adaptations and the fine translations and commentaries of Arthur Waley. Since Zeami's time, a few new plays have been written and certain changes in dramatic approach have been made; but on the whole *Noh* has altered little. Unquestionably, the *Noh* dramas of Japan are today the oldest major theatre art, both literarily and dramatically, still regularly performed. For this reason they have perhaps been unduly emphasized by Western scholars, to

SCENE FROM SAGI, A NOH PLAY

Player: Roppeita Kita

the extent that *Noh*, to most Westerners, means either all or the best of Japan's theatre. Neither is true.

Had it not been for Zeami, even more than his father, *Noh* would hardly have merited the enduring attention it has received. Zeami, after improving the aesthetic principles underlying his father's creations, changed the *saru*, "monkey," of the word *Sarugaku* to *saru*, a meaningless ideograph but respectable at least by being part of the first character of *Kagura*, "god."

Zeami's new and polished form of *Sarugaku-no-Noh* was finally called merely *Noh*, and in dictionaries of the 15th century, *Noh* is the only word to be found for drama.

The ideograph *"Noh"* by itself means skill, faculty or power. To be more explicit about the various aspects of *Noh*, today the art and performance is more precisely known as *Nohgaku* ("skill-music"). *Yokyoku* is an alternative generic word for *Noh* drama in general. *Utai* is a word for the text of any specific play of a specific school.

In all, there are about two hundred and fifty *Noh* plays still in existence. Of these scarcely half are normally performed. *Noh* is grouped roughly into five main classifications, according to the subject matter or central character of the play. These five classifications are *Shin*, "God," *Nan*, "Man," *Nyo*, "Woman," *Kyo*, "Madness," and *Ki*, "Demon." In practice these groupings mean:

1. God plays (Examples: *Takasago, Tamura, Yumiyahata.*)
2. Warrior-ghost plays (Examples: *Atsumori, Yashima, Sanemori, Utoh.*)
3. Women plays (Examples: *Tohoku, Hagoromo, Kikitsubata.*)
4. Plays of Insanity—women, however, are usually the protagonists; (Examples: *Mochizuki*, the most famous of revenge plays in *Noh, Dojoji, Sumidagawa, Ataka,* adapted in Kabuki and called *Kanjincho.*)
5. Demon plays (Examples: *Nomori, Tsuchigumo, Momijigari.*)

Plays which do not fall precisely into any of these categories are lumped in category No. 4, which may also be called *genzai mono* ("contemporary plays of the era"). No. 4 is actually a completely miscellaneous group.

A congratulatory dance-play *Okina,* a sort of ritual of longevity, must precede any proper performance of a full *Noh* series. These dance-plays have many variants, a good number of which have been adapted as *Kabuki.* In general the pattern of their action is the same. A star actor without make-up slowly enters the stage; from a black and gold lacquer box, tied with thick purple cord, he removes the bearded wooden mask of a face withered with age. This represents *Okina,* a symbol of long life. The actor ties the mask to his face and intones strange, rune-like words which were originally in a corrupt form of Sanskrit that had reached Japan via Tibet, but are now incomprehensible. At the same time he dances a slow and dignified series of movements, carrying in one hand a fan. The musical accompaniment is provided by two drums and a flute.

After this opening section, Senzai (literally "1,000 years"), a bright but reserved character, enters. He is invariably dressed in an elaborate costume of blue on which the white stork, a symbol of good fortune and eternity in Japan, has been embroidered or woven. Senzai dances in a somewhat more lively mood. Then enters Samba, a comic, semi-mystic figure, dressed in a conical hat of black and silver with a large red dot painted on it, and grand brocaded clothes. He carries the Buddhist *juzu,* or handbells, which he rings in somewhat sacrilegious mock piety. Samba capers about the stage in a virtuosic swift dance of youthful abandon. Symbolically, *Okina* dances represent three stages of man's existence on this earth, and are presumably rites to enhance the possibility of a long life. This connection of *Okina* with the sacred is further illustrated by the custom that all major theatre-houses in Japan are "dedicated" upon completion of their construction by an opening performance of one of the *Okina* dances.

The order for a series of *Noh* plays in a day's performance was formerly determined by the traditional classifications listed above. One play from each group was performed in succession as a series of six plays, including *Okina*. The idea was that such a sequence of different dramas of different types offered sufficient variety and suited the time-schedule for a full day's program.

Today, however, due to considerations of time, this prescription is not observed. With the advance of mechanical civilization in Japan, leisure has become rarer. Audiences now are impatient and unwilling to sit all day on the mats of a *Noh* theatre. In addition, new refinements and traditions have been added through the years, and the present detailed perfection and precision have greatly lengthened the actual performing time of any single *Noh* play. It is impractical to follow the traditional order in its entirety; but two plays from the same classification are rarely played successively in today's abbreviated programs.

The formula for the construction of all *Noh* dramas is rigid. No matter how the individual content of each play differs, the outline of the play's framework is invariable; it is something remotely parallel to the "well-made play." Instead of three acts, each *Noh* play has three sections called *Jo, Ha* and *Kyu,* a beginning, a middle and an end, a convention already found in *Bugaku* dances.

The primary point to be remembered in the analysis of a *Noh* play is that action is generally recollected and that the plot hinges on an event that has already taken place in the past. This means that the dramatic situation is not necessarily acted realistically before one's eyes. Rather it is poetically recalled and discussed by the characters and chorus, and their movements become dreamlike glosses to the idea carried by the words.

Each character introduces himself (and others, if necessary) by words, so that an actual dramatic situation on the stage to serve this purpose becomes inessential. Each character also lays the setting in words because *Noh* is enacted on a bare stage with only a pine tree painted on the permanent wooden backdrop. In addition, a chorus to the side and musicians at the back of the stage further contribute an explanation of the situation, mood, feelings or action by words and musical sounds.

A skeleton outline common to all *Noh* dramas is as follows:

Jo—the opening section starts with the entrance of the side-character or foil (*waki*). He introduces himself by name, rank, and states his purpose for appearing. There ensues a "travel song" (*shidai,* or more commonly called, *michiyuki,* "road-going," especially in *Kabuki* where it is also a familiar convention). During the "travel-song," which is sung by the chorus, the side-character moves, and it is understood that he has reached his destination. The protagonist (*shite*), who may also be accompanied by followers (*tsure*), then enters; he is frequently a character in disguise. The protagonist and the side-character converse (*mondo,* literally, "questions and answers"). Through their conversation the plot is laid, and the audience is informed of all events and tensions necessary to the theme of the play.

Ha—during the middle section, the protagonist dances what is technically called *kuse* (derived from a folk dance of the period, *kuse-no-mai,* now no longer practiced). The dance usually represents in stylized action a physical re-enactment of a prior event. He retires from the center of the stage. A comic interlude (*ai-kyogen*), but performed by extraneous characters who speak in informal, colloquial language, then follows.

Kyu—the final and most dramatic section is when the protagonist re-appears; this time in his true colors; often as a ghost or demon. He dances a climactic dance, resolving the plot, and the play ends. Performers, chorus, and musicians silently leave the stage.*

In the course of *Noh's* long existence through the centuries, it has been subjected to the whims and tastes of a variety of different patrons. As a result, specific styles of performing and certain emendations of texts developed. *Noh* finally settled into five basic schools (*ryu*) called, *Kanze, Kita, Hosho, Komparu,* and *Kongo.* The various performers and their families guard the traditions pertaining to each of the schools and rigorously adhere to their hereditary trade secrets. Star actors of one school may, on occasion, perform in another school's

---

* For those who wish to pursue the mechanics of *Noh's* construction, Noel Peri's book, *Le No,* in French, is virtually exhaustive and definitive.

production. The repertoire of each school is, for all practical purposes, the same, but costumes, texts, and details of acting vary.

A sixth school arose in the late 19th century, the Meiji Era. During this period the military government of the shoguns was overthrown. Since *Noh* had long been a primary pastime of these shoguns, the newly-risen anti-shogun factions advocated its abolition and to a serious degree actually enforced it. The five basic schools disappeared underground, but an erstwhile pupil of the *Kanze* school, named Umewaka, created a new school and fairly openly sustained the tradition of *Noh.* Gradually as the atmosphere of reconstructed shogun-less Japan cleared, the other schools came back to life. Under the patronage of a few wealthy aristocrats they have resumed their former prestige and dominance.

Today, the Umewaka school may be forced to cease its performances. Through intrigue and pressure the large *Kanze* school is now making every effort to get the Umewaka "secessionists" back into their fold. If they succeed, the Umewaka school will have to forfeit its royalties, rights, and honoraria.

The language of *Noh,* even to educated Japanese, is virtually incomprehensible when heard, largely because of the archaisms and partly because of the chanted, sing-song declamation. At *Noh* programs, most of the spectators bring scripts which they follow as assiduously as the action of the performance itself.

The sentences of exaggeratedly polite syntax are complicated by obscure Buddhist references, derivations from the Chinese, and phrases from now-forgotten poems and songs. In view of the fact that *Noh* was the plaything of elegant nobles, and that the subjects of the plays often concern personages of high rank, emperors, and gods, it is natural that the grammatical construction should be excessively elaborate. For example, the question "What is your name?" in *Noh* can be as lengthy and convoluted as the following: *"On namae wo uketamaritaku zonji tatematsuri soro."* While this series of honorifics, post-positions, desideratives, etc., cannot be literally translated

[19]

into English, one can still see the complication of the language by contrasting it with the simplest form of asking a person's name in modern Japanese: *"namae wa."*

Noh dialogue is in *sorobun,* a fast-disappearing, formal and quasi-poetic language used mainly for letter writing and documents requiring special verbal elegance. Its syntax requires that sentences end in *soro,* commands in *soraye,* questions in *soroya.* Hence its name of *soro-bun.* *Sorobun* is weighted with a special vocabulary, and the meaning of its sentences is, to a certain extent, dominated by its syntax. Its oblique formalism often renders a fairly simple thought complex and vague. Unfortunately for future students of *Noh,* the problem of comprehension will be almost insurmountable. *Sorobun* will soon become entirely obsolete, particularly if the language reforms proposed after the war, and unofficially but urgently pressed by the Occupation authorities, are put into effect.

Noh is performed in a specially constructed theatre, rather like a house and garden within a house and garden. The stage, which is covered with a peaked roof, extends frontally into a gravel garden pit which separates the audience from the stage. A passage-way (*hashigakari*) off to one side of the stage is the only means of entry and exit for the performers. This passageway, so indispensable in one form or another to Japanese theatre, had a direct influence in the development of *Kabuki's* passageway through the audience, the *hanamichi.*

There are numerous conventions governing the production of *Noh.* They are rigidly followed, and account for much of the 15th century flavor which still continues into the 20th century. All the roles are played by males. Men, however, even when playing female roles, speak in their natural voices. Women, demons and ghosts are invariably masked. The mask in Japan stems from *Gigaku,* but *Noh* masks are much smaller and cover only the area of the face itself. The un-made-up ears and throat of the actor are usually visible. The actors who do not wear masks appear without make-up. Wigs are occasionally used with roles requiring masks.

Emperors and high personages are played by young boys. The reasons for this are various. One is that an adult appearing in such exalted guise bears a moral responsibility beyond the powers of a lowly actor. Another reason is that representation on stage of high rank prevents a performer from being active or free enough in movement to be a leading character (*shite*). Consequently roles depicting such personages are incidental and passive. They serve as causatives (*waki*) to the main action of the play. If adults appeared in the roles of such important people, their realistic, physical presence alone would overbalance and overpower the actions of the lead character. Still another reason is that the "cult of youth" (*shudo*), a euphemism for homosexuality, was abnormally prevalent during this period of Ashikaga rulers (14th-15th century). Patrons delighted in seeing their favorite boys act in reserved and graceful parts of dignity. Their beauty fitted such roles; their lack of skill denied them any more active or theatrically essential participation.

In keeping with the flamboyance of Japan's stage and national dress, *Noh* costumes are brilliant, with variegated colors, and luxuriously embroidered and brocaded with silver and gold. Performers all wear formal white bifurcated socks (*tabi*), except comic characters (*kyogen kata*) who wear yellow.

An uncostumed chorus at the right of the stage intones a description of the action. They sing in perfect unison, confining themselves to a basic interval of a fifth which is filled with various melismata. Musical instruments consist of the hand-tabor held over the shoulder and struck with the palm of the hand; a hand drum balanced on the knee and played with two drum sticks; and a high sharp flute.

Noh is an exceedingly slow and deliberate style of drama. Each step of the foot and each gesture of the hand are carefully measured and stylized. Maximum economy of gesture and movement and complete restraint characterize a performance. A step can mean a complete journey; the lifting of the hand, weeping; the merest turn of the head, negation. *Noh* abounds in understatement. At first it appears to be a sort of intellectual exercise, like deciphering a cryptic code. Once its conventions take on meaning, its impact as an emotional experience is strikingly great. The curious enjoyment of a *Noh* performance lies in the fact that afterwards, in retrospect, after the strain and chore of following minutely its poetry and its elusive gestures are over, the lyric overtones penetrate and move the spectator's heart.

7.

Noh's Import. In the history of the Japanese theatre it has often happened that when techniques and forms, originating either with the people or coming from abroad, reach a certain stage of advancement, they find themselves the property and possession of aristocrats. *Noh* began as a popular amusement performed for the public on temple grounds. The nobility and their higher vassals lost little time in adopting it as their private entertainment. At first it served as a means of raising funds for public and private works. After taking *Noh* from the people, the nobles organized subscription performances (*kanjin noh*) to which paid attendance by commoners was compulsory.

In later eras, the people were deprived of *Noh* by law. In the long reign of peace known as the Tokugawa Era dating from the 17th to the 19th centuries, it was a punishable offense for anyone but samurai or warriors to witness *Noh*. One recorded example during this period tells that some commoners secretly erected a *Noh* stage in Yoshiwara, a flourishing center of the gay quarters of Tokyo. They disguised it by covering it with straw mats by day and held their clandestine performances at night. When the authorities heard of this, they completely destroyed the house and fined the "criminals" severely.

Although the people suffered from the nobles' selfish patronage and abuse of their prerogatives, *Noh* itself profited as an art form. Artists were for once afforded a stable livelihood. Playwrights, who were usually also performers, were given an insight into the actual world about which they wrote. Elegance and cultivation penetrated this originally crude art product. It is undeniable that the present grace of *Noh* and its scholarship are purely the result of its contact with and dependence on the aristocracy it entertained. If *Noh* had been left in the hands of the illiterate populace, it would not even have been recorded in writing. Inevitably it would have changed, become corrupted, and would finally have disappeared like the numerous other folk dances and dramas. The people of Japan created, but it was their aristocracy which preserved their achievements, at least in the theatre.

There was, however, one serious disadvantage. *Noh's* intimate connection with the aristocratic classes, and the fact that it was completely under their aegis, meant that it concentrated on refinement, rather than on growth or development along broader lines. It lost all contact with the people, and for lack of stimuli devoted itself to preserving its own traditions, and thereby limited its subject matter. *Noh* in some respects turned into a sort of ceremonial court music with tenuous stories, exclusively for the shogun and his retainers. Players were given an honorary rank of *samurai*. Patronage caused *Noh* to develop its present excessively cryptic understatement. Yet somewhere in this technique a reality is created, but it is as bodiless as an echo. Originally it was considerably more natural than it is now. The years have widened the gulf between it and its origin, and have intensified its artificiality and museum-like mustiness.

Although commoners wrote *Noh* plays, the tastes and yearnings of their noble audience determined the content to a great extent. At the time of *Noh's* height in the 15th century, the aristocracy had a genuine need for *Noh*. With its quietness and its dignified movements, it provided an emotional outlet compatible with the reserve and austerity which custom forced on Japan's well-born. Its sexlessness, for instance, impinged at no time on the moral code or arbitrary rules of decorum of the various courts which made it welcome. The spiritual necessity for nobles, and by extension for their guardians, the warriors, to have an entertainment such as *Noh* is apparent by looking at the history of the times.

During this turbulent Ashikaga period, the country was split between the Northern and the Southern Dynasties, each with its own emperor. Constant civil strife was waged among rising or resisting warring barons who gave allegiance to either one or the other side. Suffering surged over the country. Warriors were continually faced with the metaphysical problems of life and death, and the moral questions confronting men in battle. The spiritual solace of Buddhism, as depicted in *Noh,* satisfied a dual need, that of relief from temporal reality, and that of reassurance as to man's ultimate salvation.

Around twenty per cent of *Noh* plays remaining today, and certainly the best masterpieces, are the warrior-ghost plays (*shuramono*), in which a dead warrior returns from limbo (*shura*) and begs the living to pray for him. Such plays give us a clue as to the warrior-audience's attitude of mind towards their problems. Although play-acted on a stage, they still must have represented a very real part of what troubled the warrior in ordinary, daily life.

A typical example of this type of play is *Atsumori,* written by Zeami. Its story is simple.

Kumagai in battle has killed Atsumori, a young enemy general, coincidentally the same age as his own son. The horror of this premature killing (the boy was only sixteen) and Kumagai's ensuing hatred of battle lead him to take the tonsure, that is, shave his head and become a priest. He devotes his life and remaining years to prayers for the repose of Atsumori's soul.

The actual staging of this drama begins with the entrance of the priest (formerly Kumagai, but who, with the change in his life, has taken the holy name of Rensho). He is on his way to make a pilgrimage to the death-place of Atsumori. Near the spot, he meets some grass-cutters returning from work. As they talk to him, unaware that he is Kumagai, they recall the story, and express their resentment at the untimely death of Atsumori. They leave the priest. Shortly after, one of the grass-cutters reappears in masked form. He now represents the ghost of Atsumori and re-enacts his death scene. In a dialogue between the priest and Atsumori's ghost, and with interpolations from the chorus, the theme of forgiveness is developed. In life Kumagai was an enemy, but in death the two are friends. Crying "Pray for my soul," the ghost of Atsumori disappears, leaving the grieving priest.

This sort of play is essentially one of comfort to the warrior. It assures him that he has a future life, that prayer expiates sin, that the circumstances which determined the side for which he kills are fortuitous, that all resolves into peace if prayers are frequent and fervent.

It is interesting to note that in contrast to the warrior-ghost plays, the vast majority of *Noh* plays have no warrior roles at all. They consist of escapes into a world of fantasy or religion, or are merely instructive, visual representations of past history necessary to the education of 15th century aristocracy.

In recent times, when Japanese expressed the fear that war would destroy their culture, propagandists seized upon *Noh* as an example of a dramatic form born of wartime. The bulk of *Noh*, however, is not concerned with war. Those plays that do in fact deal with battle, like *Atsumori,* are ultimately a protest against wars and their tragedies. Assuredly, had a similar art form been attempted during prewar years, those selfsame propagandists would have been the first to suppress it. As *Noh* is permeated with Buddhist teachings, its content can scarcely be involved in justification of war. It is also significant that since Japan's recent defeat, there has been a considerable revival of *Noh,* particularly among the young student groups who before the war regarded it as a somewhat laughable relic of antiquity. . .

Noh's subject matter is concerned with the after-life, the sin of killing, the transience of this world, the power of Buddha, the evil of lust. Its characters, humble or high, are concerned in some way with a priest or god, and throughout there is hatred of killing. One of the most moving of all dramas is *Utoh* or *Birds of Sorrow,* also by Zeami and beautifully translated by Bruce Rogers and Meredith Weatherby.* In it a priest conjures up the ghost of a simple hunter who returns to this life to re-enact the agonies of hell which he must endure for having spent his life in killing.

Noh of the 15th century served as a spiritual release from the bloodiness of the times, as *Kabuki,* born in the 17th century time of peace, perhaps served as an outlet for a lust of blood and lingering, overshadowing instincts to murder.

8.

Kyogen, Comic Interludes. Kyogen are an adjunct of *Noh,* and are short comic plays interspersed between *Noh*'s heavier items. The proportion of *Kyogen* to *Noh* is two *Kyogen* to five *Noh* dramas. In shorter programs, one *Kyogen* for two *Noh* is usual.

Kyogen's primary origin is found in the earliest types of *Sarugaku. Sarugaku's* primitive realism and humor, which became etherealized beyond recognition in *Noh,* were retained in *Kyogen.* In the same way that *Sarugaku* developed as an interlude between *Kagura* dances in shrines, *Kyogen* similarly were comic interludes to relieve the strain of prolonged Buddhist temple services. They were adapted to *Noh* to serve precisely the same purpose. During *Noh* programs, they are used as comic relief from the sobriety and length of formal *Noh* programs.

Kyogen literally means "mad words," a term which well expresses the frivolously madcap quality which pervades their humorousness. The designation originally derived from a famous prayer-like poem of the Chinese poet Po Chu-i (772-846 A.D.) which reads to the effect that by the power of Buddha, even a fool's mad words can be transformed into a "paean of praise."

Although *Kyogen* characters and plots, costumes and actions are 15th century in spirit, the language is not. *Kyogen,* lacking the pat-

---

* *Birds of Sorrow,* Bruce Rogers and Meredith Weatherby, Obunsha, Tokyo, 1947.

ronage of scholars, were transmitted orally, unlike *Noh* dramas which were written down immediately upon conception. Not until the 17th century were *Kyogen* recorded on paper. Two centuries of oral transmission changed the language. What we see today looks like the 15th century, but sounds more 17th century.

Kyogen are always short, vastly humorous, and require at most two or three characters. They are not accompanied by music, nor have they a chorus to explain the action. Their subject matter is an excellent commentary on conventional 15th century life. One sees the superstitions of the simple folk held up to ridicule, lords mocked by their servants, and the emotions and passions of men and women depicted so naturally that even today, to people of any country, *Kyogen* are amusing and credible. Their universality was often proven after the war at the performances for Allied personnel. These monthly programs were arranged at the time theatres were "off limits" to members of the Occupation. It was at first considered a delicate choice to perform for foreigners so archaic a form as *Kyogen,* even in an enlivened form as *Kabuki* adaptations. However, they were always successful, and were probably the most popular of any type of theatre selected.

There are about one hundred and fifty different *Kyogen* remaining. A third of them involve the characters of a feudal lord (*daimyo,* literally "great name") and his servant who is always named Taro-kaja. If a second servant is required as an additional foil, he is called Jiro-kaja. The lord is invariably made ridiculous, but usually turns out to be right in the end. In the 15th century this was a theatrical necessity. Noble spectators could laugh at themselves while knowing full well that all would end without embarrassment. Meanwhile the commoners could laugh at the nobles without fear of consequence. Another third of the *Kyogen* mock Buddhism, the religion at that time almost universal among nobles and the upper classes.

Kyogen composers, among whom none stands out and few are known by name, were commoners actually writing for ordinary people. *Kyogen's* historical importance lies in the fact that it was Japan's first drama of social protest in contrast to *Noh's* resignation. *Kyogen* thus prepared the coming of *Kabuki*.

9.

Musical Story-Telling—(Forerunner of Bunraku and Kabuki). Sung and spoken recitation to instrumental accompaniment is a form of musical story-telling which has become pretty much a thing of the past in the Western world. Chanters of the *Iliad* and *Odyssey* in ancient Greece, minstrels of Europe with their metrical romances, strolling and strumming musicians, ballad singers with accompanying harps, lutes, lyres, and guitars, have for the most part disappeared from our life. They only remain in our minds as a bygone, primitive combination of music-making and story-telling which subsequently developed into maturer, separate forms, such as song, novel, opera, or chorus.

In Japan, as in all of Asia, musical story-telling is very far from being an outdated entertainment form. Especially in Japan, it is very far from being homespun or primitive, and its popularity is amazing. Each day on any of the numerous Japanese radio stations, an hour at least is devoted to these dramatic, half-sung, half-recited narratives with samisen accompaniment, called *naniwabushi*. Ubiquitous variety halls (*engeijo*) and temporary theatre-stalls which spring up overnight in the poorer districts of the cities, feature at least one or two such recitations in their sporadic nighttime performances of mixed entertainment.

In Japan's history, the first musical story-telling was performed by blind, itinerant priests who accompanied themselves on an instrument something like a lute (*biwa*). By the 14th century this occupation spread to secular chanters. They gave their recitations on street corners or wherever crowds gathered, and used taps of the fan to punctuate their meaning.

The greatest source of material for these performers was provided by Japan's two great historical romances, *Tale of the Taira Clan,* (*Heike Monogatari*) and *Tale of the Rise and Fall of the Taira and Minamoto Clans* (*Gempei Seizu Ki*), both written in the 12th century. The scope of their influence is roughly analogous to that of the *Iliad* and the *Odyssey* in Western literature. *Tale of the Rise and Fall of the Taira and Minamoto Clans* alone totals forty-eight volumes. Japan's classical stage is also deeply indebted to these literary works. Approximately one-fourth of the Bunraku Puppet Theatre and Kabuki repertoire is based on incidents drawn from the long struggle between the Minamoto and Taira.

The enormous acclaim given these tales and the dramas derived from them is not hard to explain, for the stormy period of the 11th and 12th centuries forms one of history's most vivid chapters. The colorful personalities and variety of situations detailed in *Tale of the Taira Clan* and *Tale of the Rise and Fall of the Taira and Minamoto Clans* offer an inexhaustible supply of material for talented storytellers or dramatists.

The basic theme of both works is the struggle of the Minamoto clan in its rise to power, and the crushing defeat of the gentle Taira clan. Inherent in such a dramatic situation are two fundamental characteristic aspects of Japan's theatre: respect for power and sympathy for the weak. The Japanese responds equally to both. His lot in life has generally been one of subservience to power, and so he identifies himself with the weak in his theatre. Such situations are as sure-fire with Japanese audiences, as the Cinderella-success type of story is with American movie audiences. It is significant that for eight centuries these stories have captured and held the imagination of the Japanese people.

Until a sort of three-string guitar (*samisen*) was imported from China through the Ryukyu Islands in the 16th century, flutes and drums were the backbone of Japan's secular and popular music. The new instrument gave minstrelsy and dance a very great stimulus, and has remained the most important single musical instrument of Japan to this day. With the samisen, immediate progress was made in the art of recitation and story-telling. In addition to rhythmic punctuation and tuneful melody, the samisen allowed simple two- or three-tone harmony and all manner of sound effects. The emptiness of fan taps on the one hand and the faint, feminine lilt of the priests' lutes on the other, were overcome by the resonant timbre of the samisen, and disappeared from the art of story-telling.

Shortly before the introduction of this instrument, a long masterpiece for story-telling was written, *The Tale of Princess Joruri in 12 Parts (Joruri Junidan Sochi)*. It provided a perfect vehicle for storytellers and their accompanying samisen players. The combination attained such popularity that *Joruri* became the standard word for this new art. Today the word *Joruri* applies specifically to musical dramas which developed from this style of chanting, and which retain for their accompaniment a combination singer-narrator and one or more samisen players.

Joruri is still a vital and active force in Japanese theatre arts, particularly in her two greatest drama forms, the puppet theatre and *Kabuki*. The very substance of the puppet theatre is recitation. Such a device obviously solves the problem of the dolls' muteness. The narrator tells and sings the entire story and delivers speeches for all the puppets. So taxing are the demands on the voice, replacements are often necessary. The greatest reciters reserve their appearances for only the climactic and best passages from the long dramas.

The reciters of the puppet theatre are greatly respected and the stage names of the foremost performers are conferred by members of the Imperial family. It was interesting to note that when, after World War II, the Emperor was allowed to visit the theatre for the first time in his life, he chose to see the Bunraku Puppet Theatre of Osaka. His selection was primarily determined by his desire to hear Yamashiro no Shojo, the greatest *joruri* singer of Japan, whose title and name had been awarded to him by Prince Takamatsu, the Emperor's brother.

FROM UTAURA, A NOH PLAY
Player: Minoru Kita

Photos by Nippon Photo Works Ltd. Co.

OKINA, A NOH
CONGRATULATORY DANCE
OF LONGEVITY

In Kabuki, the reciters to the side of the stage are less dominant than in the puppet theatre, and *joruri* itself is somewhat modified since the actors themselves speak the actual dialogue. However, the reciters still serve a variety of essential purposes: as a voice of conscience like a Greek chorus; as a substitute for the soliloquy so necessary in Elizabethan drama; as a medium for informing the audience of facts necessary to understanding the setting, plot, or prior events bearing on the immediate moment in the drama; and as a rhythmic, musical accompaniment intermittently freeing the actors to dance.

The hold that this musico-dramatic-recitative art form has, both in its concept as sheer story-telling (*naniwabushi*) and in its more highly evolved theatrical expressiveness as found in the puppet theatre and Kabuki, testifies to the fact that Japan's inner theatrical and dramatic taste is very much older than the modernity of her buildings and her outward civilization lead one to believe. Her long isolation protected her ancient drama, and the spectator today has the historical privilege of witnessing a theatre too highly evolved in artistic achievement to be considered primitive, but yet sufficiently uninfluenced and uncorrupted by modern changes to be dominated by its beginnings. The result is that both in the puppet theatre and in Kabuki, a spectator has not only an aesthetic reaction to arts which have reached perfection through centuries of laying subtlety upon refinement, but he is simultaneously transported backward into time, not merely by subject matter or by setting and costume, but by style of acting, type of text, forms of staging, and fundamentally by the very basis and nature of the entire art form itself.

10.

Bunraku, the Puppet Theatre. To use the word "Bunraku" in designating the puppet or doll theatre of Japan is technically incorrect, although permissible in accordance with modern day custom. *Ningyo shibai* (doll theatre) or *ayatsuri shibai* (manipulation theatre) are the only precise appellations. *Bunraku* is derived from a puppeteer named Bunrakuen, who built his own theatre in the middle of the 19th century. In 1872 a manager for Bunrakuen's theatre, named Okura, established a rival theatre in the gay quarters of Osaka, and called it Bunraku-Za, literally, Literary Pleasures Theatre. The name was immensely successful. Of all Japanese puppet theatres in history, and the maximum number throughout Japan at any one time was never more than twelve, only one—the Bunraku-Za of Osaka—has survived the vicissitudes of history and the changing tastes of modern Japan. Shochiku Company, Inc., which has controlled puppet performances since 1909, is mainly responsible for Bunraku's existence. Through adroit financial manipulations of their massive combine of various theatrical enterprises, Shochiku's Bunraku has been sustained. By 1914 there was no rival puppet theatre in Japan. Since that time, the word "Bunraku" for all practical purposes has come to mean the puppets, the theatre, the repertoire, and that type of art which utilizes puppets to enact dramatic narratives.

Puppets were introduced into Japan in the 9th century. As their handlers were foreigners, the social status of puppeteers for a long period of history was, officially, that of outcasts (*hinin*). Puppets were of the Punch-and-Judy type, manipulated by hand. For centuries their function was limited to simple stories to amuse children and occasional performances at festivals.

Towards the end of the 16th century in the twin cities of Osaka and Kyoto, a samisen player named Menukiya Chozaburo and a puppeteer named Hikita joined forces. They created a new kind of theatrical entertainment in which the puppets were used to perform actions described by the musical story-telling accompaniment of *joruri*.

Shortly after, the next step in the historical growth of puppet drama was made in Edo, now called Tokyo. A renowned *joruri* chanter, Satsuma Jo-un, originated a new style of recitation. It was characterized by violence and bombast. He chose as his central character, Kimpira, a legendary hero of bold and fierce nature whose supernatural exploits demanded a most vigorous declamation and

[32]

singing. Satsuma Jo-un recognized in the puppets their capability of performing the humanly impossible and fantastic actions. Later, this style of singing, when combined with the puppets, came to be known as *Kimpira Joruri*. It is said that the puppets were so violently thrown about the room that replacements were constantly needed. Satsuma Jo-un also in some of his impassioned declarations would become so carried away that he would reach over and crush the head of the nearest puppet.

This form of entertainment was in great demand. Love of violence had become characteristic of Edo (Tokyo), the residence of the ruling shogun and military center for all Japan. *Kimpira Joruri's* influence continues even today in that type of Tokyo Kabuki known as *aragoto* (literally, rough business) or plays of bombast and heroics. In contrast, gentle and artistic Osaka and Kyoto continued peacefully, far removed from the roughness of the capital city. There the puppets were elevated to a position of great literary and artistic perfection.

The year 1685 marks the establishment of the Takemoto-za (theatre) in Osaka. This was the foundation of the superlative art known today as Bunraku. Three men combined their genius and were responsible not only for the success of the Takemoto-za, but for the tremendous rise and advance of the puppet theatre as an institution in Japan's theatrical life. The first was Takemoto Gidayu (1651-1714), a farmer's son who refined the singing and chanting style of *joruri*. His style became so popular that even today his name, the word *gidayu,* is synonymous with *joruri*. The second was Tachimatsu Hachirobei, an expert puppeteer—the puppets were still on a one-puppet to one-man, hand-operated basis. The third was the greatest playwright of Japan's history, Chikamatsu Monzaemon (1653-1725).

As these men devoted their genius to the theatre, and as followers, imitators, and collaborating playwrights began pouring out plays and recitations, the capabilities and manipulations of the puppets advanced enormously. By 1730 the eyes and eyebrows moved. By 1733 individual fingers were articulated. By the following year the stomach of the dolls could swell, and a man was assigned to move the left foot. In 1747 devices were contrived to make the ears move. To the great puppeteer Yoshida Bunzaburo whose descendants are still stars at the Bunraku-Za in Osaka today, goes the credit for establishing a system of three men to one puppet. From 1734 up to the present, it has been standard practice for a leading puppeteer to hold the doll by the back and operate the right hand, head, and eyebrows, a second man to operate the left hand, and a third man to manage the feet. In the case of female dolls, which have no feet, the third man operates the skirts so as to give the impression of walking, leg movement, etc. This complicated manipulation of the large and skillfully constructed puppets has led the Japanese puppet theatre to a unique position in world theatre forms.

It is astonishing how the puppet, about one-third the size of a man and requiring three full-sized adults to move it, can take on almost human life. In performances today the leading operator dresses in flamboyant and luxurious formal costume (*Kami-shimo*) of the Tokugawa Era. The subsidiary operators are dressed in black with a hooded flap hanging over their faces to make themselves less conspicuous. Within a few minutes of the start of the action the operators are completely forgotten by the audience.

By the middle of the 18th century, puppet theatres completely overshadowed the Kabuki of human actors. Government restrictions had given death-dealing blows to the live actors. Kabuki lost its best actors. Untrammeled creative genius had become concentrated in the puppet theatres. In order to compete, Kabuki borrowed more and more liberally from the puppets. The actors took plots, imitated the puppet movements, and adapted wholesale styles of declamation and *joruri*. The result was successful. However much the public liked to see puppets act as humans, they were more delighted to see actors perform as puppets. By the end of the 18th century, the dominance of the puppet theatre was broken. Kabuki re-established its supremacy, and it has lasted to the present day as the major force of Japan's theatre.

Since the histories of the puppet theatre and Kabuki are inextricably interwoven, and since today's Kabuki has arrogated to itself virtually the entire puppet repertoire, plays and playwrights of Bunraku are dealt with in the following pages as a part of Kabuki.

II

Kabuki–Japan's Popular Theatre

1.

Meaning of the Word Kabuki. By the 10th century A.D., scholars from China began to flood Japan. They brought with them religious tenets, cultural influences, and most important, a workable means of writing. For the first time in history the Japanese were able to record their own original tongue.

The ideographs of written Chinese were not merely phonetic or alphabetical. They were capable of representing, if only approximately, sounds of a foreign language, but because they were fundamentally pictures or drawings, the ideographs in themselves conveyed images and ideas. They could also be combined and compounded to create further concepts. In this way, the native Japanese language, already rich in its own right, greatly enlarged its vocabulary. From the characters the Japanese also extracted a simplified script which could be used in conjunction with the Chinese to express the grammatical terminations and postpositions of the spoken language.

One of these Chinese word-compounds in current use by the 16th century was *kabu* (song, *ka*; dance, *bu*). The Japanese added to this their own ending *su* (meaning "to do"), and arrived at a verb meaning "to sing and dance" (*kabusu*).

At the same time there was also a common and somewhat vulgar colloquialism pronounced *kabuku*. It was a verb with a variety of meanings which nowadays in modern Japanese requires two separate words to explain it, *fuzakeru* and *shareru*. In English the concept requires even more words to communicate its full significance. Roughly, the now obsolete word *kabuku* meant to frolic, disport oneself, flirt, dress a little over-smartly. To complicate the matter further, etymologically *kabuku* derived from *katamuku*, literally, to slide downhill, and by inference therefore, contained the sense of to decline or degenerate.

When in the late 16th century a type of risqué dancing was created, the Japanese of the time dubbed it a form of *kabuku*, and shortly after its appearance, made from the word, a noun, *kabuki*. As its popularity and artistic merits began to command widespread attention, the colloquialism *kabuki* was elevated in writing by the scholarly Chinese characters of *kabu* (from *kabusu*, to sing and dance). To this was arbitrarily added an ideograph pronounced *ki* and incidentally suggesting the idea of "skill" or "trick." *Ki* at this time was written with the radical, or first half of the character representing "woman," significant perhaps of the woman who originated the art of *Kabuki*. In the 19th century this radical of the ideograph was changed—belatedly, as women had not performed *Kabuki* for centuries—to simply "person."

Fusing the words *kabuku* and *kabusu* to represent the art of Kabuki and dignifying it with ideographs was something of a linguistic accident. The original slang *kabuku* with its rather unflattering connotation of riotous behaviour was exactly what people in the early 17th century meant when they said "Kabuki."

However, today what is known as Kabuki is a broad concept. It is elegantly written, with characters which mean "song-dance-skill." In effect the meaning covers a combination of words and music, of dancing and movement, all skillfully executed. Kabuki eventually became the most important theatrical art of Japan, and until the late 19th century, it stood in the minds of the people as the entire theatre of Japan.

With the influence of the West and new types of theatrical performances in Japan, the meaning of the word Kabuki became more

[38]

restrictive. It now refers to a specific and particular type of classic theatre, and communicates the synthetic idea of a special and rarefied style of acting, certain types of plays, and a set and inflexible repertoire. The last successful additions to the now standard list of Kabuki plays, which totals around three hundred and fifty pieces, appeared in the late 19th century. Since then Kabuki has become completely crystallized, or "fossilized" as certain critics prefer to say.

2.

O-Kuni's Kabuki. In former days the great temples of Japan combined elements of both the Shinto and Buddhist religions. They often joined their separate theatrical media and dispatched temple dancers annually for the purpose of soliciting contributions and funds by performances throughout the country. These dancers, the progenitors of today's temple girls, or *miko,* who carry on the tradition of *Kagura* dancing, were as often as not prostitutes for the corrupt clergy.

One day in 1586 a dancing girl, claiming to be from the great Shrine of Izumo in Central Japan, performed outdoors in the dry bed of the Kamo River. There between the banks of the river which divides the city of Kyoto into two halves, and between the two thickly populated sections of the town, she was reasonably remote from police surveillance. The place of her performance was in a way unfortunate. For centuries actors of the Japanese stage were dogged with the epithet, "things of the river bed" (*Kawara mono*), although their popularity as actors was not affected by their lack of social standing and immoral origins. Nothing was known about the girl except that her name was O-Kuni and that she was thought to be the daughter of a blacksmith named Nakamura Sanemon.

O-Kuni began her performance with a "prayer dance" (*nembutsu odori*). She began like a priest with an incantation, "Man is mortal. Money is nothing. Believe in Buddha." At intervals she tapped a bell in her hand as if executing a conventional ritual. As the performance proceeded she filled in all manner of erotic by-play quite removed

[39]

from any religious context. It is highly doubtful that O-Kuni was really attached to a temple at all; but since money could only be charged for a public performance at that time if it was for religious purposes, her motives seem obvious.

Reports have it that O-Kuni was plain in looks, but of exceptional cleverness. The scattered and conflicting references to her in historical documents of the period certainly indicate an extraordinary and creative person. Her success was fantastic and immediate. As audiences increasingly demanded her appearances, she began to expand her repertoire. In addition to her solo "prayer dances," she incorporated the basic theatrical relation of Noh, that is, leading character (*shite*) and a causative character or foil (*waki*). The first result was a dance in which she appeared as a man dashingly sporting two swords at her (or his) side and made impassioned love to a courtesan. Her originality and unusual flavor, in the true sense of *kabuku,* attracted many people who wished to join her troupe. They mainly were women who danced as men, and men who danced as women.

O-Kuni's group also attracted writers of comic interludes (*kyogen*) who sought freer expression than Noh and its patrons allowed. They introduced into O-Kuni's Kabuki a third element from Noh, the follower (*tsure*). She turned him into a comic character and called him Saruwaka. Through Saruwaka, O-Kuni restored to Japan's theatre the lusty, comic mimicry which had started with *Sarugaku. Sarugaku,* by its incorporation into Noh and by losing contact with the common people, had lost these qualities of abandon. The tradition was only faintly and with great restraint and decorum carried on in *Kyogen* interludes.

Saruwaka's portion of the performance developed into a full-fledged, individual type of dancing within Kabuki. Now it has degenerated into a handful of incomprehensible, archaically funny fragments. Some of the older actors of Kabuki today still remember them, but they neither perform them nor transmit them to pupils. With the death of the great Nakamura Ganjiro twenty years ago, the leading actor of the Osaka Kabuki stage, hereditary knowledge of Saruwaka and the right to perform it ended.

With the added fillip from *Kyogen* writers, O-Kuni became even bolder and took over Noh's drums and flutes for her musical accompaniment.

Gradually as her popularity continued to increase her themes grew more elaborate and eventually developed into playlets. Some of these were based on famous stories of historical events, such as the dramatic and long-plotted revenge of the two Soga brothers against their father's wicked murderer. Others borrowed from the popular romances of musical story-tellers. Particularly suitable to O-Kuni's taste were episodes from the life of the handsome and admired warrior-hero of the Minamoto clan, Yoshitsune, and his accomplished dancer-concubine, Shizuka. In one ancient painting, O-Kuni is even shown dancing as a Christian with a cross around her neck, which is reminiscent of the then recent persecutions of the Portuguese fathers and their Japanese votaries. On this theme she must have exploited drama and pathos to the fullest, although the actual story of her dance is unknown.

At the conclusion of O-Kuni's programs, she held a "general dance" (*so-odori*), in effect a type of lively curtain call for the entire troupe, but one in which spectators could also participate in whatever manner they saw fit. Such abandon was the essence of the word *kabuku* in the Japanese mind.

O-Kuni began to require a larger stage. She performed on the noble and sacrosanct Noh stage of Kitano in Kyoto. Because of this honor she was given, or more likely arbitrarily took, a new name and added a title, Kitano Tsushima-no-kami. Her leading subordinates followed suit and added *Tayu* after their names. The titles of *tayu* and *kami* were stolen directly from the honored singers of musical recitations (*joruri*) and of the puppet theatre. Leading singers of the period were given official ranks of *tayu, kami,* and *jo* in order of increasing importance. Because of these titular ranks the best singers were considered respectable human beings and allowed to appear with propriety before their superiors by birth.

O-Kuni too, after assuming the rank of *kami,* performed before the upper classes. In certain annals of the period, credence is given to the rumor that she had on one occasion appeared before the Emperor in Kyoto. Specifically known is an incident in 1603 when the mighty warrior and enemy of the Tokugawa shoguns, Toyotomi Hideyasu, gave her a necklace of crystal beads in his beleaguered castle in Fushimi, Osaka. In 1607 she appeared before the Tokugawa Shogun in Edo (Tokyo). It is also written that she performed before "tens of thousands" and that even the Noh stage was no longer adequate for her troupe and her devotees.

Performances were all in the open air. Even when performing on Noh stages, the roof covered only the stage. From O-Kuni's performances before vast audiences, the word "shibai" (literally, on the grass) arose. In modern Japanese the word "shibai" now means theatre of any type or kind, but of course in origin it primarily signified Kabuki.

The large crowds witnessing her performances meant the mixing of peoples from various stations of life, and often the result was bloodshed, as social resentments came to the surface. Foreigners, who were of no social position whatever, also evinced interest in O-Kuni's performances, and an early painting of the period, in an illustrated book called *Kabuki Soshi,* shows them conspicuously among the spectators. Increasing interest on the part of nobles and warriors, who were not permitted to be in public with commoners, caused the construction of special screened boxes (*sajiki*) at the sides of O-Kuni's stage. This architectural addition made the first step towards the construction of a closed theatre-house where audience and actors were both under cover.

The jumble of miscellaneous references to O-Kuni in various accurate and inaccurate documents contributed to considerable difficulty in deciphering her true story. Until very recently it was thought that she had met the glamorous warrior, Nagoya Sanzaburo, in Kyoto, and that he had joined in her performances and ultimately married her. Various accounts that have recently come to light scotch that rumor. The famous Sanzaburo was certainly killed in a samurai brawl before O-Kuni had even danced that first dance in the river bed of Kyoto.

Such an invention about the two is understandable and even a sympathetic one, regardless of the annoyance of the historian. Sanzaburo was noted for his heroic exploits; O-Kuni had exhibited an exciting new art. They were the two most romantic names on the lips of people during the period dating from 1569 to 1614.* O-Kuni dancers coming on the heels of Sanzaburo's untimely death used him as a favorite theme. It was natural for rumor to wed them. Precisely at the time that the figure of Sanzaburo first entered the O-Kuni dances, the noun Kabuki (derived from the colloquial verb *kabuku*) was specifically applied to O-Kuni's type of dancing. There is still a large body of later Kabuki plays about the two personalities. They are studied as literature now, and are known as the Fuwa Cycle of plays, but are rarely performed on the stage.

3.

Pleasure Woman's Kabuki. The date of O-Kuni's death is a mystery. The majority of documentary evidence and the consensus of scholarly opinion place it somewhere around 1610. The exact date is further obscured by the fact that at least two other women assumed the name of O-Kuni around this time.

After O-Kuni's death, many imitators arose and their popularity continued to spread. At first this new type of imitation Kabuki was known as *Woman's Kabuki* (*Onna Kabuki*). Later it came to be known as a compound word, *Pleasure Woman's Kabuki* (*Yu-jo Kabuki*). Despite the fact that men continued to be in many of the troupes, the emphasis of the performers and spectators was on the

---

* Called the Keicho Era. In accordance with all Japanese chronology, each era is named after the death of an emperor who is given a posthumous name, by which both he and the era are subsequently known.

women and the pleasures they offered both during and after the theatre.

During the period of *Pleasure Woman's Kabuki* the samisen was introduced into the performance. This was the chief theatrical progress made; for despite a few inchoate histrionic advances, *Pleasure Woman's Kabuki* was primarily a vehicle for prostitution. The girls of the troupe were available after the performances to the wealthier spectators. The dances requiring women and men to be disguised as the opposite sex in a Kabuki-esque, off-balance spirit, also involved some abnormality. The grim fact remains that the majority of the dancing groups consisted of nothing more than prostitutes of one sort or another, who used O-Kuni's original creation as a means of exhibiting their talents in order to sell their charms. Their popularity was very great. In 1610 it is known that no less a lord than Date Masamune, subsequently eulogized in Kabuki as a great and regal feudal lord, brought an entire troupe of *Pleasure Woman's Kabuki* to his domain in Sendai, Northern Japan.

The flagrant immorality of these Kabuki types became too much for the Shogunate which was responsible for the order and morality of the country. Thirty-three years after Kabuki's inception, in 1629, it was officially banned. *Pleasure Woman's Kabuki* and indeed any appearance of women on the stage were forbidden, and until the 19th century the ordinance remained tacitly in effect. This censure was not designed to strike at the material of the Kabuki plays, although certainly some of the performances parodied officials, but rather it was to safeguard the morals of the warrior or *bushi* upon whose virility and moral integrity the defense of the military governors depended.

Kabuki was primarily designed to appeal to and was performed for commoners, townsmen, and merchants, the three rather humiliating social classifications of the masses of people of Japan, registered in official documents as *heimin, chonin,* and *shonin*. Individuals were not allowed to rise from these groupings into higher classifications.

But the warriors quickly responded to O-Kuni's type of art. They had wearied, like modern spectators today, of their sanctimonious Noh plays. The ruling Shogun himself had at least once commanded O-Kuni to perform for him, but when his warriors began weakening themselves with Kabuki performers, drink, and the theatre, his indiscretion was no longer justifiable.

Until the appearance of O-Kuni, the only dramatic expression of the Japanese common man for two centuries had been sacred dances in temples, folk dances at festival times, and the annual subscription performances of the nobles (*kanjin noh*). Direct responsibility for this lack lay with the ruling classes whose one concern had been civil wars and the welfare of the warrior class. Until O-Kuni there had been no time to allow the people an art.

The final establishment of a stable and consecutive series of military rulers, the Tokugawas, at the beginning of the 17th century, inaugurated an unprecedented reign of three centuries of peace. In this atmosphere of calm, the artistic impulses of the people burst into expression.

The emptiness which the people had felt in their lack of a theatre was undoubtedly responsible for the contagious success of O-Kuni and her imitators. Eagerness for stage expression had been pent up, and once released, even the mighty Shogun was powerless to suppress it. Persecution and censorship, though often merciless, could no longer seriously check the growth of the popular drama, Kabuki.

4.

Young Man's Kabuki: Such was the drive to dramatic expression on the part of the people that when *Woman's Kabuki* was forbidden, handsome young men took over the performances. Still another form of Kabuki evolved—*Young Man's Kabuki (Wakashu Kabuki)*. These young men, or *wakashu* as they were called, were identifiable by a long forelock which they assiduously cultivated as a mark of youth, beauty, and grace. *Wakashu* is still a current word and refers specifically in present-day *Kabuki* to young man roles. The wigs for these parts carefully preserve the tradition of the heavy forelock.

Wakashu literally means "young group," but in this era it applied exclusively to those youths who lived at the side of the warriors. They sat with the older men, danced for them at banquets, carried their swords for them on formal occasions, and in the battlefield, where women were not allowed, served as catamites. The nearest approximation to the word for "homosexuality" at this period was *shudo,* the "way of the youth," an equivalent adjunct of *bushido,* the "way of the warrior."

At the time of the establishment of an ear of peace, the Tokugawa Era, many of these young men found themselves without employment. The stage provided an easy solution to all their problems of livelihood, training, and inclinations.

Already as early as 1617, a troupe of these youths had been organized by Nippon Dansuke, a former actor-manager of an O-Kuni Kabuki troupe in Osaka, either in anticipation of the eventual extermination of Woman's Kabuki, or in order to cater to the specialized tastes of some spectators. In 1624 Saruwaka Kanzaburo, most brilliant of the troupe managers of the time, who had borrowed his name from the comic and licentious Third-man role in O-Kuni's early Kabuki, established a theatre in Edo (Tokyo) and called it the Saruwaka-Za. In the troupe there, he included a number of young men or *wakashu.*

Most of the *Young Man's Kabuki* vehicles concerned humorous aspects of sodomy, but some of them showed an increasing complexity of dramatic interest. Two of the more advanced of the *Young Men's Kabuki* performances are described in a document called *Mirror of Art* (*Gei Kagami*). *Mirror of Art* was written sometime after 1652, the time of the eventual ban on *Young Man's Kabuki.* But the writer, Tominaga Heibei, is recalling some of the earlier performances he witnessed at the time *Young Man's Kabuki* was in vogue and permissible. As Tominaga Heibei was a writer

BUNRAKU DOLL DANCE

(from Yoshitsune Senbon Zakura)

himself, in fact the first playwright of Japan ever to call himself one on a program, he was especially careful in recalling the stories of plays he saw.

The first play described is *The Ronin's Wine Cup* (*Ronin Saka-zuki*). (By way of explanation it should be mentioned that a *ronin* is a lordless knight, or a retainer who is no longer in the pay or keeping of a superior warrior.) A paraphrase of the story will give some indication of the kind of material that was employed.

While a retainer, accompanied by his men, is riding on horseback, he happens to see a ronin wearing a sedge hat. The ronin bows down with his hands on the ground. He turns out to be an old friend of the retainer; but once when he had tried to intervene and prevent their mutual lord and master from committing some misconduct, he had incurred the lord's great displeasure. For his presumptuous interference in his lord's behavior, he was discharged and forced to become a ronin. On hearing that a former friend and erstwhile fellow-retainer was to pass through the town, the ronin has appeared to renew the acquaintance. Both friends weep. The retainer gives the ronin a fan shaped like a wine bottle, and a cup. They symbolize the congratulatory cup of wine to be drunk together when the ronin is accepted back into the service of the lord. The ronin accepts these presents with joy, and pretending drunkenness from imaginary wine poured from the fan, dances in glee.

Another of the *Young Man's Kabuki* performances related in the *Mirror of Art*, is called *A Visit to a Courtesan*. Here the story is of an entirely different sort, and the audience's reaction to it is also recorded.

An introduction was given, "Now begins a visit to a courtesan." Then the lover Murayama Hachirobei appeared. He was dressed in white silk with the pattern of deer's antlers with a bee on it. He wore, hilt downwards (to show he was on pleasure), a long sword at his side. With his left elbow stuck out and with a fan in his right hand, he strutted from the side-passage (the *hashi-gakari* of the Noh stage) to the center of the stage. He struck the hilt of the sword with the fan and cried out, "Oho, I am the visitor." Here the spectators hailed him unanimously, saying, "Here has come an expert visitor!" They were so noisy that it took some time for them to be quieted.

The host of the house appeared from the opposite entrance and was dressed in a worn-out blue skirt (*hakama,* worn over the bottom part of the kimono for formal dress). Over his shoulder hung a towel. In his hand he carried a shell-spoon. Unctuously he cried, "Welcome to you, sir!" Again the spectators shouted, "That's the host! Look at his face! See how funny!" They laughed so boisterously that the actor could not give his next speech.

When they became a little silent, Hachirobei said, "Has the girl not come yet?" "She is coming; soon she will be here," answered the host. And looking towards the entrance passage, he cried, "Look! look! She is there!" Then the people stood and looked at the curtain breathlessly.

A girl (a young man, of course) in beautiful kimono of golden patterns entered. Her hair was covered with gay paper and smartly groomed in the fashion of the time ("as wigs were seldom used in former times," the writer adds). She approached her lover saying, "Welcome to you, my lord," and took his hand. The people again laughed out, much delighted. At every action they laughed and applauded.

Then the host passing a wine-cup said, "Girl, dance for him and let him feast his eyes and ears." At this, musicians entered, began to play, and the girl danced.

Although the *Young Man's Kabuki* playlets described in the *Mirror of Art* are naïve as drama in our eyes today, they do contain three very important elements of a nascent drama: order, gradation, concentration. Obviously they were the genesis of the much later and more fully developed Kabuki.

The majority of performances of *Young Man's Kabuki,* in contrast to those recounted in the *Mirror of Art,* however, made little effort to improve Kabuki as a drama. The primary aim was to display the beauty of the boys to the customers. The immorality and license of *Young Man's Kabuki* quickly came to be regarded unfavorably by the government. A series of restrictive measures were put into force. In 1636 any luxury in the theatre was prohibited. In

1642, a celebrated actor, Sakon Murayama, star of *Young Man's Kabuki* and first of the great players of female roles (*onnagata*), appeared in the military capital of the Shogun in Edo. As a result of his notoriety, all players of women's roles were barred from the stage. The clever Saruwaka Kanzaburo, however, managed a year later to persuade the authorities to restore permission, for *Young Man's Kabuki* could not exist without these performers. In 1644 fights over the subject matter of plays forced the government to condemn the use of any but fictitious names in theatricals. In 1646 in a vain effort to keep the warriors out of the theatres, the practice of screened boxes, where people could secretly see but not be seen, was discontinued upon order. In 1648 the practice of homosexuality (*shudo*) was forbidden by law. In 1652, the Shogun, becoming interested in this new headache, ordered a command performance. But *Young Man's Kabuki* had already by then become an uncontrollable source of trouble to the government. The warriors were even fighting over the boys in the theatres.

In the same year, 1652, *Young Man's Kabuki* was formally banned. All actors were ordered to shave their distinguishing forelocks. Dancing and music were prohibited from the stage. Theatricals were confined by decree to scenes of mime with stories (*monomane kyogen zukushi*, literally imitation of things or events—plays—series). The use of the word *kyogen* here is not to be confused with the comic interludes of Noh. By this time the word *kyogen* had come to be a generic term for any acted scene or playlet except those of Noh which were called by that name only. The word is still used in the sense of any play today.

Once the young men shaved their forelocks, the youth of the actors and their amorous charms were gone. Older men joined Kabuki troupes, and *Men's Kabuki* (*Yaro Kabuki*) immediately came into being.

5.

Men's Kabuki. Men's Kabuki (*Yaro Kabuki*) is the real basis of the

Kabuki which we see today, although modified by centuries of growth and development. The groundwork and frame of modern Kabuki dates from this time. Without sex and physical beauty to sustain *Men's Kabuki,* and impelled by the dramatic yearnings of the people at large, it developed into a true art form.

"Yaro" in modern Japanese has the meaning of rogue or brute, but in this period of the early 17th century, it simply stood for "man." Eventually the word was dropped, and *Men's Kabuki* became known simply as Kabuki.

Governmental oppression and interference of the various original types of Kabuki, far from weakening the people's theatre, actually quickened its development. The barring of women from the stage in 1628 only made male actors concentrate on make-up, costuming, and refinements of gesture, in order to create the greater illusion and appearance of women. Aristocrats with their Noh may have been content with the actor's merely putting on a woman's mask and still speaking in his natural voice, but this was not enough realism for the commoners. As a result, the artful use of the falsetto came into practice. With the loss of their forelocks, the actors needed wigs to hide their shaven heads. Deprived of music and dancing (although only temporarily, as the ban was not feasible for any length of time against the will of the people), the actors concentrated on speech and drama. Real fundamentals of the theatre, such as disguise, imitation, deception, story and mime were given a new and mighty impetus. Suppression of *Young Men's Kabuki* raised Kabuki from the sensuality into which it had fallen and upon which it had depended. The ban forced *Men's Kabuki* to focus on genuine theatre.

As a result, in 1664 in Osaka, the first complete play of more than one act (*kyogen tsuzuki*) appeared. Written by Fukui Yagozaemon, and called *The Outcast's Revenge* (*Hinin no Adauchi*), it was the story of a man who disguises himself as a beggar to revenge the accidental killing of his father. Plays of several acts and scenes quickly followed from the pens of other playwrights. The changes of scene required by these new plays, which had a continuous story divided into different acts, led to the invention of a curtain. By using the curtain, the stage of Kabuki became independent of Noh's stage, and scenery was introduced.

Within the space of 70-odd years, O-Kuni's elementary dance-dialogues had grown into a soundly based, individual theatre. For hundreds of years to come it was to continue and develop.

III

Genroku Kabuki

1.

Genroku Era. The initial forms of Kabuki in the light of later history seem little more than a primordial groping towards the direction Japan's theatre was to take. When *Men's Kabuki* set the basic pattern, Kabuki grew by leaps and bounds into a major art form. In a matter of thirty or forty years from the inception of *Men's Kabuki,* the essence of Kabuki clarified itself and theatre in Japan was established among the people for all time. A peak, a first stage of perfection for Kabuki, was reached in the Genroku Era.

Genroku is a magical word and communicates to the historian the idea of one of the most fabulous periods of Japanese national existence. The nature of the people of the Genroku Era and the historical and social atmosphere of the time are at the center of Kabuki's meaning and significance today. Much has changed in the course of almost three centuries; but the appearance, the mood, and the manifest quality of Kabuki are inseparable from this period in which its essential qualities were first determined.

Technically, Genroku is the name given to the 16-year period from 1688 to 1703, during the reign of the fifth of the Tokugawa rulers or shoguns, Tsunayoshi. But Genroku has a broader sense. The color, activity, and artistic and social development so characteristic of those sixteen years also extended before and beyond that brief period. Genroku in this broader sense also includes the periods of rule called Empo and Kyoho. Altogether the three periods included in the larger concept of Genroku date from 1673 to 1735, a total of sixty-two years.

Even more than a mere period or trio of periods of history, Genroku has come to signify a brilliant étape of the culture and civilization flourishing under the Tokugawa rulers. In theatrical history it is vital, because during this time Kabuki took definite shape, and in competition with it the puppet theatre rose to great heights. The spirit of Genroku, which can be epitomized by calling it the moment of awakening of the common man in Japan, was crystallized in these two popular theatres. Kabuki, and its companion piece, the Bunraku puppet theatre, are precise embodiments of the Genroku temper and tenor.

In order to understand the implications of Genroku, the social and political life of the Japanese nation at that time must be examined. The Tokugawa Era came to birth through the power of the sword, wielded by the samurai class. Both economically and by virtue of their traditional position within the social order, they were the superiors of the masses. Their motto for centuries had been to respect agriculture and to despise gold.

The political doctrine of the day was based on the Confucian principle of governing so as to suppress luxury and to encourage frugality. The first Shogun of the Tokugawa regime, Ieyasu (1542-1616), although he is to this day always depicted in Kabuki plays as a cruel and ruthless overlord, actually gave a measure of freedom to his subjects. The historical situation was a curious one, and the ineluctable facts of the era made it impossible to follow the advice tendered him.

Through weapons peace had been achieved. A powerless emperor had been sequestered in Kyoto. In a final gesture of ridding temporal government of the emperor's spiritual hold, the capital of the country was moved from Kyoto to Edo (Tokyo). The conquered feudal lords were required to send there a certain number from their courts for a period of time each year, as a gesture of allegiance and to enable the Shogun to exert a more direct control. In order to ensure the loyalty of the various traitorous barons, the Shogun was forced to maintain an elaborate and luxurious capital.

The palace of the Shogun could only remain a center of control if it was prosperous and attractive. The warriors (now with no wars to fight) and the people at large would remain peaceful and docile only if given pleasure. Consequently, restaurants, brothels, theatres, and music were allowed throughout the land, despite the fear that in such hedonism insolence lurked.

The peace the sword had brought began to destroy the very social structure the warriors had fought to establish. The common people began to rise in the world, and money became a more important weapon than a sword. Numerous reasons account for this change. Once released from the long years of bloody civil strife, the attention of the people turned from hardship to comfort. Despite the new military situation with its ramifications in the economy of the country, the samurai class continued to make the very serious blunder of exacting taxes from the peasantry and ignoring the artisans and merchants. They did this simply because, according to the warrior's code, the military was supposed to look down on tradesmen. Concentrations both of wealth and of population in the castle towns resulted in a shift from a land economy to a money economy. Soon the situation became such that no exchange of commodities was possible without an intermediary merchant. In 1695, the Shogunate, in an effort to save the tottering state economy, recoined all the money. The new money lacked value or security and the result was inflation. It ended by the near-collapse of the samurai and their permanent financial dependence on the merchants.

Merchants gained further control over the samurai by engaging in transactions involving rice tickets. Feudal lords reckoned their fortunes in bales of rice rather than in amounts of money. As the need for money, as opposed to rice, increased, the merchants bought and resold these rice tickets. Unfortunately, lords were strictly limited in the amount of rice they were entitled to; but there were no limitations to the profits the merchants could make in bartering and exchanging these rice incomes. The warrior's standard of living gradually became more and more incompatible with the new, inflationary black-market economy of Genroku.

Genroku produced several millionaires among these merchants, including figures whose names are now romantic, such as Kibun, Naramo, Narayasu, Ishikawa Rokubei, Yodoya Tatsugoro, and Ibarakiya Kasai, who all furnished the subject matter for Kabuki dramas. Their luxurious lives matched that of the Shogun himself, and filled the poor feudal lords with bitter resentment. The merchants for their part gave the idle and poor warriors the outward respect and deference demanded by law. In their hearts, however, they loathed them and reveled in being their financial superiors.

During this period of rising merchants and declining samurais, Edo (Tokyo) and Osaka (together with nearby Kyoto) were the chief centers of activity. Osaka was a town of production, and Edo a consumer. Osaka was the creditor; Edo, the debtor. The great fire of 1657 in Edo ruined theatre business temporarily, and many of the artists went to Osaka where the greater commercial prosperity made an art center far superior to Edo. Edo was the military center of Japan and was filled with lords and samurais who were almost hostages. There, citizens were less aware of the reaches of their power. The warrior still remained comparatively more predominant. Osaka, however, had been a town of simple people from its beginning. It was uninfluenced by the samurai's morality and ethics, and commerce and business activities were naturally the main tastes of the people.

There is, at least to the Westerner, a curious aspect to the Genroku period. Despite the ferment of activity, it led to no fundamental structural upheaval as might have been expected. The awakening of the people and the development of art in the Genroku period have sometimes been likened to the Renaissance in Europe. For the Renaissance, reason was the guiding principle. Its primary aspects were self-consciousness, a discovery and emancipation of the individual—in other words, respect of individuality and a demand for liberty. But the basis of Genroku culture was an unconscious and instinctive emotionalism. There was a kind of liberty, but it was the liberty to pursue pleasures. There was emancipation to a certain extent, but it was emancipation of the emotions from narrow moral restraints. There was the desire for equality, but for equality in the pleasure districts only. Although the social structure which placed merchants beneath warriors continued and the merchants outwardly adhered to it, they knew that financially they were far superior. Even if they had to bow to the samurai in the streets, it was certain that they could afford the best courtesans and the greater luxuries.

One similarity with the European Renaissance was that the standard of education rose. Common men began to study both Chinese and Japanese classics. However, in Japan, the Confucian and Buddhist traditions were so strong that the people did not explore further fields of knowledge. There was no development of science, philosophy, or even of a revolutionary spirit to throw off existing shackles.

Genroku was a period in which unconscious and blind emotions of a people reacted to an economic transformation of the state. The citizens had real power but no thought of class struggle. Instead of revolt, the people sought only the release of their emotions in the pleasure districts and theatres where commoners and samurai were on equal terms. They were content with an emotional explosion (primarily shown in their theatre) which relieved the tension and resolved the need for direct action. The political rule of the military classes continued to exist. In Genroku society, irrationality, conventionality, and formality were harmonized. And in these respects, Genroku was vitally different from the humanistic Renaissance. Despite the power of gold, the pressures of society retained their hold over the people.

The most brilliant manifestation of Genroku, one common both to Edo and Osaka, was the birth of citizen art. The period abounds in great names of Japan's cultural history. Among actors, there were

Ichikawa Danjuro I, Sankata Tojuro, Mizuki Tatsunosuke, and Yoshizawa Ayame; among musicians, there was Takemoto Gidayu; among novelists, Ihara Saikaku and Eshima Kiseki; among playwrights, Chikamatsu Monzaemon; among poets, Basho; and among painters, Hishikawa Moronobu, Ogata Korin, and Hanabusa Itcho. The preponderance of talent in the theatre, however, resided in Osaka and Kyoto.

The history of the patronage of Japan's theatre was a continuous downward progression. The highest level of the country, the Imperial Court, sheltered *Bugaku* dances. The next layer, the aristocratic samurai, supported Noh dramas. And now, in Genroku, the people had their own Kabuki. For the first time in history, the commoners had sufficient wealth to sustain the luxury of an art and to produce their own popular dramas, on a rich and flourishing level. In Genroku there were four theatres in Edo, three in Kyoto, and at least four in Osaka. Of these one in Kyoto was the largest and measured over 16,000 square feet in size, about one-fourth of the size of the present-day Kabuki-Za in Tokyo. Hundreds of spectators witnessed Kabuki each day. The actors numbered altogether more than three hundred, and the staff of actors and musicians for each theatre averaged around seventy. In addition, there were the puppet theatres.

The exuberance of the common man in Genroku and the thriving growth of his entertainments conflicted with the government's desires. As can be imagined, the artistic expression of a people long oppressed by the samurai would by nature be antagonistic to the oppressors and would glorify their own cause. The very existence of Kabuki had been a worry to the government from the beginning, and with the rise of the commoners in Genroku and the social significance of the people's drama, these worries increased. But the government was powerless. The revered scholars of Chinese learning, Sorai Ogyu and Shundai Dadai, while condemning Kabuki for influencing social life in the wrong direction and corrupting morals, praised it along with the licensed brothels, as a political and economic advantage. Shundai in his famous treatise *On Economics,* wrote, "Amusements are a symbol of peace, and depression a symbol of decline. People who otherwise would commit crimes have a means of livelihood. Gold and silver coins circulate through the places of amusement; otherwise they would stagnate in the hands of the rich." The military was eager that those coins should not remain exclusively in the hands of the commoners.

The government maintained censorship and supervision over the theatres. It took every excuse to punish the theatre and theatrical folk. In 1711 when a scandalous love affair (later glorified in a Kabuki dance) between a court lady named Ejima and a handsome Kabuki actor called Ikushima reached the ears of the government, stringent action was taken. Theatres were forbidden to have roofs, screened boxes, or second and third balconies. Patrons were not allowed to see actors personally. The backstage became a forbidden area.

These limitations retarded the progress of the theatre-house in Japan, but scarcely affected the art of either Kabuki or the puppets. The people were irrepressible and the theatre continued to advance despite restrictions imposed on it by the government.

2.

Osaka (Kyoto) Theatre. The fundamental difference between the temperament of the military capital of Edo and the commercial centers of Osaka and Kyoto was clearly reflected by their respective theatres. These latter places were by far the more important area of theatrical activity. From there Japan's best plays and playwrights issued.

Of all the stars in Genroku's constellation of great men, unquestionably the brightest was the playwright Chikamatsu Monzaemon (1653-1725). His works burn with the glow of Genroku spirit and are the quintessence of the Osaka-Kyoto type of theatre. The Japanese are fond of referring to him as "Our own Shakespeare." Certainly he was the most graphic writer of plays in Japan's history and without question he has remained her greatest dramatist so far.

As with Shakespeare, our knowledge of the actual details of Chikamatsu's life is very sketchy. Historians have pieced together enough of his life to know with some degree of reliability that he had once served in a minor capacity in a samurai household, although his own origins were humble; that he had for a brief period of time been a Buddhist priest; and that he had given up writing plays for Kabuki in Kyoto in order to join the Takemoto-Za puppet theatre in Osaka.

It was a fortunate decision for him, in the middle of his life, to quit Kabuki altogether. He moved to Osaka in 1685 and devoted himself to composing for the puppets. He combined his talents with those of his friends, the puppeteer Tachimatsu Hachirobei, and the master-singer Takemoto Gidayu, founder of the Takemoto-Za.

The position of a playwright in the Kabuki world was a subservient one. Writers were treated as little more than property men. Those actors who wrote their own plays were congratulated on their acting in them rather than on the writing. During Genroku when the Kabuki actors became petted and spoiled by the adulation of the public, temperament and off-stage histrionics must have been more than Chikamatsu could bear. Actors frequently changed lines, ordered scenes written in, altered meanings, and ignored nuances of character delineation. Chikamatsu, while writing for Kabuki, was scarcely more than a tailor of words, at the mercy of difficult customers who wanted him to make them appear better than they were.

When Chikamatsu went to the puppet theatre in Osaka, he at last found the freedom his genius needed. He was the master, and the puppets had to follow to the letter what he wrote. He was also freed from the normal limitations of human acting. If he liked, he could give his imagination full play and disregard the possibilities of live actors. But he carried with him to the puppets one important quality from Kabuki. This was a sort of gentle humanity characteristic of the art of the leading actor of Kyoto, Sakata Tojuro (1647-1709). Sakata Tojuro had appeared in some of Chikamatsu's plays and had brought to them soft, warm, and responsive interpretations. Sakata Tojuro's taste in the theatre, like Chikamatsu's, was towards roles of courtesans, or of affectionate warriors—as the Japanese say, "thick and rich scenes of love and lovers' quarrels." Chikamatsu was greatly influenced by this actor, and in taking his style of performance to Osaka with him, infused the stiff and lifeless puppets with greater humanity and life than they had ever known before. Chikamatsu's plays and Sakata Tojuro's influence set a style which became characteristic of Osaka and Kyoto theatres alone.

Chikamatsu's familiarity from youth with the functioning of the house of samurai aided him in producing plays with insight into a variety of ways of life and experience ordinarily denied to a commoner. His learning as a priest gave him the advantage of both Japanese and Chinese scholarship. His long training at the hands of the actors with their demands for tailor-made dramas also developed a discipline and craftsmanship that served him well when his genius was released to write for the puppets. His enormous capacity for observing the world around him and for recording it expressively infused his plays with tremendous interest. Whatever animation the dolls may have lacked was amply supplied to the audience by the richness of Chikamatsu's libretti—particularly when helped by the power of Takemoto Gidayu's accompanying singing and dialogue, and Tachimatsu Hachirobei's skillful manipulation of the puppets in sensitive obedience to the words and music.

Chikamatsu's stories were usually written in the 7-5 syllabic meter (*shichi-go cho*), a rhythm in which lines of seven syllables are alternated with lines of five syllables. This meter may be compared in its popularity in Japanese theatre with that of dactylic hexameter in the ancient epic poetry of the West. Chikamatsu's language is always that of the people of the day, and is filled with subtleties of the dialect of the Osaka-Kyoto districts. It is rich in snatches from popular songs, a wide range of scholarship, detailed descriptions, and plays on words. Plays on words and puns have fallen out of favor in the West. But in

Japan, as in the Orient in general, the pun is one of the most interesting ways of handling words. The pun in Chikamatsu's plays is as familiar and pleasing as rhyme is in Western poetry. It adds meaning within meaning and varies the thought of a sentence subtly, quickly, and effectively. Chikamatsu usually used the pun with great seriousness and produced a moving and special flavor. The humorous uses of the pun are numerous. Often Chikamatsu employed them in the middle of a tragic moment, as a leavening turn of phrase to give momentary relief from the mounting tension of the drama. Many of the allusions and references now are too subtle for modern audiences, as scholarship in Genroku's time was different from today's.

Chikamatsu's plays speak with eloquent authority of Genroku. Their vivid descriptions tell more of the people's thoughts, desires, and innermost qualities than do the most carefully preserved documents of the day. Chikamatsu chose his characters from all walks of life. His heroes and heroines are smugglers, farmers, courtesans of the gay quarters, warriors, tradesmen, townsmen, and even emperors. True to his sympathy for the common man, he often makes him win out over his superior, a samurai. He makes him succeed in tasks of honor—contrary to the idea of the day that nobility and valor were the exclusive prerogatives of the warrior class.

In the same way that Chikamatsu ennobled the simple man, he at the same time reduced the great to their essential humanity. Emperors as subject matter, for example, had always been treated delicately in Noh dramas. Some scholars interpret this as an indication that even the shoguns, who seized control of the country and flouted the emperors, still regarded them as holy and apart. Such was, however, not the case with Chikamatsu. Long before the rescript of abdication of divinity was urged by the Occupation forces in Japan, Chikamatsu had already considered the Emperor as human. In all thirty-three of the plays of Chikamatsu in which an Emperor appears either as a major or minor character, he is always depicted as a nor-

BUNRAKU KUMAGAI DOLL HEAD

mal, suffering man. Like everyone else of the period, the Emperor too
had had a share of hardship.

In all, Chikamatsu wrote around a hundred works for the Takemoto-Za. The bulk were historical pieces (*jidai-mono*) dealing with
heroes and heroines of history. They were not, however, his best or
most popular plays. Among his greatest, and those still in the repertoire of Kabuki troupes today, are his domestic plays (*sewa-mono*)
concerned with happenings and persons in ordinary daily life. Here
Chikamatsu's perspicacity and ability to hold a mirror up to life, display themselves to fullest advantage.

Chikamatsu was the first playwright of Japan to transfer actual
events of the day to the theatre. He made the theatre a kind of living
newspaper at the service of the illiterate populace. The domestic plays
are a lively portrayal of Japan in the Genroku Era with its problems,
pleasures and gossip. For example, there was the problem of smuggling which continued despite the severe punishments for the crime.
In 1718 five law breakers were caught smuggling tiger skins and
medicinal carrots from Korea. After having their noses cut off as
punishment, they were banished from Osaka and fled to the island of
Kyushu in southern Japan. In the same year, a beautiful courtesan in
Hakata, Kyushu, drowned herself after her lover had been executed
for smuggling. Before the year was out, Chikamatsu combined these
two events on the stage in a masterpiece called, *Kojoro the Courtesan
of Hakata and Her Pillow of Waves* (*Hakata Kojoro Nami Ma-
kura*), more commonly called, simply, *Kezori,* after the name of the
leading character, a heavily bearded smuggler.

Chikamatsu's version of the events is as follows:

Soshichi, a young and handsome merchant from Kyoto, boards a pri-
vately-owned ship sailing for Hakata, Kyushu. The bearded ship owner
is named Kezori Kuemon. One day at sea they discover that they are
both in love with the same courtesan, Kojoro, in Hakata. While the boat
is anchored off the coast, Soshichi accidentally discovers Kezori and his

crew engaged in smuggling. The men throw him overboard so that he cannot betray their secret. Soshichi is, however, miraculously saved from drowning.

When Soshichi finally arrives at Hakata, he finds Kojoro, the courtesan, with Kezori. Kezori generously accedes to Kojoro's preference for Soshichi. He offers Soshichi enough money to redeem Kojoro from the gay quarters on condition that he join him in his smuggling. Out of love for Kojoro, Soshichi consents.

Soshichi's father hears that his son is a smuggler and disinherits him. Soshichi sets out to make amends with his father, but is captured by the police. He commits suicide and Kojoro weeps over his body.

The staging of the first act of *Kezori* is a high example in Japanese stagecraft and must be described in some detail. The entire stage is filled with a full-size replica of a wooden junk. The bow and stern almost extend into the wings. The backdrop behind the deep stage is a dark blue curtain on which a full moon slowly rises during the progress of the act. The floor of the stage and the *hanamichi* passageway are covered with billowing cloth painted blue and white to look like waves and ripples. The smugglers pass their goods from the deck of the junk to a waiting rowboat at the side of the ship. Soshichi puts his head out of the cabin window midway down the side of the junk, and Kezori sees him from his vantage point above on deck. The smugglers throw Soshichi overboard at the stern of the ship. The audience only sees him flung from the junk. Kezori, in order to make sure that Soshichi has drowned, peers over the side of the ship into the sea. When Kezori goes to the bow, the junk slowly revolves on the stage. When the bow projects directly out into the audience, he makes a stylized gesture and pose indicating that he is certain Soshichi has drowned. Kezori and his smugglers go below. Soshichi suddenly appears struggling and swimming out of the waves on the *hanamichi*. A rowboat appears and the exhausted Soshichi is hauled aboard. The boat is rowed along the passageway and disappears into the dressing room at the back of the theatre.

Chikamatsu tried his hand at telling the story of the forty-seven *ronin*, whose famous revenge story, now familiar under the title of *Chushingura*, took place in 1701. But the authorities were sensitive about the rights and wrongs of the event and the play was suppressed. The expectation of probable censorship of the play apparently hampered Chikamatsu, because his version was not a good play and has never been performed since.

All the sensational events of the peaceful days of commercial Osaka found their way in some form or other to Chikamatsu's pen. Among his domestic plays the most frequent theme is that of lovers who commit suicide together. This type of play is referred to as *shinju-mono,* or plays ending with a lovers' double suicide. Whenever such events occurred in real life, Chikamatsu quickly adapted them to the stage. As a result, it was said at the time that these suicides became a fashion and greatly increased in number. But these in turn only provided more theatrical material for Chikamatsu.

One of the most famous of these suicides immortalized by Chikamatsu in his *The Courier on Love's Path to Hell (Meido no Hikyaku)*, is the story of Umegawa and her lover Chubei. The play was written in 1706 and is familiarly referred to as *Ume-Chu,* from the first letters of the two lovers' names.

The story briefly is as follows:

Chubei, a money carrier for an express agency in Osaka, is betrothed in accordance with his parent's wishes. He has continued, however, to frequent the gay quarters in order to be with his beloved courtesan, Umegawa. Hachiemon, a wealthy merchant, is also in love with Umegawa. He arranges to buy Umegawa from her bondage. One day Chubei, while on an errand to deliver some money, stops by to see Umegawa. He learns of Hachiemon's plan to buy her.

Chubei is taunted by Hachiemon. In his desperation he is driven to break the seal of the official funds he is carrying. This of course is a grave offense. He opens the bag of money and ransoms Umegawa.

The two lovers then set out for Chubei's birthplace. He wishes to see his aged farmer-father for the last time. En route, while Chubei is away, making arrangements at the local inn, Umegawa sees an old man in some distress. She assists and comforts him, and in the course of conversation discovers he is Chubei's father. She does not let him know that she is Chubei's wife or of the tragic events surrounding their lives. Chubei enters and the father and son embrace. The police arrive. Umegawa and Chubei flee to commit suicide together.

Chikamatsu's lovers are always faced with a problem surmountable only by death. The lover is in some way forced to violate the law for the sake of his sweetheart, and rather than face punishment and the consequent separation, they die together. In some of the plays, a commoner loves a girl above him in station, and they cannot gain permission to marry; or the lover is unable to ransom his courtesan from the gay quarters and is driven to theft. As a result, inevitably the lovers vow to die together. Although to us double suicide may seem a convention of Chikamatsu's writing, to the people of Genroku it represented a real and actual occurrence. The causes and occurrence of each suicide were similar but the details, the people, and the circumstances were different and subject to a wide variety of treatment.

In another of the famous suicide plays, *The Double Suicide at Sonezaki* (*Sonezaki Shinju*), the story is handled as follows:

Tokubei, an apprentice clerk in an oil seller's shop, exchanges vows of love with O-Hatsu, a courtesan. In spite of this, his employer (who is also his uncle), Hiranoya, arranges a marriage between Tokubei and his wife's niece who has a large dowry. Hiranoya's avaricious wife privately settles the marriage endowment and takes the dowry in advance. Tokubei later manages with great difficulty to extract the dowry money from his aunt and intends to return it and end the question of the distasteful marriage.

On his way to return the dowry, Tokubei is accosted by his friend, Kaheiji, who asks to borrow the money. His friend is so insistent that Tokubei cannot refuse. Later, however, Kaheiji fails to return the money as he has promised, and pretending ignorance of the whole matter, publicly denounces the honest Tokubei. Tokubei is discredited.

His uncle demands a repayment of Tokubei's indebtedness as an apprentice. The only way he can repay his uncle is by going through with the arranged match—a situation he tried to avoid in the first place. Rather than do this, he and his beloved courtesan O-Hatsu hasten to Sonezaki forest and commit suicide there together.

The social attitude of Genroku is reflected in Chikamatsu's plays, particularly in these suicide pieces. The characters are tormented by pressures of society. In all his dramas, love or passion is the motivating force, gold is the direct cause, but it is always the social structure which is the element that drives the characters to their doom.

In *The Double Suicide at Sonezaki,* outlined above, this is clearly illustrated. At one point the uncle says to Tokubei:

"Since you love O-Hatsu you won't marry your aunt's niece. Very well! I won't compel you. So instead I must ask you please to pay your debt to me by the 7th of April. Settle your balance with me or I will drive you away from Osaka forever."

Accordingly, Tokubei complains to O-Hatsu:

"If I am driven from Osaka, I will have no opportunity to meet you. Even though my bones be crushed and thrown into the river, I will not part company with you" [and he weeps].

Not only has Tokubei no will to live nor ideas on how to overcome the difficult situation, but he bends immediately to the pressure of society and cannot stand against it.

Again, at the time that Tokubei is fraudulently accused by Kaheiji, Tokubei does not try to prove his innocence. He is shamed by the incident. He feels guilty and the pressures of society force him to decide to commit suicide with his lover.

Another example of this sort of succumbing to external forces appears in the latter part of the *Woman's Suicide of Nagamachi (Nagamachi Onna Harakiri).* Jingoro is in difficulty over his lover's theft of a sword. When thinking about fleeing the city with his lover, he complains to himself:

[67]

"If the neighbors report that I have left town without official permission, my position among the townsmen would become unbearable."

Due to the power of the social unit, so fantastic a reason constitutes a motive for suicide.

In the main act of *The Double Suicide at Ikudama* (*Ikudama Shinju*), the story of which is virtually the same as *The Double Suicide at Sonezaki,* a similar attitude of subservience is shown. Saga, a courtesan, elopes with Kaheiji, a chinaware shopkeeper. On the way she says to her lover:

"If we are caught and punished, perhaps people will blame you, saying that you, Kaheiji of Osaka, hesitating to commit suicide, lived in misery while owing a heavy debt to the brothel. As my sister has said, it would be a disgrace to your family. So we should decide to die together at once."

Thus people were not only keenly alive to criticism from neighbors, but the pressure of society was such that if a debt could not be settled, persons were not allowed to live.

Later in this play, Saga finds that Kaheiji's father is trying to compel her lover to marry another woman. She deplores the idea of giving up Kaheiji, but she admits the financial and moral reasonableness of the father's wanting his son to marry well. She accedes mournfully, saying, "Our decision to die together was made only too late."

Kaheiji is finally given some money by his father and he is delighted to see the end of his troubles. But Chosaku, a rascal, arrives on the scene and forcibly takes the money which Kaheiji deserves "in the name of God and Master." Kaheiji cries that he will arrest the villain and starts to pursue Chosaku. But the servants of his landlord appear at the door saying "Kaheiji, you are too impolite.* You have just now returned after a long absence, and yet you dare to commit violence. We will give our sentence tomorrow. Until then you will be confined." They shut him inside and surround the house with sticks in their hands. "We will watch you until sunrise." Kaheiji asks them to listen to his story and tries to escape, but

* This may sound weak in English, but it has tremendous impact on a Japanese audience even today. Manners have remained a supreme factor in Japanese life.

all in vain. In Genroku, the public was adamant and ruthless in subordinating individual freedom to the power of the group as a whole. It was small wonder that the lovers could not live in opposition to the pressures of society. Finally Kaheiji and Saga manage to commit suicide at the shrine of Ikudama.

In one of Chikamatsu's last plays, *The Woman's Murder and The Hell of Oil* (*Onna Goroshi Abura Jigoku*), these pressures are again clearly stated. O-Sawa wants to force her son Yohei to start a new life and to give up his dissolute ways. She terminates his family ties forever, and says:

"Oh dear Yohei, you are mean; teaching you with words is like asking a stone to answer a riddle. Get out! Get out! If you won't move, I will gather the townsfolk and drive you away."

Then Yohei who is a "reckless fellow without fear," is horror-stricken. Even he, a rascal, is terrified by the words "gather the townsfolk and drive you away."

Later in the same play, Yohei is asked to pay a debt. If he fails to pay within the day, the matter will be made public to the townsfolk. So he feels compelled to raise the money. He tries to borrow from O-Yoshi, a woman who has once befriended him. He explains how he has been cheated:

"The amount on the promissory note is a pound of silver coins. Actually I borrowed only a few ounces. I am obliged to pay the amount shown on the note. If I can't pay, it will be made public not only to my parents and brothers, but also to the five elders of both towns. I can't raise the money by any means. And now I have decided to commit suicide."

O-Yoshi rejects his request. Yohei murders her and takes the money.

Chikamatsu faces a difficult task in dealing so frequently with the fairly rigid formula he created for himself in the lovers' double suicides. His difficulties as a writer about the human beings of his day and age were further increased by the peculiar makeup of Genroku society where the social structure imposed specific types of behaviour

[69]

on the people. But it is precisely through these restrictive conventions that his genius comes out. His characters are always deeply human and moving; and although to the Westerner they may seem motivated by almost inhuman reasons, their personalities are alive, real, and pathetic. For this reason, the names of Chikamatsu's characters are still in the hearts of the people of Japan, even in the provinces where they are known only as stories, and where the people have never actually seen the plays on the stage.

Nowhere does Chikamatsu create more moving characters than in his *Bridge to Heaven by the Suicide at Amijima* (*Shinju Ten no Amijima*); more commonly called simply *Kamiji,* after Jihei the paper merchant and hero of the play. In *Kamiji* all of the characters are tormented by their own natures and the impossibility of reaching satisfaction.

Jihei is deeply fond of his two children and greatly respects his wife, O-San. But he falls passionately in love with Koharu, a courtesan. Their love is so profound, and the situation so fraught with inner conflicts, they resolve to die together.

Jihei's wife, O-San, goes to Koharu and asks her to give Jihei up for the sake of his family life. Koharu consents. In order to terminate the relationship, she pretends to have an affair with Jihei's older brother. Jihei tries to kill her but the brother prevents him. Jihei returns home brokenhearted.

O-San, the wife, realizes, on thinking it over, that Koharu's real intention is to commit suicide. She then decides that Jihei and Koharu should be together, since in separation their lives are crushed. O-San pawns her wedding clothes in order to procure the money to buy Koharu from her debt at the brothel. But O-San's father, meeting her on the way to the gay quarters, forces her to return home with him and frustrates her attempt to help Koharu.

To make matters worse, Jihei gets involved in a fight with a samurai villain and kills him.

That night, Jihei and Koharu flee to Amijima where the tragic double suicide is reluctantly carried out.

[70]

BUGAKU, THE CLASSICAL COURT DANCE

In all the domestic plays of Chikamatsu, the pressure of society revolves around a matter of money and is connected with love. The individual is inexorably forced to his death. The characters of Chikamatsu's plays and of many other Japanese dramas are motivated by inner urges of the individual; but outside pressures in the end are always stronger. The individual is a victim of circumstance, and not completely responsible for his own tragedy.

This attitude of mind is actually not too remote from that of the present-day Japanese. Their obedience to the pressures of society makes them fight a war fanatically and immediately after to obey the Occupation implicitly. One finds this quality in a wide range of circumstances, from mothers who quiet and control their children by saying, "People will laugh at you," to prime ministers who threaten the nation with phrases such as "The eyes of the world are upon Japan." The famous phrase "to lose face" means in essence the bending of the individual to the pressure of society.

This succumbing to outside influence, this lack of self-determination, may make Japanese drama seem empty to the Westerner who does not recognize these qualities within his own society. The characters are, in one way, like automata responding to arbitrary orders issued by society. But a dramatist's final aim can scarcely be more than to depict life as he sees it, and to record nature as he understands it. Life was like these plays in Chikamatsu's time. As an artist of Genroku, Chikamatsu has no superior.

In the recurrent theme of the double suicides and the pressures of society on the individual in Chikamatsu's plays, a dramatic formula was created which was to influence the Japanese theatre for centuries. This formula is sometimes described by the phrase, "the obligation-versus-humanity conflict" (*giri-ninjo*). In these conflicts the hero is torn between his sense of duty and the dictates of his heart. Sometimes one, sometimes the other wins out; but the result is usually death either way. There is rarely a reward for him.

Criticism has been leveled at the Japanese theatre (as literature) for its seemingly repetitious use of plot situations reducible to the obliga-tion-versus-humanity conflict. Certainly Chikamatsu and many sub-sequent playwrights depended heavily on this facile convention. However, important as such plays were and characteristic as they are of certain aspects of Japan's theatre at large, they do not by any means comprise all the repertoire of Kabuki and the puppet theatre. There existed in Japan even in Chikamatsu's time, comedies, farces, dances, and, most numerous of all, classical plays—the form of drama known as the "revenge plays." None of these is concerned with the theme of obligation versus humanity.

Revenge plays together with the obligation-versus-humanity plays undoubtedly dominate the theatrical scene of Japan. The reason for this is that they both, like all classical dramas of the world, deal fundamentally with the question of right and wrong. In them right must triumph over wrong. But the problem of each is quite different.

Revenge plays are the simplest and most elementary form of pre-senting right and wrong. They are based on man's instinct—the only primitive one containing the possibility of complete drama—to pro-tect loved ones, and by extension, to repay harm done to them. The bad is clearly the harm-doer; the good is that which destroys the bad. The course of action is obvious. The plot progresses by the efforts of the good to wipe out the evil.

Plays of the obligation-versus-humanity category are more compli-cated and advanced than the revenge plays. The opposing poles of good and evil are intangibles. Obligation is the element which the group, religion, or the state has arbitrarily designated as the path to be followed—in short, the pressure of society in some form. The op-posing element to this is man's inherent humanitarianism which either resists the obligation or suffers by complying with it. The con-flict lies in whether or not to conform to social requirements when they run counter to human feeling. What the individual wants or does is always in conflict with what he should want or ought to do. The plots of these plays progress through the devious ways the values of good and evil affect and determine the action of the individual. Here an emotional and mental conflict is placed within a single individual, and becomes the focal point of the dramatic situation. In revenge plays the interest is in the action of one man against another in the cause of clear-cut righteousness and in order to mete out justice.

The formula of obligation-versus-humanity, as it is employed in complex drama such as Kabuki and the puppet theatre, is far from a simple convention. The basic opposites are subjected to numerous variations of treatment. Their conflict falls into about five main types of treatment: 1) duty is made to symbolize the bad and humanity the good; 2) humanity is the bad, duty is the good; 3) the evil of refusing to carry out one's obligation is justified by the higher good of humanity and righteousness; 4) the audience is deceived about which course of action has been taken, i.e., whether the hero has performed the duty or followed his heart; 5) action is compelled by outside causes, and the characters are helpless victims of the forces of good and evil, with no direct responsibility for their fates.

Vulnerable as the plots of Japan's classical theatres may be on the grounds of logic and orderliness and repetitious as they often are—and there are reasons for all these as we shall see later—there is considerably more substance to them than the obligation-versus-humanity formula implies. The struggle or compliance of human nature with its obligation to God, cause, kindred, or society, is in any event not only the kernel of the work of Chikamatsu Monzaemon and the other playwrights of Japan, but pretty much of life itself.

3.

Edo Kabuki. Chikamatsu, writing for the puppets, and Sakata Tojuro, acting his gentle roles for Kabuki, dominated the theatres of Osaka and Kyoto. Edo (Tokyo), however, was simultaneously developing its own special type of theatre. There was a constant interchange of actors and plays between Edo and Osaka especially by means of guest appearances and road companies, but the cultures of the two places were dissimilar. Osaka was typified by its stories of love and "dramas of gold." But the townsmen of the military center of Edo craved another kind of satisfaction in their theatre. Their chief delight lay in the plays and acting of Ichikawa Danjuro the First (1660-1717), a dominant and determining genius both as playwright and actor of pure Kabuki. His name even today ranks highest in the hierarchy of traditional actors' names.

Ichikawa Danjuro appealed to the taste of his audience. He gave full play to violence and fantasy. His plays concerned martial arts. His heroes were superhuman characters who lopped off the heads of many opponents at a blow, who lifted houses with one finger, and who crushed temple gates with bare hands. No feat of bravery or strength was too great for Danjuro or the stagecraft of the day. His themes were woven around the heroes of legend, history, and the era in which he lived. The lives of simple folk did not concern him in the least.

Danjuro, like most of the people of Edo, was immensely drawn to the superman puppets of *kimpira joruri*. He incorporated into his plays their tales of the heroic exploits of the mythical figure of Kimpira and copied certain aspects of the wild acting style of these puppets. In doing so he created a new kind of acting in Kabuki which became known as "rough-house" (*aragoto*). The word arose to show the contrast with the "tear-jerkers" (*nuregoto*) of Osaka.

The difference between Osaka and Tokyo Kabuki is still a marked one. An Osaka actor today would be criticized were he to attempt to perform one of Danjuro's *aragoto* type of plays. Osaka actors resent Tokyo actors' performing Chikamatsu's domestic plays, or for that matter, any play borrowed by Kabuki from the dolls. They consider such plays their special field. However, Tokyo actors continue to perform a large part of the Osaka repertoire, which is fortunate as Osaka Kabuki is in a dangerous state of deterioration. It has verged on complete collapse since the death of Nakamura Baigyoku in 1948 and the prolonged illness of Nakamura Enjaku, the two greatest actors of Osaka in our generation.

Aragoto was and still is today a peculiar and typical expression of Genroku culture. As a theatrical device it is wonderfully effective, and constitutes one of the chief flavors of Kabuki acting. It is both a type of play and a style of acting unique in the world's theatre history.

Aragoto is a theatrical exaggeration characterized by its three indispensable aspects: 1) bombastic words, often of no meaning; 2) elaborate and far-fetched make-up; 3) expansive gestures and motions.

Typical of *aragoto* are words like *tsu-ga-mo-ne* and *i-ya-sa*. In themselves they have neither meaning nor sense. They are merely expletives which the actor shouts in a long drawn-out shriek at decisive or important moments of the play. In effect, they are vocal displays of power, might, or rage.

Expletives of this sort also appear in phrases. One such phrase is *Yattoko totcha untoku na.* Like the shorter words, this is also meaningless. The phrase originally derived from a laborer's lifting chant in Eastern Japan. It is used in *aragoto* to indicate a tremendous exertion of strength. Whenever an action is supposed to require a mighty effort, the actor cries out at the top of his voice *Yattoko totcha,* and as he completes the action he continues: *untoko na.* The phrase is used to give grandiloquent majesty to the hero's movement even when he executes such simple actions as lying down, sitting, or walking off the stage in an exit. However, no action of an *aragoto* character can be simple; all his movements are tremendous and sweeping.

Make-up for *aragoto* plays is peculiar and has a special name, *kumadori.* The actor draws thick streaks of red, black, brown, or indigo lines on his face. The formulae for applying the various make-ups, each of which is reserved for the particular character it is associated with, are traditionally handed down from generation to generation by actor to son or disciple. It is a custom for the actor after a performance, to press a cloth over his face, remove it when the paint is clearly transferred to the cloth, autograph it, and give it to his favorite patron as a souvenir.

The various make-ups have meanings. A red line drawn under the eyes and extending to the temples indicates beauty and bravery. If a parallel red line, from the top of the eyebrows to the roots of the hair, is added, it means fierce bravery, or the inflamed intensity of a strong man driven to action. Indigo lines or admixtures of black and red lines under the eyes and on the cheeks shows wickedness or double-heartedness. In certain roles, the entire body is painted with circular thick red lines, vaguely following the outline of the muscles. Nowadays, to save time and trouble, actors, instead of painting their bodies, wear tights and flesh-colored cloth on which these lines have already been drawn. To add to the fierceness of their appearance, the skin-like coverings are stuffed with cotton to make the actor look larger.

Probably these *aragoto* make-ups originally came from China. But the Chinese cover the entire face and obliterate the bony and muscular structure. Japanese make-ups always follow the facial outline. It is popularly thought that Danjuro created the make-ups after looking at the red streaks at the heart of a white peony flower, and there is a well-known poem to this effect.

The purpose of this kind of make-up is to show the blood vessels of the face distended by anger or intense excitement. These make-ups since Danjuro's time have become more and more stylized and elaborate. They are now also used for ghosts and demons, not necessarily connected with *aragoto* plays, in order to increase the awe of their countenances.

The third of *aragoto's* characteristics, the expansive gesturing, is derived from one of Danjuro's main contributions to Edo Kabuki—his adaptation of "chivalrous commoners" from Genroku life to the stage. During Genroku there rose a special type of man known as a "chivalrous commoner" (*otokodate* or *kyokaku*). They were men from ordinary walks of life but who were excessively masculine, beautiful, brave, and amorous. They were a little like Robin Hood in that they protected the weak. They always stood up against the warriors, and excelled them in their own games of swordsmanship and fearlessness. To the people they represented a form of extra-legal protection for their rights. They were in fact a safeguard and means of redress against samurai and their abusiveness.

Particularly in Edo, a city swarming with warriors, the public's admiration for these "chivalrous commoners" was unbounded. They were the most heroic figures of the day, and their outlandish affectations were among the most exciting aspects of Genroku life. They used a particular strutting gait when they walked through the streets. Their air and manner was that of a permanent challenge to any oncomer. Their mannerisms were eminently suitable for *aragoto's* pompous exaggerations.

Danjuro in his plays adapted their insolent parading and their swinging arms into dance-like gestures. The result was *roppo*. *Roppo* is the quintessence of *aragoto* movement. The word literally means "six directions," i.e., North, East, South, West, Heaven (up) and Earth (down). It implies that within any given movement in *roppo* style, these six directions are contained. The result of the expansive gesticulation is that, to the spectator, the actor appears like a giant moving in all directions at once. While making an entry or exit in *aragoto* plays, *roppo* is always used.

As curious as the *roppo* mannerisms appear to us today, they are not, as one might think, entirely a relic of the past, preserved by the stage. Two elements in contemporary Japan still affect this kind of brazen extraversion in typical *roppo* spirit. One is a body of hoodlum students in the cheaper universities and the other a group of district bosses (*oyabun*) in certain of the slum areas of Tokyo. They affect the same boastful spirit of the "chivalrous commoners" in Genroku, and are quickly recognized by their walk and peculiar gesticulation. The democratic spirit of "commoner protecting fellow-commoner" has rather changed into that of "rowdy showing off," but still it is difficult not to admire the undercurrent of both pride and revolt in these modern not-so-chivalrous commoners.

Danjuro is known to have written altogether around one hundred and fifty plays. However, the actual texts of only fifteen are known today. One of these, *Kagemasa's Interpellation of the Thunder (Kagemasa Ikazuchi Mondo)*, written in 1700, is of particular importance. It is typical of Genroku thought and feeling, and full of Danjuro's flair for the fantastic. The play is not performed today, but it is the genesis of the famous *Wait a Moment (Shibaraku)*, one of the most popular and characteristic plays of Edo Kabuki still surviving.

Synopsis of the play:

Act I

Secret Arms for the Felicitous Day

Minamoto-no-*Yoriyoshi*, the Shogun and military ruler of the land, has three sons: Hachiman-Taro-*Yoshiie;* Kamo-no-Jiro-*Yoshitsune;* and Shinra-Saburo-*Yoshimitsu*. On New Year's Day at a certain shrine, Yoriyoshi gives a banquet to celebrate the coming of age of his second son, Yoshitsune.

Fujiwara-no-*Munehira*, once Yoriyoshi's enemy but now one of his chief vassals, in honor of the occasion presents the son, Yoshitsune, with a set of armor. To test the hardness of the armor, the warriors stab at it with knives and shoot arrows at it. The armor is unscratched.

Kamakura-no-Gongoro-*Kagemasa*, the hero of the play and the role performed by Danjuro I, appears with a chest of arms to offer to the son.

Yoriyoshi calls out, "How good of you to bring a chest of arms as a token of your good wishes for my son. The letters on the chest read, 'Secret Arms for the Felicitous Day.' Open the chest at once!"

On opening it the assembly finds only a merchant's ledgerbook (*daifukucho*) and an abacus board, the Japanese counting machine. The lord and his followers cry in unison, "Behold a ledgerbook instead of arms."

Munehira steps forward, saying, "Kagemasa, you must be drunk. Are you serious? How can an abacus board and a ledgerbook serve as a helmet and armor? Your joke has gone too far! Now be off! How ridiculous!"

Kagemasa smiles, "Munehira, however clever you may be, yet you are lacking. I have offered the 'Secret Arms for the Felicitous Day' to be deposited as a family treasure for our lord. You ridicule me instead of applauding my action. The arms *you* brought are indispensable for a soldier who guards a barrier, but *my* gift is armor worthy of a general."

Munehira: "How can you call a ledgerbook the greatest arms of all Japan? Tell me the reason!"

Kagemasa: "Don't interrupt. Now hear me out! The word Dai-fuku-cho (ledgerbook) is divided into three parts, namely: the emperor; the subjects; and the land. (N. B. The following is a rather forced interpretation. Dai-fuku-cho is an ordinary word, literally written "great-lucky-book." Its ordinary interpretation would merely imply happiness at a full and thick ledger; a symbol of thriving business.)

"*Dai* is nothing but a general term for heaven and earth. It is written by combining 'one' and 'man.' *Fuku* is happiness and its left part means 'to indicate.' This signifies that the grace of one man is shown over the people. The body of the letter is an area of a rice field. According to ancient books, the subjects are the children of the land and the legs of the country. Truly the August Virtue of His Majesty is so vast and boundless as to swallow up China and India, to say nothing of this Abundant Reed-Plain Land (N.B. A classical term for the mainland of Japan) at one gulp. Lastly *Cho* signifies eternity. From the one emperor in the highest to the common people in the lowest, those who stand at the head of others are called 'chiefs,' the right hand part of the letter. The left part of this letter is 'breadth.' This means when the people are well-fed, they are content, the reign is peaceful, and the country is enriched. In governing people, first comes administration by civilians, and in turbulent days, military rule takes its place only in order to defeat the enemy. This is an eternal truth throughout all countries and all ages. On careful consideration, it is known that it should be forbidden to assume military power except in wartime. You know how peacefully Chinese warriors and statesmen, such as Ryoho, Shibo, Goshi, Sonshi, Taiso, Risei, and Onko governed their people! An old poem tells us that the people are the wall and the castle; kindness is our friend, and hate our foe. As there is a will, so there are ways; and if our mind is wrongly displayed, we will behave outrageously. In Buddhism the three treasures are Buddha, Tenet, and Priest. In Bushido, Wisdom,

[79]

Benevolence, and Valor are honored. And so it is with the people who have three treasures of their own. They must pay special attention to the shelf for the family gods, to the fire of the oven which is the sign of the prosperity of the country, and to the Merchant's Ledgerbook. This is the mystery of the three letters of *Dai-Fuku-Cho!* This is the opening ceremony of the chest of armor! Happy New Year of the Dragon! Is it not correct that I have offered the chest of 'Secret Arms for the Felicitous Day'?"

Kiyohara-no-*Takehira,* the Emperor's personal envoy to the Shogun, chances to appear. He glances at the arms box and learns that the assembly is celebrating Yoshitsune's coming of age. Takehira offers as his gift a treasured sword. Kagemasa stops him saying that a sword is unnecessary to the Minamotos since they already have "secret arms." Outraged, Takehira denounces Kagemasa as a traitor and tries to kill him with the sword. Kagemasa grasps it and breaks it in two. Munehira, who had presented the armor at the beginning of the play, intercedes and stops the quarrel. After this the entire company leaves.

Later, Yoshiie, the eldest son arrives on the scene which has taken place before a shrine, and flirts with a woman of a nearby tea-house. Onoe, Yoshiie's sweetheart, breaks in upon the scene and reproaches him for his unfaithfulness. Yoshiie apologizes. The girl of the tea-house turns out to be the half-sister of Kagemasa, Oshu. She is desirous of meeting her half-brother, and flirted with Yoshiie as a pretext, so he could arrange the meeting. Yoshiie promises to introduce Oshu to Kagemasa, as he will soon be returning to the shrine.

Towards evening, Yoshiie's two retainers, Sakata *Ichimaru* and Watanabe-No-*Azuma-no-suke,* arrive to meet their lord. They happen to stop before the two wooden guardian statues of the God's Gate. They playfully splash water on the statues which to their amazement complain, "How cold!" They throw a sandal at one statue which then exclaims, "It hurts!" Sakata and Watanabe are about to shoot the statues when they reveal themselves to be Takehira (the Imperial envoy) and Munehira (who had presented the armor). These two had disguised themselves as statues, lying in wait to kill Kagemasa. Takehira and Munehira fight against Ichimaru and Azuma-no-suke, the retainers.

In the midst of the fighting a superman appears and fells Takehira and

Munehira. He announces, "I am Bishamon (Vaisravana) from Mount Kurama and have come to arrest these two guardian statues." Bishamon takes off his helmet and reveals himself as Kagemasa. When he is about to kill Takehira and Munehira, Yoshiie and Oshu appear and stop him. Kagemasa forces the two villains to carry Yoshiie's trappings as lowly footmen.

Act II

In accordance with Munehira's advice, Yoriyoshi, the Shogun, takes his third son, Yoshimitsu, to Tetsuryuji Temple. He wants to force him to enter the priesthood so that he can pray for the repose of the departed souls of persons he, the father, has killed in battle. Yoshimitsu opposes his father. Yoriyoshi is angry with him for his disobedience.

Usui-No-*Ikkaku*, Yoriyoshi's follower, brings him two picture puzzles which he has found in front of the temple. One picture is an image of Yoriyoshi with a sword in his mouth and the other is an image of Munehira drinking water out of his hands at the top of a waterfall.

The high priest of the temple interprets the meaning by saying that the first picture signifies that Yoriyoshi will rule the world and the second that Munehira is of great loyalty in his service to Yoriyoshi.

Ikkaku opposes the priest, expressing his opinion that Yoriyoshi will not rule the world as the Minamoto clan can easily be overwhelmed and that the second picture denotes a conspiracy on the part of Munehira, because the waterfall signifies the "source of water," literally "Minamoto," and he is shown drinking from it.

The priest states that the pictures were brought by Miura-No-*Tamemune*. Munehira points out that Tamemune is a brother-in-law of Takehira, who rose in revolt against Yoriyoshi.

Tamemune appears on the scene and offers Yoriyoshi a sacred tree. Instead of appreciating his kindness, Yoriyoshi orders Tamemune to interpret the picture puzzles. Tamemune calls Munehira a traitor and the two begin to quarrel. Yoriyoshi concludes that Tamemune had arranged the picture puzzles. Yoriyoshi and Munehira retire. Yoshimitsu appears and sympathizes with Tamemune.

Munehira reappears and says that it is the will of the lord that Tamemune kill himself by harakiri. Tamemune devises a trick. He makes his servant shake the sacred tree and hiding behind it, he pretends to be the god of heaven. Munehira runs away in fright.

Tamemune returns home and tells his wife, Shikitae, that he has incurred the displeasure of his lord. The couple prepare to start on a journey.

Act III

A year has passed. Kagemasa and Tamemune are making a trip throughout the country. In the gay quarters of Kyoto, Kagemasa is accosted by a courtesan. She is Oshu and introduces herself as Kagemasa's younger sister. She presses him to ransom her. Kagemasa asks Tamemune to help him. He recounts how his father, Kagemitsu, had had an affair with a courtesan at the battle-field of Akita and Oshu is their child.

That night Kagemasa and Tamemune go to visit Kagehisa, Kagemasa's younger brother. Unaware of his relation to Oshu, Kagehisa has been her lover. At the moment of Kagemasa's arrival, the younger brother is about to kill Oshu because he believes her unfaithful and inconstant. Kagemasa prevents the murder and explains the story of how they are brother and sister. Kagemasa disowns him for this incest. Ashamed of their unlawful love, Kagehisa retires to a monastery and Oshu commits suicide.

Act IV

Kagemasa and Tamemune continue their journey. Onoe, Yoshiie's sweetheart, and Shikitae, Tamemune's wife, join them. They take a night's lodging at a wayside shrine where they all dream the same strange story.

In the dream, Kagemasa makes illicit advances to Shikitae who runs to her husband for safety. Tamemune reviles Kagemasa for his immorality. Kagemasa kills Shikitae out of spite. Kagehisa, Kagemasa's disowned brother, appears disguised as a traveling monk and separates Kagemasa and Tamemune. Having killed Shikitae, Kagemasa commits suicide. Tamemune and Kagehisa die, stabbing each other with their swords.

The four awake from sleep and wonder at the bad dream.

The younger brother Kagehisa appears, Kagemasa forgives him, and the breach between them is mended.

Munehira and his men arrive to arrest Kagemasa and Tamemune.

Yoshitsune, Yoriyoshi's second son, comes on the scene to fight against Munehira. Kagemasa and Tamemune join Yoshitsune and finally kill the wicked Munehira.

Act V

Yoshimitsu, Yoriyoshi's third son, and Ikkaku his follower, disguised as traveling priests, knock at the door of a hermitage where Kagehisa has devoted his life to prayers for Oshu. The door is opened by Oshu and she leads them to Kagehisa. Kagehisa questions them as to who led them to his cell. They answer that it was Oshu. Kagehisa tells them of the death of Oshu. Kagehisa throws a written pledge which he exchanged with Oshu into the fireplace and out of the smoke the image of Oshu appears. She tells them that she is an incarnation of Samantabhadra and had assumed the form of Oshu.

Many unusual occurrences take place within the Imperial Palace. A tremendous clap of thunder rends heaven and earth. Takehira, Kagemasa's old enemy, shoots an arrow at the thunder. Kaisan, a high priest, exorcises in vain. Kagemasa looks up at the sky and discovering Munehira's ghost in the air, challenges him to a fight. Kagemasa orders his brother, Kagehisa, to kill Takehira. Kagemasa kills the ghost of Munehira.

Yoriyoshi transfers the headship of the Minamoto family to Yoshiie, his first son. Peace and prosperity reign over the Minamoto Clan.

Although to modern eyes this play appears rough, badly organized, and erratic, it was a "finished" play as far as Danjuro was concerned. Already by 1697, under the title of *Sankai Nagoya,* Danjuro had conceived the material for the first act of *Kagemasa's Interpellation of the Thunder.* The second act of *Sankai Nagoya* shows a heroic commoner, Banzaemon, who has dedicated a Merchant's ledgerbook as a votive offering at a temple. Dazai-no-jo, the villain, starts to remove it and replace it with a sword. At this point Banzaemon stops him, calling out, "Wait a moment!" (*shibaraku*). *Kagemasa's Interpellation of the Thunder* is a reworking of this theme.

Danjuro's son, Danjuro II (1688-1758), who carried on his father's *aragoto* tradition of bombastic acting, revised the two plays under the title of *Everybody's Ledgerbook* (*Bammin Daifukucho*).

[83]

At the first performance, his opposite player was the distinguished actor of villains' parts, Yamanaka Heikuro, who out of jealousy held the young Danjuro II in contempt. Before the performance began they had mutually agreed upon their cues. When Heikuro was to place his hand on the ledgerbook to remove it from its place of offering on the shrine, Danjuro II was to call out from off stage, "Wait a moment!" Heikuro, to spite the youth, said his lines, but failed to put his hand on the ledgerbook. Danjuro II was angered and refused to speak out. The silence was embarrassing and Heikuro said, "What now? Shall I tear down the ledgerbook?" At this point, Danjuro II called out, "Wait a moment," but did not appear. Once again there was an awkward silence. "Who the devil has called out, 'Wait a moment'?" shouted Heikuro. Danjuro II merely repeated the words, "Wait a moment." Then Heikuro, beside himself in rage, screamed, "And what is meant by 'Wait a moment'?" At this point Danjuro II calling out, "Wait, wait, wait," rushed down the *hanamichi* passageway onto the stage. According to the critics of the day in the Kabuki picture-book commentaries, the angry faces of Heikuro and the young Danjuro matched each other in inflamed passion. The effect was "like a struggle between a tiger and a dragon." The performance from all accounts was a huge success. Applause was heard as far as the teahouses in the neighboring streets.

This was so dramatic that the many repetitions of "Wait a moment!" are still retained in the one-act play performed today. *Wait a Moment* is one of the *aragoto* pieces now included among the "18 Favorite Plays" (*Juhachiban*) of the Ichikawa Danjuro family. In the play the commoner's insult to the warrior and his regard for the merchant's ledgerbook as above the samurai's sword have now lost their importance. The large ledgerbook is still indispensable and is in full view in the center of the stage, but it is merely a stage property and is not referred to in the course of the dialogue. The plot now goes as follows. A lord who has usurped the rule of the country and wears the high crested headdress of the Emperor orders the beheading of some innocent people. As they are about to be killed, "Wait a moment" is heard offstage. The *aragoto* element of the play with its gestures, bombast and turgid prose-poetry, however, has remained in the play since Danjuro's time.

Obviously *Kagemasa's Interpellation of the Thunder,* and even its several derivatives, including today's "Wait a Moment," are very far from literary masterpieces. Their significance is in the fact that they reveal what the Edo public liked in and wanted from Kabuki. The irrationality, the confident belief in the supernatural and complete abandon of the heroes such as Kagemasa and Banzaemon reflect the yearnings and aspirations of the commoners.

Aragoto as a form of acting is an expression of the impulse of the people to become supermen. It is an outlet for the instinct to throw off the shackles of oppressive government. Man's desire to control his fate and rule his enemies is vicariously satisfied in *aragoto.* All that the common man could not hope to accomplish in real life was fulfilled for him by Danjuro's creations. Good always triumphed. Wicked warriors were always destroyed. The heroes were gods or god-like chivalrous commoners, or noble warriors. Such plays were full of social conscience. As with the changing times they lost their necessity and no longer afforded release to the common man, they ceased to be important in the theatre and the plays themselves descended into a curious jumble of nonsense and stylization. In the form they now appear, *aragoto* plays delight not for their literal meaning, but for their characteristic quality of acting, which is exclusive to Kabuki. By all odds, for sheer acting, they are the most exciting part of all Japanese theatre.

One of Danjuro's plays has however continued to be performed even today in more or less its original form. It is a traditional play for the month of January, and is always performed with star players in even the subsidiary roles. It is called *The Confrontation of the Soga Brothers (Soga no Taimen).*

Synopsis of the story:

Asahina is a retainer of the ranking lord Kudo Suketsune. He is also a friend of the Soga brothers, Juro and Goro, whose father was murdered many years ago by Lord Kudo. He arranges for the brothers to be received in audience by the lord.

The scene opens showing an assembly of lords gathered to pay homage to Lord Kudo on his day of formal audience. Asahina goes to the *hanamichi* passage-way and calls out for the brothers to present themselves. They appear bringing the traditional New Year's gifts. Goro, the impetuous brother, wanting revenge at once, presses to attack Lord Kudo; but his younger brother restrains him. Lord Kudo, in conformity with the protocol of New Year's audiences, offers them a congratulatory cup of wine. Juro drinks, but Goro crushes the cup in his hands. He openly declares Lord Kudo to be his father's murderer and publicly proclaims his desire and intent to take revenge.

Lord Kudo scornfully tosses them two wooden tickets to a hunting contest to be held at the foot of Mt. Fuji later in the year. At this time he will give the brothers their opportunity to take revenge. They agree to meet at that time.

This play may seem to lack in dramatic interest in comparison with Western plots, but the undercurrents in the play, from a Japanese standpoint, are extremely interesting. The custom was that revenges must be publicly declared. The standard of honor and chivalry of the time also required that the enemies confront each other and make known their intention. However, on formal occasions and felicitous days, violence was not tolerated. Forbearance was essential and the struggle of the brothers to maintain the protocol and suppress their burning anger makes throughout the play a series of climactic rises and falls in tension.

The tradition of Edo Kabuki and its illustrious creator, Danjuro I, is perpetuated in a collection of plays called "The 18 Favorites." They are full of *aragoto,* weird make-ups, and *roppo.* Today in Japan if one asks, "What is Kabuki?," the majority of Japanese would answer, "The 18 Favorites." So popular have these plays been throughout their history, that the word itself (*juhachiban*) has come to be a colloquial expression for anything favorite.

"The 18 Favorites" is a set of plays compiled by Danjuro VII (1791-1859). They represented the best plays and performances of the Ichikawa family since the first Danjuro in Genroku. In reality there are only sixteen plays in the list, although originally they must have numbered eighteen. Of these sixteen, the majority are known only by name. As a rule, until the 19th century texts for Kabuki were not written down in permanent form. The result has been that many plays were lost. Danjuro VII started a series of "New 18 Favorites," but only went so far as to select two before his death. Danjuro IX (d. 1903) inherited the task and the number of "New 18 Favorites" reached thirty-two, although the term eighteen was retained.

The stories of the known "18 Favorites" are as follows. The plots of some of them are thin; their charm and enduring quality is in their performance.

I *Narukami:*

Saint Narukami has made a petition to the Imperial Throne which has been refused. Therefore he uses his magical power of prayer to stop all rain throughout the country. Narukami's virtue is so great that even the elements obey him. The farmers are hard pressed, and the country is on the verge of ruin. Princess Taema, of the Imperial household, volunteers to sacrifice herself by going to Narukami's mountain retreat and to break his spell by seducing him.

Women are banned from the area, and she is refused entrance by two comic priests who stand guard as Narukami prays. She begins to tell them a story. Narukami overhears it and his interest is aroused. At last he draws near her. She begins to complain of a pain, and the climax of the play is reached.

Narukami: I am a doctor as well as a priest. My hand is enchanted. It cures such an attack. I will touch you. (He places his hand on her shoulder.) Are you better now? Has the pain left you?

Taema: Somewhat.

Narukami: The pain is in your stomach. There is a convulsion to the right. I assume women's sicknesses are all to the right. What have I felt? (He draws back startled.)

Taema: What? What have your fingers felt?

Narukami: I have placed my hand on a woman for the first time in my life. On the chest, I found two soft things, like pillows, with small tips, hanging. What are they?

Taema: Master, don't you know? They are called nipples.

Narukami: Nipples? By them was I fed by my mother when I was a baby. I had forgotten them and their benevolence. How strange that a priest should forget the instrument of nurture to which he owes his very life! (He reaches further within her clothing.)
They are flexible. Beneath the nipples is the pit, where lies your illness. Are you better now? Beneath the pit is the umbilicus. It is also called the navel. On either side of the umbilicus are the two centers of feeling. (*tensu*). Slightly beneath the umbilicus is the center of breath (*kikai*). Beneath it is the center of health (*tanden*), beneath it is the center of spirit (*imbaku*). Beneath the center of spirit, there is Paradise.

Taema: Master!

Narukami: I implore you. I cannot contain myself. Worldly passion (*bonno*) is the Bliss of Buddha (*bodai*). I do not need the highest passions now, give me the lowest.

Taema: Narukami, master, have you . . .?

Narukami: Lost my mind?

Taema: Surely you are not serious. This is because . . .

Narukami: You accuse me of violating Buddha's commandment?

Taema: More than that; you are a Buddhist priest . . .

Narukami: I am corrupt. I am corrupt. I have fallen into hell. But there is my bliss.

Taema: Your Holiness!

Narukami is turned into a devil. The Princess cuts the sacred straw rope guarding his mountain retreat and lending efficacy to his prayers. The rain falls.

[88]

II *Fudo:*

The ghost of Narukami haunts Princess Taema. Through the miraculous power of the God Fudo, the ghost is exorcised.

III *Kenuki* (The Hair Standing on End):

Nishiki-no-mae, a young maiden of exalted rank, betrothed to Bunya-no-Toyohide, is mysteriously ill. Bunya's minister, Kumedera Danjo, visits her and finds that her illness consists of her hair standing on end. He divines that someone had oiled her hair with a pomade kneaded with iron-filings. They are attracted to a huge magnet hidden in the ceiling, and so her hair stands up. Danjo tests his deduction by hair-tweezers which are also attracted to the ceiling. He kills Yatsurugi Gemba, the villain, and her disease is cured. Toyohide forces Ohara-no-Mambei, another villain, to confess, and recovers from him a slip of paper on which one of the great Komachi's odes has been written. Thus he retrieves the treasured heirloom of the Ono family.

IV *Yanone* (Arrowhead):

Soga Goro is sharpening an arrow. As it is New Year's Day, a friend brings him a present of a *Takara bune,* a painting of a ship laden with treasures. According to custom, if one sleeps with the *takara bune* under one's pillow, the first dream of the New Year will be felicitous. As Goro sleeps, his brother Juro appears in a dream and asks him to come save him from mortal danger. Goro awakens and rushes to the door. A seller of horseradishes passes by. Goro fights with the horseradish seller and steals his horse. Brandishing a large horseradish as a whip for the horse, he rides down the *hanamichi* to the rescue of his brother.

V *Kanjincho* (The Subscription List):

N.B. *Kanjincho* is unquestionably the greatest musical dance-play in the entire Kabuki repertoire. *Kanjincho* is a play of three movements and moods. It contrasts three elements: drama, pathos, and humor. From an actor's standpoint, *Kanjincho* is designed to show the hero's brilliance, his knowledge of Buddhism, his ability to dissemble in time of danger, his devotion to his lord, his ability to drink yet remain alert, and finally his knowledge of the graceful art of dancing. It is adapted from the Noh play *Ataka* which was written in 1465 by Kanze Kojiro. The adaptation was made by Namiki Gohei III, the Kabuki playwright, especially for Danjuro VII.

Kanjincho tells the story of Lord Yoshitsune, who, having been falsely suspected of intrigue by his jealous brother, the Shogun, is fleeing with a handful of his devoted followers from the capital. The Shogun has established barrier stations throughout the country in order to capture the party. At the suggestion of the loyal retainer, Benkei, Yoshitsune has disguised himself as a coolie accompanying a group of itinerant priests (*yamabushi*). They reach Ataka, a barrier station under the charge of Togashi, a highly trusted vassal of the Shogun.

Part I   The Dramatic

Togashi enters. He explains that by order of the Shogun, he is to prevent any itinerant priests from passing the barrier station.

Yoshitsune, disguised as a coolie with his face hidden by a deep peasant hat, enters with his retainers. They wish to fight their way through the barrier station. Benkei stops them and Yoshitsune orders them to follow whatever instructions Benkei gives.

Benkei approaches the barrier keeper and asks to pass. He says that the party is composed of itinerant priests roving over the country soliciting contributions for the reconstruction of their home temple which has been ravaged by fire. Togashi refuses, saying that all itinerant priests are suspect and they are to be killed.

Benkei orders the followers to hold a Buddhist service for the repose of their souls, since death appears inevitable.

Togashi interrupts Benkei saying that if he is collecting funds, then he must have a subscription list. He asks him to read it.

Benkei pulls out a blank scroll and brilliantly imitates the formal and obscure liturgical language necessary for such a document. Togashi is still suspicious.

A. The Questions and Answers (Mondo)

Togashi, wishing to test Benkei further, asks him a series of questions dealing with abstruse aspects of Buddhism. These Benkei answers without hesitation and shows the profoundest knowledge of the subject.

Togashi is filled with admiration at Benkei's learning and offers him presents as his contribution to the reconstruction of the temple. Benkei accepts only the cloth, and asks that the other presents be left to be picked up on their return.

B. The Beating (Chochaku)

The party is permitted to pass. One of Togashi's retainers spots Yoshitsune as too beautiful and gentle to be a real coolie. Togashi stops them. Yoshitsune's retainers thinking the life of their lord is in danger, start to fight. Benkei with great difficulty restrains them.

Benkei then beats Yoshitsune with his priest's stick, reviling him as a nuisance and the cause of trouble for the party.

Togashi now knows full well that the coolie is in reality Yoshitsune; but he is astounded that Benkei would go so far as to strike his lord—the one tenet of loyalty never to be broken by a subordinate.

Benkei pretends that he will kill the coolie. Togashi stops him, saying that his own retainer had made a mistake in suspecting the party. Togashi knows that by letting them pass now he is being disloyal to his lord, the Shogun, and eventually will pay for it with his life. He suppresses his tears and leaves the stage.

Part II   The Sentimental

Yoshitsune and his party proceed a short distance. Benkei humbly apologizes to Yoshitsune for having struck him and describes his emotions at having to strike his beloved lord. It was only, however, in order to make the deception perfect. Yoshitsune extends his hand to Benkei. This gesture is equivalent to an embrace and for the superior to touch the person of the inferior in ancient Japan denoted love and affection of the deepest sort. Benkei is overcome with joy.

Benkei dances a descriptive re-enactment of the various hardships which they have borne together—all as a result of the suspicions of the Shogun. The party weeps.

Part III   The Comic

Togashi calls out to them and reappears on the stage. He offers Benkei a parting drink of wine. Benkei greedily drinks the entire cask of wine. Benkei complies with Togashi's request to dance the Dance of Longevity. Although drunk and dancing, he is ever mindful of his responsibility to his lord and party. In the course of the dance, he secretly signals the party to be on their way, out of danger, in case Togashi changes his mind.

Part IV The Roppo

Benkei and Togashi bid farewell, and the curtain is drawn, leaving Benkei alone on the *hanamichi* passage-way. Benkei bows in gratitude and relief at having successfully passed this most dangerous of barrier stations. Then he executes an elaborate, stylized, dancelike *Tobi-roppo* (literally, "flying in six directions") which represents Benkei's joy and haste to catch up with the party.

VI *Sukeroku:* Because of the importance of this long play as a pure example of Edo Kabuki, and for its sheer dramatic interest and colorful portrayal of Genroku Japan, a full translation is contained in the Appendix.

VII *Wait a Moment* (*Schibaraku*): The story has already been given.

The remainder of the "18 Favorites" are preserved in name only: *Fuwa, Kagekiyo, Kanu, Nanatsumen, Kedatsu, Kamabige, Zobiki, Oshimo Doshi,* and *Jayanagi*.

4.

Return to the Puppets. The puppet theatre was an older historical development than Kabuki. It had attracted many meritorious playwrights who wanted to avoid the constant difficulties of writing for arrogant Kabuki actors. With the deaths of Sakata Tojuro and Danjuro I, some of Kabuki's vitality disappeared. The puppet theatre began to dominate the theatrical scene. It gained such popularity that Kabuki, in order to continue, was forced to borrow its material and adapt it. From this time onward, the interchange between Kabuki and the puppets increased steadily.

It was Danjuro himself who in the year of his death, 1717, made the first direct borrowing from the Osaka puppets. He made over Chikamatsu's historical play *Kokusenya* into a Kabuki play, and played the leading role, the hero Watonai, in *aragoto* style. This was an important moment in theatre history for Japan. It was the first time that a well-written puppet play had been used in the Kabuki theatre. It was also a wedding of Osaka's and Edo's best talents.

The play *Kokusenya,* written in 1715, casts an interesting light on Japan's attitude towards China at the time. It is still performed today in its weird costumes—Japanese versions of Chinese costumes of the period.

The story is as follows:

The Ming Dynasty in China has been overthrown. The Ming princess, Sendan, flees to Japan. There she is saved by a gallant hero named Watonai. Watonai's father was Roikkan, an old retainer of the Chinese Ming Emperor. His mother was Japanese. Watonai and his parents return to China in order to restore the Ming Dynasty.

The chief Chinese general of the anti-Ming faction is called Kanki, and has pledged himself to the invading Tatar king. His wife, Kinshojo, is Roikkan's own daughter and Watonai's sister. The family ask her to help their cause. She is to plead with her husband to assist them in restoring the Ming Dynasty. Watonai waits on the bank of the Yellow River to learn the answer as to whether she is successful in persuading her husband. The agreed-upon signal is that if the husband refuses, she will drop powdered rouge from the castle window into the river water.

As Watonai waits, he sees the river turn red. He then forces his way into the castle singlehanded, only to find that Kinshojo has killed herself. The dilemma of choosing between her family and her husband was too much for her. The coloring in the river was not the signal, but her life's blood. Watonai's mother kills herself in grief over the daughter's death.

General Kanki, much moved by his wife's intensity of feeling, resolves to enter the war on the side of Watonai. Together they defeat the Tatar army and restore the Ming Dynasty.

A still closer connection between the puppets and Kabuki was started in the same year as the performance of *Kokusenya,* by the appearance in Edo of Tachimatsu Hachirobei, the puppeteer. He gained fame there not only for his skill in manipulating the dolls, but also by teaching some of the Kabuki actors how to move, particularly when playing soft love roles. His gentle movements of the puppets had contributed substantially to Chikamatsu's popularity in Osaka.

The Takemoto-Za puppet theatre, first established at the end of the 17th century, had by the first half of the 18th century reached a fantastic degree of popularity in Osaka. In competition, a rival puppet theatre, the Toyotake-Za, set up operation across the street. This new theatre started as the result of a quarrel. Toyotake Wakadayu, a disciple and protege of the *joruri* singer, Takemoto Gidayu, fell out with his master, probably over his ambition to have more leading roles to sing and recite. Toyotake Wakadayu quit the Takemoto-Za, and taking with him Ki-no-Kaion (1663-1742) as chief writer, established his own theatre. A curious vying for popularity between the two theatres ensued. If Chikamatsu had a success at the Takemoto-Za, Ki-no-Kaion followed with a play on a similar theme at the Toyotake-Za. Although this does not speak well for Ki-no-Kaion's inventiveness, his excellence as a craftsman, judging from his surviving plays, cannot be denied. Both theatres prospered side by side for many years.

The years 1723 and 1724 saw the retirement from writing of both Chikamatsu and Ki-no-Kaion. Following in their wake, a large number of excellent writers appeared. The chief writers for the Takemoto-Za and the Toyotake-Za, respectively, were Takeda Izumo (1691-1756) and Nishizawa Ippu (1665-1731). These successors had as additional work the duty of managing the theatres. The heaviness of these non-writing tasks and resultant lack of time for writing precipitated the custom among playwrights of "joint compositions" (*gassaku joruri*). Texts were no longer the responsibility of one playwright. The chief writer worked with his confrères and students to produce a single play. *The Chronicle of the Alphabetical Rise and Fall* (*Hiragana Seisuiki*) written around 1739, is the combined effort of as many as five men: Takeda Izumo, his son Takeda Koizumo, Namiki Senryu, Miyoshi Shoraku, and Asada Kahei.

The theatres of Japan until the 19th century opened at dawn and closed when darkness came. As a result, programs and plays were of great length. In addition, programs changed every two weeks on the average. To write such long plays, a large number of writers were needed. The practice of joint composition was both necessary and practical. Each act in Japanese drama includes three parts: *kuchi* (mouth), *naka* (middle), and *kiri* (cut), (the *Jo-Ha-Kyu* formula); and each of these parts is equivalent in length to an act of Western drama. Although plays were usually written in five acts, this actually meant a possible fifteen acts in our sense of the word. Such massive dramatic structures could not possibly have come from a single pen, nor could a consistent standard of excellence be maintained. Subsequently uneven and inferior acts were dropped from the repertoire of Kabuki and puppet companies. The custom of performing excerpts from these long plays came into being.

Posterity has suffered from this habit of performing segments of plays. Many passages and texts have completely disappeared and cannot now be reconstructed. In recent times the parts performed are sometimes so truncated that without extensive program notes or considerable prior theatrical experience it is impossible to follow the gist of the play. This abbreviation is partly excusable because of the fact that there is a tremendous amount of repetition in classical plays of Japan. In the old days, throughout the entire day spectators drifted in and out of the theatres. It was customary for the plays to begin each act with a recapitulation of the story of the preceding action. These are now deleted because modern audiences give less divided attention. Also, as the repertoire became more familiar and traditional, many among the audience began to know the plays by heart.

A most felicitous example of how joint composition worked in actual practice is seen in the story of the writing of *The Lustrous Imparting of Sugawara's Calligraphic Secrets* (*Sugawara Denju Tenarai Kagami*), one of the perennial masterpieces of Kabuki and the puppets.

The play came to be written because of some financial difficulties of the Takemoto-Za in 1746. Takeda Izumo, Namiki Senryu, and

Miyoshi Shoraku, the theatre's three leading writers, in desperation at their plight, went together to pray at a temple. They chose a temple in Kyoto dedicated to Sugawara Michizane, the patron saint of Calligraphy. On their return to Osaka the three, suddenly and simultaneously, so the story goes, conceived the idea of writing a play on the life of Sugawara Michizane.

The historical facts of Sugawara's life in themselves tell the tragic story of an innocent man's fall from high favor, and offer an excellent source for dramatic incident and material.

Facts of Sugawara's Life:

Sugawara Michizane was born in 845 A.D., the only son of the scholarly family of Koreyoshi (812–880). From youth he evinced a talent in poetry. In 877 he was granted a Doctorate in Literature. In 891 he was appointed Director of the Imperial Treasury Bureau. The Emperor Uda took him into his confidence and appointed him one of the court lecturers. At this time Sugawara wrote *A Condensation of the National History* (*Ruiju Kokushi*). The Emperor Uda suggested that he accept the high government position of Privy Councilor, in order to check the power of the Fujiwara family.

In 897 the Emperor Uda abdicated and the throne passed to his 13-year old son, the Emperor Daigo. Sugawara, as Home Minister, together with Shihei Fujiwara, the War Minister, were the young Emperor's advisors. In 900 the Emperor secretly asked Sugawara to be Chief Counselor to the Throne. Sukawara declined to accept the appointment. Shihei begrudged Sugawara's great favor. Shihei and his ally, Fujiwara Kankon, charged that Sugawara was exhorting Prince Tokiyo, the younger brother of the Emperor, to seize the throne. Emperor Daigo believed the false charge and degraded Sugawara to a minor post in Kyushu. His relatives were also lowered in rank. In Kyushu he confined himself to his home. In 903, at the age of 59, he died broken-hearted.

He was well known as a man of virtue. He had excellent talents and a thorough knowledge of Confucianism, although his faith was Buddhism. He was one of three great calligraphers of Japan. His art of penmanship is called the "Kanke" style of writing. After his death many catastrophes occurred in Kyoto, and Shihei died. The people of the time referred to these terrors of the earth as the "curse of Sugawara."

In 923 Sugawara was given posthumous honors of reinstatement and was appointed to the senior grade of the second court rank. In 993 he was elevated to senior grade of the first court rank and also to the rank of Chief of the Supreme Council. The people later deified him at a shrine in Kitano near Kyoto, the Imperial capital city. He is even today worshipped as God of Calligraphy and Patron Saint of writers.

Into these historical facts, the three authors wove a contemporary event. The then recent birth of triplets in Osaka had attracted wide public attention. The governor of the area had rewarded the mother with a special grant of money. So the heroes of the new play were to be represented by triplets, colorfully named Matsuo-maru (pine), Umeo-maru (plum), and Sakura-maru (cherry). In order to tie the cast of characters into an integrated whole, the writers made the triplets the retainers of the three central characters of the plot: Sakura-maru was an aide to Prince Tokiyo, the Emperor's brother; Umeo-maru was the trusted follower of Sugawara; and Matsuo-maru was a vassal of the villain of the play, Shihei.

The writers decided upon a single common theme to appear throughout each of the three main acts which they would write. The chosen theme was the separation of members of a family, *nikkotsu no wakare,* literally, "the parting of flesh and blood." Miyoshi Shoraku's act (*Domyoji Temple*) is the parting of Sugawara from his daughter. Namiki Senryu's act (*Celebration of the 70th Birthday*) contains the parting of Sakura-maru, the youngest of the triplets, from his family and wife through death. Takeda Izumo's act is the celebrated *Village School* (*Terakoya*) which was performed by Ichikawa Sadanji in Russia in 1923, and which also was adapted by John Masefield into English as *Pine* and performed both in England and America. In this act, Matsuo-maru, the first of the triplets, parts from his only son by sacrificing him.

Summary of the main scenes of *The Lustrous Imparting of Suga-*

wara's Calligraphic Secrets performed today in Kabuki and the puppet theatre:

1—*The Palanquin Package* (*Kamo Zutsumi*)

Sakura-maru acts as a go-between in arranging a secret meeting between his lord, Prince Tokiyo, the Emperor's brother, and Princess Kariya, Sugawara Michizane's daughter. They both arrive at the trysting place in palanquins.

2—*Impartating Scene* (*Denju no Ba*)

(N.B.—The title of the play is derived from this act.)

Some years before, Takebe Genzo had been Sugawara's favorite retainer and calligraphy disciple, but because he became involved with one of the palace ladies, Sugawara reluctantly dismissed them both.

Sugawara now summons Genzo in order to impart the secrets of his calligraphy to him. Genzo copies two of Sugawara's poems perfectly. Sugawara is delighted, but nevertheless dismisses him again. A summons from the Imperial court comes, and Sugawara learns that he is to be exiled in disgrace due to the calumny of Shihei.

Genzo kidnaps Sugawara's son and heir, Kan Shusai, so that he will not suffer at the hands of the enemy.

3—*Domyoji Temple* (*Domyoji*) by Miyoshi Shoraku.

On his way to his place of exile, Sugawara stops to bid farewell to his sister Kakuju.

Princess Kariya, his daughter, arrives in the hope of seeing her father before he leaves. Kakuju beats her because the downfall of Sugawara was the result of her action. (It was on the basis of Princess Kariya's intimacy with Prince Tokiyo that Shihei, the villain, had based his calumny. The malicious rumor which the Emperor was finally persuaded to believe was that Sugawara was plotting to marry his daughter to the Prince and then dispose of the Emperor, thereby clearing the way for his own son-in-law to become Emperor.)

Some of Shihei's men kidnap Sugawara in order to kill him secretly, but by a miracle the man they have taken turns out to be a stone.

Sugawara at last sets out in safety. Kariya tries to bid him farewell, but he refuses to recognize her. He fears that to acknowledge her would involve her in his punishment, and she would be seized as an accomplice in the false plot.

4—*Stopping the Carriage* (*Kuruma-biki*)

(N.B.—This scene is performed in *aragoto* style.)

Since the triplets, Matsuo-maru, Umeo-maru, and Sakura-maru, were retainers of Shihei, Sugawara and Prince Tokiyo respectively, they were deeply concerned in the causes of their masters. Umeo-maru and Sakura-maru sympathize with each other and bear resentment against Matsuo-maru whom they feel has taken part in the wicked Shihei's plot against Sugawara. By chance the two brothers encounter Matsuo-maru and Shihei as they are on their way to a shrine in Kyoto. They stop the carriage and fight with their brother.

5—*Celebration of the 70th Birthday* (*Ga no Iwai*) by Namiki Senryu.

Shiro-dayu, the father of the triplets, is celebrating his 70th birthday. The triplets and their wives attend. Umeo-maru and Matsuo-maru continue their fight.

Sakura-maru commits *harakiri* out of guilt and in apology for having been the cause (by acting as a go-between for Tokiyo and Kariya) of the downfall of Sugawara.

6—*The Village School* (*Terakoya*) by Takeda Izumo.

Genzo, the disciple in calligraphy of Sugawara, and his wife, Tonami, are protecting Kan Shusai, Sugawara's son, at their small school in the country. Shihei learns of this and sends Matsuo-maru and another retainer to bring back the head of the boy. Matsuo-maru determines to betray his lord. In order to right himself with his brothers and to serve on the side of righteousness, he secretly sends his own son, Kotaro, to the school to be enrolled as a new pupil on this day.

Genzo takes advantage of the child's resemblance to Kan Shusai and gives his head to the two retainers. Matsuo-maru, who is required to inspect the head for identification, falsely states that it is Kan Shusai's.

Matsuo-maru resigns from Shihei's service and becomes a priest to pray for the soul of his son whom he has sacrificed.

[99]

7—*Tempai Mountain* (*Tempai Zan*)

Umeo-maru goes to Sugawara's place of exile in Kyushu and informs him of Shihei's rise to power. Sugawara dies of bitterness.

The ghosts of Sugawara and Sakura-maru haunt Shihei at the Imperial Palace. Kan Shusai and Kariya take revenge and kill Shihei.

Sugawara is posthumously cleared of guilt and is deified.

The Lustrous Imparting of Sugawara's Calligraphic Secrets was tremendously successful. The Takemoto-Za was saved from financial worries and subsequently produced a series of dramas unparalleled for theatrical excellence in the history of Japanese drama. The succeeding plays today comprise the nucleus of the standard Kabuki and puppet-theatre repertoire. The three greatest of these are called "The Triumvirate of Masterpieces" and comprise, in addition to *The Lustrous Imparting of Sugawara's Calligraphic Secrets*, the celebrated *Yoshitsune and the Thousand Cherry Trees* (*Yoshitsune Sembon Zakura*) written in 1747, and the perennial *Chushingura* written in 1748. Because of the dramatic importance of these plays, and because of their continued popularity even today, they merit somewhat detailed summaries.

Summary of the main scenes of *Yoshitsune and the Thousand Cherry Trees:*

Background to the story: The Taira Clan, once the rulers of the country, are finally crushed by the Minamoto Clan, which has assumed their power. However, two of the defeated Taira generals, Tomomori and Koremori, flee to safety. The responsibility for their escape fell on Yoshitsune, the chief commander for the victorious Minamoto Clan. Yoritomo, now Shogun of the country and elder brother of Yoshitsune, as a result of jealousy and intrigue, uses the escape of the enemy generals as an excuse to confine Yoshitsune to his palace in Kyoto and thereby prevent him from rousing sufficient popular support to undermine his power.

Yoshitsune and the Thousand Cherry Trees deals primarily with the the trials Yoshitsune suffered because of his wicked brother's machinations. Into these are woven the events which befall the two Taira generals and their families. One point in connection with the play needs explanation, at least for the Westerner. The fox in Japan is considered in folk lore to be a magical animal who can at will assume human form. In Kabuki fox roles are performed as double roles; sometimes the actor appears human, sometimes in the guise of a fox. When representing a fox, the role is generally played in *aragoto* style, with a highly painted make-up symbolic of the fox-fires (*ignis fatuus*) with which the fox is always associated in Japanese fairy stories, and with nervous, animal-like gestures.

1—*The Messenger Kawagoe* (*Kawagoe Joshi*)

Kawagoe Taro, a messenger from the Shogun Yoritomo, appears at Yoshitsune's palace in Kyoto and demands the head of Yoshitsune's wife. Shortly after, Tosabo Soshun, also sent by Yoritomo to harass his brother Yoshitsune, attacks the palace. Yoshitsune flees.

2—*The Gate at Fushimi Shrine* (*Fushimi Torii*)

Yoshitsune is to embark for the southern island of Kyushu. His beloved concubine, Shizuka, has accompanied him to the Fushimi shrine where they are to part. He gives her as a token of his affection a precious hand-drum which she is to play to pass away the lonely hours of their separation.

Yoshitsune entrusts Shizuka to the safe-keeping of one of his most trusted retainers, Tadanobu. In fact, this Tadanobu is a fox who has assumed human form. The real Tadanobu is, unbeknown to Yoshitsune, seriously ill in his native village. As Shizuka and the fox-Tadanobu exit, the latter executes an elaborate *roppo* in *aragoto* style.

3—*Daimotsu Ura*

At the point of embarkation, the inlet of Daimotsu Ura, Yoshitsune and some followers prepare to board ship. The ship is owned by Tokaiya Gimpei. Gimpei, it turns out, is in reality the chief of the defeated Taira generals, Tomomori. He takes advantage of Yoshitsune's presence on shipboard and tries to kill him. He fails in the attempt and is gravely wounded by Yoshitsune and his followers.

Tomomori, as head of the Taira Clan, has in his custody the young Emperor Antoku* who represents the symbol of the Taira's erstwhile power and who would be placed on the throne were the Tairas ever to regain control of the land. He now realizes the hopelessness of the Taira cause and, filled with admiration for Yoshitsune, he hands over the young Emperor. Tomomori then ties himself to the rope of the ship's anchor. He tosses it overboard, and its weight pulls him into the sea.

4—Travel Dance (Michiyuki)

The lovely Shizuka is on her way to rejoin Yoshitsune. She pauses in a forest to rest, and idly begins to play the precious hand-drum. Suddenly from nowhere, Tadanobu (the fox) mysteriously appears.

The pair dance together, describing their journey and recalling their beloved lord, Yoshitsune.

The climax of the dance is a "recital of a past event" (monogatari) in which Tadanobu describes in dance the death of his brother during the decisive battle in which the Minamoto Clan achieved victory.

5—Konomi

Koremori's wife, Wakaba no Naishi, with Rokudai Gimi, her son and chief heir of the Taira family, are fleeing in disguise. They are attended by Kokingo, a retainer. On their way, they encounter Gonta, a village rogue. He robs them of their purses and discovers who they are. For the sake of the reward, he informs the authorities who send men to capture them. Kokingo is killed after a long fight, but the mother and son escape.

6—The Sushi Shop (Sushiya)

Gonta's father, Yazaemon, keeps a shop which sells sushi (a sort of rice sandwich). Koremori, one of the defeated generals of the Taira Clan, is hiding there under the name of Yasuke. He pretends to be an adopted son of the shopkeeper.

O-Sato, Yazaemon's daughter, falls in love with Yasuke. She does not

* For some years before and during the last war, Japan's militarists allowed no depiction of an emperor on the stage. This affected a large number of Kabuki and puppet plays. Under the regulation, the role of the child Emperor Antoku was altered to that of a young princess indirectly related to the Imperial family and therefore a precious hostage of the Taira Clan.

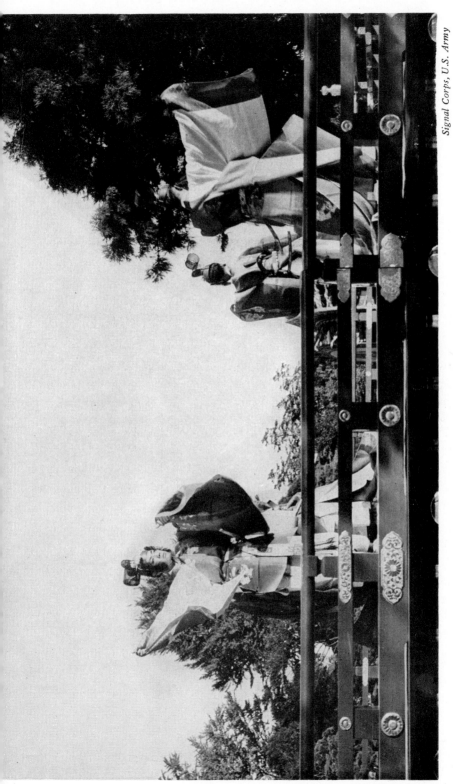

BUGAKU DANCE PERFORMED FOR ALLIED PERSONNEL

know that he is already married, above her in station, and that their marriage cannot take place.

Gonta decides to reform. In penance for his past wickedness, he sacrifices his own wife and child as substitutes for Koremori's wife and child. Yazaemon not knowing of the substitution, kills Gonta for having worked against the Taira cause.

Kajiwara, the Minamoto general responsible for capturing the last remnants of the Tairas, secretly wishes to protect Koremori. He accepts the substituted heads of Gonta's family as those of the Taira mother and son.

7—*Shino Kiri*

Shizuka with her guardian, the fox-Tadanobu, arrive at the retreat of Yoshitsune. The real Tadanobu appears. Yoshitsune and Shizuka give the hand-drum to the fox-Tadanobu in reward for his protection of her during the journey. The skin of the drum is that of the fox's parents and that has been his reason for such devoted service and the cause of his mysterious appearances whenever Shizuka played the hand-drum.

The real Tadanobu discovers several enemies around the retreat and a fight ensues.

In the following year, the triumvirate of playwrights, Takeda Izumo, Namiki Senryu, and Miyoshi Shoraku, produced yet another masterpiece, *Chushingura*. It is to this day the crowning work of Japanese theatre and its importance not only to Japanese theatre, but to the outside world is such that it requires special attention. The full title of the play is, *Kanadehon Chushingura* or *The Alphabetical Storehouse of Exemplary Loyal Retainers*. The word "alphabet" in the title refers to the fact that each of the forty-seven lordless knights or ronin used as code a letter from the forty-seven syllables of the Japanese alphabet.

A skeleton-outline of the eleven acts of the play is as follows:

Act I

Two lords, Enya Hangan and Wakasa-no-suke, assemble with other vassals of the Shogun Ashikaga Tadayoshi at Hachiman Shrine prior to the court reception for the Imperial Envoy to the Shogun. Hangan's wife is asked to identify a helmet which the Emperor had once given in battle and which on definite recognition is now to be enshrined. After she has identified the helmet, Moronao, a wicked lord of high rank and chief of court protocol, makes advances to her, which she rejects. Wakasa-no-suke accidentally finds him trying to embrace her. Moronao vents his rage on Wakasa-no-suke.

Acts II and III

Honzo, Wakasa-no-suke's loyal retainer, fears that his rash lord will attempt to repay the insults of Moronao. Under the guise of paying Moronao for instruction as to the etiquette of receiving the exalted Imperial Envoy, Honzo hands Moronao a large sum of money. Honzo hopes this will placate Moronao in the event Wakasa-no-suke attempts revenge. Wakasa-no-suke, ignorant of this arrangement, enters the palace to kill Moronao. Moronao apologizes, pleads for his life and is most abject before Wakasa-no-suke. The matter passes off.

Hangan enters and is abused by Moronao. Since he has not given a sufficient gratuity to Moronao for instruction in etiquette, Moronao refuses to teach him and mocks him about his wife. Hangan is driven to such desperation that he draws his sword and wounds Moronao. He is stopped from killing him by Honzo.

Meanwhile Hangan's retainer, Kampei, is making love to O-karu and is not at his lord's side in this hour of need.

Act IV

As Hangan has struck a superior within the walls of the palace, his punishment is that he must commit harakiri. The Shogun's envoys come to witness his self-execution. Hangan patiently waits for his devoted chief retainer, Yuranosuke, to arrive. Finally after he has stabbed himself, Yuranosuke enters. The dying Hangan asks him to complete his unfinished action and to kill the wicked Moronao. He hands him the dirk with which he has stabbed himself.

Yuranosuke surrenders Hangan's goods, property, and castle to the Shogun's messengers. The loyal retainers vow to take vengeance when the time is ripe, and they disperse.

Act V

Kampei has become a hunter. At night in the woods he meets two of his former fellow retainers. He asks to join the league pledged to avenge the death, despite his remissness at the time of his lord's need. They refuse him indirectly, not trusting him fully, and indicate that money might be welcome in order "to build a monument to their lord."

Kampei's father-in-law is returning from Kyoto where he has made arrangements to sell his daughter, O-karu, now Kampei's wife, to a house of prostitution. This money he hopes to give Kampei so that he can contribute it and somehow ease his deep sense of guilt for failing his lord. He encounters the wicked Sadakuro, a former retainer of Hangan's who refused to side with his lord and his loyal retainers. Sadakuro kills Kampei's father-in-law with his sword and robs him. At this point Kampei, who is pursuing a wild boar, fires his gun and mistakenly hits Sadakuro. He is horrified at his error, but robs the body of the money.

Act VI

The proprietor of the brothel in Kyoto has come to take O-karu away from Kampei's house. Kampei returns and refuses to relinquish her because he cannot believe she has been sold by her father. The dead body of her father is brought in and as the cloth in which the money was wrapped by the Kyoto proprietor is the same as that which Kampei robbed from a dead body the night before, Kampei assumes that he has murdered his father-in-law. He is speechless from grief, and O-karu is taken away.

O-karu's mother reviles him as her husband's murderer. Two loyal retainers arrive and join in the rebuke. They refuse his money, saying that their dead lord could find little joy in money stained with the blood of a murdered father and touched by the hand of a thief. Kampei in sorrow commits harakiri. Later, too late, it is discovered that the father was murdered by a sword, not a gun. Kampei's innocence is proven. As he dies he is allowed to join the league of loyal retainers and seals the document with his blood.

Act VII

Yuranosuke, the chief retainer, pretends to have forgotten the revenge, and has given himself to wine and lust. O-karu, Kampei's wife, has become a leading courtesan in the gay center which Yuranosuke frequents. She inadvertently reads a letter revealing the plot of the *ronin* to wreak vengeance. Yuranosuke discovers that she knows these facts and offers to ransom her without asking her to be his wife; after three days he will set her free. O-karu is overjoyed and starts to write a letter to Kampei to tell him the news.

O-karu's brother, a lower footman of the dead Hangan's entourage named Heiemon, arrives and tells her of the death of her father and Kampei. When Heiemon learns that Yuranosuke is going to buy O-karu, he realizes that it is in order to kill her because she knows of the plot. He starts to kill her so she can die by his hand rather than a stranger's, and to prove that he too is willing to go to any lengths to assist in the *ronin's* scheme to avenge the death of Hangan. Yuranosuke saves her and when he hears the touching explanation, he allows Heiemon, a commoner, to join the league.

Act VIII

Act VIII is a "travel dance" interlude (*michiyuki*) between Honzo's wife, Tonase, and her daughter, Konami. Konami has been betrothed to Yuranosuke's son, Rikiya, and the mother and daughter are journeying to Yuranosuke's house in Kyoto to prepare for the marriage.

Act IX

Tonase and Konami arrive at Yuranosuke's house, but Oishi, Yuranosuke's wife, refuses them admittance. She blames Honzo for having stopped Hangan from killing the wicked Moronao, which was the start of the trouble. Konami, who will have no other husband, prepares to be killed by her mother—hoping that in this way Oishi's heart will be touched. Oishi stops this cruel action. Honzo, the father, appears. By bribing Moronao, Honzo served his lord, Wakasanosuke, and prevented him from killing Moronao. By preventing Hangan from going so far as to kill Moronao, he thought the punishment would be lighter. In apology and to force Yuranosuke to accept his daughter, he allows himself to be killed by Yuranosuke's son, Rikiya. Honzo, before dying, hands them a map of Moronao's house.

Act X

A merchant is charged with preparing the necessary equipment for the avengers to attack Moronao's house. Moronao suspects the merchant, his men torture him, but the merchant does not expose the plan. When questioned by Yuranosuke, he speaks the famous line, "I too am a man among men," and thus becomes the forty-seventh to join the league—a tradesman once despised by the samurai.

Act XI

The loyal retainers raid Moronao's house. The villain is murdered with the very knife which Hangan used for his harakiri.

Chushingura was the source of considerable misunderstanding during the early days of the Occupation. It is the one sure-fire play to draw packed houses, and is hauled out of the repertoire whenever a producing company needs to recuperate its losses. Naturally it was the play the Japanese most wanted to put on after their disastrous losses during the war. The Occupation authorities in charge of Japan's theatre refused and negotiated for the issuance of an ordinance to ban it in perpetuity from the Japanese theatre.

To a certain degree, the Japanese themselves were to blame for the bad odor surrounding *Chushingura*.

Before the recent war, Japan's notorious Board of Information, which tried to turn everything into propaganda, hoped that *Chushingura's* popularity could be useful. First, they wanted loyalty. This was in the title: *Chushin* means loyal retainers. They wanted the spirit of willing sacrifice. This they found in the patient waiting of the forty-seven biding their time to avenge their lord. They wanted to foster a characteristic Japanese spirit. This they found in such customs as harakiri, following one's lord after his death, etc. But when it actually came to making *Chushingura* serve as propaganda, the play version and even the historical event itself were not really adequate. They made a movie called *Genroku Chushingura* and filled it with loyalty to the Emperor. (In the actual *Chushingura,* there is only one minor mention of an Emperor, in connection with a helmet which he had given, and to the Shogun's enemy at that.)

On the basis of this, during the war one of the leading American magazines reproduced a series of wood-block prints showing scenes from the play in order to emphasize the fanaticism of the Japanese. This was rather curious; it was as if the Japanese had published pictures of the last act of *Hamlet,* and said, "This is the way Westerners behave." The Occupation's attitude towards *Chushingura* might be compared to our burning Beethoven Sonatas in World War I, and avoiding Wagner operas in World War II.

The merit of *Chushingura* as a dramatic spectacle was such, however, that not even the Occupation could seriously tamper with the artistic heritage of Japan and ban the play. In 1947 the play was freely permitted to the Kabuki actors and puppets, who now give an annual performance of it in the three cities of Osaka, Kyoto, and Tokyo.

A brief analysis of the background and the actual play of *Chushingura* clears up any misapprehensions about it.

The historical facts surrounding *Chushingura* are simple. In 1701 the Shogun ordered a lord to kill himself. His offense was that he had attacked and wounded a superior within the palace, thereby breaking the rules of conduct. A year later, forty-seven of his devoted followers took vengeance upon the man who had caused their lord's downfall. A duly registered vendetta was recognized by law in Japan until the late 19th century. But these forty-seven had not only violated this law but had flouted the Shogun's decree. They were therefore subject to the death penalty.

Bursting upon the peaceful and decadent air of the Tokugawa Era, the event caught the public fancy. The Shogun was forced, in the face of public opinion, to grant them the right to die by their own hand, which was considered an honorable punishment as compared with execution as common criminals. In 1703, the forty-seven were forced to commit harakiri. Twelve days after the death of the forty-seven, the incident was dramatized under the guise of the Soga brothers' revenge by Chikamatsu. The authorities caught wind of it and stopped it some days later. Regulations were eventually relaxed and,

either openly or on the sly, various versions of the forty-seven began
to reach the stage. In all, over a hundred plays have centered around
the story.

The best of these was *Kanadehon Chushingura*. In the past two
hundred years it has, at a conservative estimate, had over four thousand performances.

It is extraordinary how this play has held its popular appeal for so
long. In the beginning in Genroku, the intrigues and scandals of in-
accessible and colorful places were naturally a source of fascination
to the common people. The story behind *Chushingura* was an historical fact, enacted merely forty years before, and well within the memory of the older spectators. There was also an erotic element in that
the whole incident started over illicit advances made to another man's
wife, and there was also a brothel scene. Further, the subject centered
around a very great problem of the day—the *ronin* or unattached
warrior whose lord had lost either his fief or his life. The *ronin* was
a displaced person, without pay or stability of livelihood. With no
wars during the Tokugawa era to give warriors employment, the number of *ronin* increased alarmingly. They became commoners, and settled down as farmers or tradesmen; but many others turned highway-
men. *Chushingura* deals with forty-seven of these men who were then
a contemporary and familiar problem.

Another source of appeal lies in the fact that in *Chushingura* there
is a deep underlying social protest. Moronao, a venal lord who goads
his inferiors with insults, is a symbol of the corruption and oppression
of the warrior class. Hangan, the hero, through an injustice of the
Shogun's has to forfeit his life. Kampei through weakness for women
fails in his duty and pays with his life after he suffers such tragedies
as his wife being sold into prostitution, thinking himself his father's
murderer, becoming an object of the contumely of his mother, and
failing in his attempt to atone for remissness by joining the league of
forty-seven (then forty-five). Honzo, the retainer, bribes Moronao to
save his own lord and is loyal according to *bushido,* but this very

loyalty causes Moranao to vent his spite on Hangan and leads to Hangan's downfall. Suffering becomes general and loyalty is its cause. The playwright is forced to kill Honzo in the ninth act, in order to appease the audience. Heiemon, a footman of lowest rank, is finally allowed to join the league. This must have delighted audiences of old. They could see themselves, commoners, joining in an event that concerned high ranks and had set the entire nation talking. In a word, the warriors suffered, the audience rejoiced. Commoners made the grade, and the audience vicariously shared the honor. Over all, the sincerity of purpose of the forty-seven men united to right an egregious wrong symbolized in the hearts of the spectators the righting of their own wrongs.

Not even the Board of Information could succeed in making any more of *Chushingura* than what it was and is today: a play which concerns the righting of a grievous wrong. In *Chushingura* we have a licentious and corrupt superior who causes the death of an innocent man. The innocent man has a devoted retainer, Yuranosuke, who, in compliance with his lord's dying wish, undertakes to repay the injustice. Yuranosuke is filled with mortification at the loss of his friend and master, and at the resultant loss of livelihood, lodging, and future security, not only for himself but for all the dependent retainers. The point here is not loyalty but human emotion. One has only to conjecture about how shining an example of "loyalty" there would be if Yuranosuke had been the wicked Moronao's retainer. *Chushingura* is a clear-cut example of the forces of good opposing evil. The good wins out, and wins directly against the bad. Yuranosuke is a symbol of good. He effects the poetic justice necessary to assuage the aroused emotions of the spectators. The dramatic interest lies in the countless hardships which the characters endure between the initial evil and the ultimate triumph of good.

In *Chushingura* the element of revenge is purely ethical. If Yuranosuke had been motivated by revenge *per se,* he would have taken it on the Shogun by whose order his master was forced to commit harakiri. This was the impulse of the other retainers who intended to resist surrendering the lord's property to the Shogun. But Yurano-suke, whose one desire was to right the wrong by revenge against the man who actually caused the wrong, stopped them by saying, "There can be no real substance in the bitterness you feel towards the Shogun." (*Iyasa, Ashikaga dono o taishite wo urami mosu suji wa gozaranu zo!*) In this connection it is interesting to note that revenge in Japan today as an actual fact is quite as rare as in Western nations.

Despite the poetic merit of *Chushingura,* its primary appeal is in the actor's particular performance of the roles. *Chushingura* with its elaborate, detailed character depiction and the enormous difficulties it poses for an actor, has become the standard play for determining an actor's rank in the theatrical world. Yuranosuke, the leader of the league of forty-seven is the highest part an actor of male roles can take; Kampei, the highest for players of handsome men; O-karu, the ranking role for players of women's parts. Spectators through the years have become exclusively occupied with how one actor, as opposed to another, does a certain role. This has even led to the tour de force of a single actor performing the leading role of each type in the best acts of the play *Chushingura.*

In Japan the relation between actor and audience is considerably more intimate than it is in the West. To begin with, there is the *hanamichi* passage-way which makes it possible literally to reach out and touch an actor in any Kabuki play. Sometimes two *hanamichis* on opposite sides of the theatre are used. Actors exchange words over the heads of their audience. Home addresses of actors are published in the cheapest of theatre magazines. Their dressing rooms are un-locked, without guard or police to protect them. In certain popular roles, such as *Sukeroku,* the costumes until recently used to be do-nated by various shopkeepers, and musical dialogue and action ac-knowledge these gifts. When actors were to eat on the stage, they sent part of the food to various fans so that they could eat together. Audiences even today call out to the actors. Only recently in a performance of *Chushingura,* fans of the leading actors competed so vociferously in praise of their favorites that a near riot took place in the Tokyo Theatre. Even today actors change their lines or directly face a favorite patron in the audience and address an apt line to him openly.

This close connection between actor and audience explains why the actor is more important than the story. The texts are in fact irrelevant because of their frequent irrationality and fragmentary nature. For instance, if a spectator looked at *Chushingura* for its plot or propaganda value, it would be impossible to admire the hero, Yuranosuke, who is stupid enough to read a secret document in a brothel, and then to try and buy the courtesan who has read it in order to kill her. Or Kampei—who kills himself without even ascertaining whether he has really killed his father or not—is no more admirable. One cannot really take Moronao seriously; he is a man who is such a fool as to beg Wakasanosuke not to kill him one minute, and then literally to force Hangan to strike at him with his sword. So the plot and motivation remain subsidiary to the artistic appeal of the whole as a play and to the individual performance of the actor. However, *Chushingura,* like any serious work of art, is, in the last analysis, its own justification and stands on its own merits in the eyes of the nation whose particular civilization produced and sustained it.

One of the co-authors of these three great masterpieces, Namiki Senryu (1695-1759), is of special interest. He was actually a writer for the rival Toyotake-Za where he wrote under the name of Namiki Sosuke, but for a brief period of six years (1744-1750) he collaborated with Takeda Izumo and his playwrights at the Takemoto-Za. In 1751 after *The Lustrous Imparting of Sugawara's Calligraphic Secrets, Yoshitune and the Thousand Cherry Trees,* and *Chushingura,* he wrote (under the name of Sosuke) a masterpiece, *The Battle Chronicles of the Two Leaves at the Valley of Ichi-no-Tani (Ichi No Tani Futaba Gunki).* One act from it, the scene at Kumagai's camp

(*Kumagai Jinya*), is today among the best of Kabuki and puppet repertoire. It is a moving story and it contains some of the most intense and powerful poetry in Japanese literature.

Background of the play:

At the time the Taira Clan was still in power in Kyoto, Sagami was a lady-in-waiting to Fuji-no-Kata,* a lady of high rank at the Emperor's court. Anyone serving within the court circle was forbidden to marry an outsider—the punishment for such an offense was death. Nevertheless, Sagami fell in love with the dashing and brilliant warrior, Kumagai Jiro Naozane (at that time, however, called Kumagai Satake Jiro). Fuji-no-Kata viewed their attachment with sympathy and aided the pair to flee to Western Japan. For this kindness the two lovers literally owed their lives to her and pledged their eternal gratitude.

At this time of parting, both Sagami and Fuji-no-Kata were pregnant, which fact probably created an added bond of sympathy between them. Fuji-no-Kata had been seduced by the Emperor himself and was subsequently married off to Tsunemori, brother of the Shogun Munemori of the Taira Clan. Their child was named Atsumori. Kumagai and Sagami's child was named Kojiro Nao-ie.

Sixteen years elapse after the birth of the children. Many changes have been wrought. The Taira Clan has been dislodged from Kyoto and forced to flee. Kumagai has taken sides with the Minamoto Clan, and has become one of Yoshitsune's ablest generals. Fuji-no-Kata's husband, Tsunemori, has become one of the generals on the side of the Tairas, protecting the Shogun Munemori and the child-Emperor, Antoku.

Yoshitsune is fully cognizant of Kumagai's debt of gratitude to Fuji-no-Kata. He also knows that Atsumori is an Imperial son (illegitimacy was not a problem in those days). And he knows that Kumagai inevitably will encounter Atsumori on the battlefield in the clashes between the clans. In view of these factors, Yoshitsune wants to free Kumagai from his responsibility as an enemy commander of taking Atsumori's life should he meet him in combat. He has Benkei, the trusted warrior priest, write a cryptic

* *Kata* is an honorific title. She is also referred to in the play sometimes as Fuji-no-Tsubone. *Tsubone* is the generic title for ranking ladies of the Imperial court.

[113]

notice-board and place it in front of a particularly lovely and young cherry tree* blooming outside Kumagai's headquarters at the battle-ground. The notice-board bears a peremptory inscription containing a triple play on words, *Isshi wo kiraba, isshi wo kiru beshi. Isshi* can mean "one branch," "one finger," or "one son." The literal interpretation would be, "Anyone cutting a branch from this tree must have one finger cut off." However, it can also be read, "If you kill a son, you must kill your own son."

Kumagai senses the various meanings which Yoshitsune wishes to convey indirectly to him by this notice-board: to enable Kumagai to repay his debt of gratitude; to excuse Kumagai from the crime of taking the life of one who is of Imperial blood; and to offer Kumagai a means out of the disgrace of sparing an enemy life. Kumagai makes his choice: to sacrifice his own son and to submit his head as that of Atsumori's.

The Story of the Play: Kumagai's Camp begins with the arrival of Sagami, Kumagai's wife, at Kumagai's headquarters in the valley of Ichi-no-Tani. Although Sagami had bravely borne up when Kumagai set out for battle with their son, Kojiro, her mother's love has overpowered her. She has come straight to the battlefield to see how her son fared in his first experience in war. She finds the camp empty, but most unexpectedly after sixteen years, she meets Fuji-no-Kata. Fuji-no-Kata has heard that Kumagai killed her son, Atsumori. She has come to avenge his murder. Fuji-no-Kata prevails upon Sagami to kill Kumagai for her. Sagami acquiesces verbally, because of her past indebtedness, and melts in tears.

A shout announces the return of Kumagai to the camp. To add to the suspense and to deceive the audience as to what course of action Kumagai has actually decided on, the *joruri* singer declaims, "Kumagai has killed Atsumori in the full flower of his youth. Does he now sense the emptiness of this dream we call life? So great and noble a warrior has at last come to know the sorrow at the core of all things." As the music continues, the curtain of the entry-box at the back of the audience is drawn aside. Kumagai begins to walk down the long *hanamichi* passage-way in silent meditation. In one hand he carries a box containing a dissevered head. In the other, he absently carries a Buddhist rosary of crystal beads. He pauses,

---

* The cherry blossom and the splendid warrior are closely linked in Japanese thought. There is a familiar proverb in Japan, "Among flowers the loveliest is the cherry blossom; among men, the warrior," which perpetuates this connection. In poetical works the cherry blossom and the "flower of knighthood" are practically synonymous.

his hand falls to his side, and the beads tinkle against his sword. The sound awakens him from his reverie. He hides the rosary and quickly enters his headquarters.

At this point it is interesting to note that even the *joruri* singing, which serves throughout as a sort of mood-setter and interpreter of the mental states of the characters, uses the name "Atsumori" and conceals from the audience the sacrifice of Kumagai's own son. The singer cooperates, as it were, in making Kumagai's ruse perfect. The preceding scene of the drama, called *Behind Suma,* portrays the actual beheading. It is so written that the audience is led to believe that Atsumori has actually been killed by Kumagai. It is only later, when Sagami confronts her own son's head that the audience really knows that it is Kojiro and not Atsumori whom Kumagai has killed.

Kumagai finds Sagami, his wife, in his battle camp. He can scarcely conceal his irritation. She might easily spoil his plot by missing their son Kojiro or by recognizing the head when the time comes for the identification.

Fuji-no-Kata rushes in from an ante-chamber, and frantically tries to stab Kumagai. He frustrates her attempt. There ensues the famous "Narration" (*monogatari*) in which with only a fan and a sword Kumagai dances-acts-recites the story of his presumed slaying of Atsumori. The action of the "narration" is symbolic. The approach of Kumagai and Atsumori on horseback is shown by twisting the open fan as if it were a recalcitrant steed. (The fan is painted with a large red circle in the center like a rising sun, the emblem of the Minamoto Clan and their characteristic battle emblem.) The swords of the two warriors are symbolized by the closed fan held at the side or brandished realistically. When Kumagai pins Atsumori beneath him, he presses the open fan to the floor. When he lifts Atsumori to his feet and asks him to flee, he holds his sword erect and brushes the dust off with his open fan. When Hirayama, a subordinate general, calls out to Kumagai from a hill to the rear of the skirmish, the actor (Kumagai) advances to the three steps (*sandan*) in the center of the stage and leading up to the raised platform (*niju-butai*) representing Kumagai's tent, and calls out as if he is Hirayama himself.

The following is a detailed translation of the section containing the "Narration."

Fuji-no-Kata

(Enters with drawn dagger) My son's enemy! Prepare to die by my hand!

Kumagai

(Instantly turns around to avert her attack and knocks the dagger out of her hand) Who calls me "Enemy"?

Sagami

She is the Lady Fuji-no-Kata.

Kumagai

(Looks at her in astonishment) Indeed it is Lady Fuji-no-Kata! I had never thought to see you again.

(He bows in obeisance to her. He returns the dagger to her and disarms himself by pushing his sword towards her. He then falls prostrate before her.)

Fuji-no-Kata

Kumagai, with cruelty and violence, with ingratitude and pride, you have killed my young son on the battlefield. Sagami—you have promised. Assist me now—Kumagai must die.

Sagami

How can I—oh, my husband——

Fuji-no-Kata

Did you lie—did you deceive me then?

Sagami

Oh—I——

Fuji-no-Kata

Then help me—help me!

Sagami

But, lady, how can I?

Fuji-no-Kata

Here is how! (She offers the dagger and presses Sagami to kill him.)

Sagami

(In tears) Yes . . .

Music (*joruri*)

"Sagami answers 'yes' sadly."

Sagami

Husband, tell me what possessed you? How could you kill Atsumori? Why should you shed Imperial blood?

Music

"Her tears prevent her from speaking further."

Kumagai

(Scornfully) A useless question, my wife! The Emperor Antoku and his followers, the Taira Clan, were our enemies. I saw no need to discriminate between Atsumori and any other enemy.

Fuji-no-Kata, be resigned to your sorrow. The events of the battlefield are inevitable.

Let me describe the battle of that fateful day, and I shall recount how it was that I killed Atsumori.

(N.B.—Here begins the "Narration" proper.)

Music

"When he says these words, he formally adjusts his position."

Kumagai

It was the sixth night after the new moon. The Taira warriors had hoped to advance by stealth and strike at Hirayama and at me. Among them was one——

Music

"—superb warrior in beaded armor of red. Even one so valiant as Hirayama had been no match for him. Towards the beach——"

Kumagai

—he fled. (Kumagai laughs.) Turn there, splendid warrior youth! Do not follow with the fleeing enemy. I am here. Come back. (Kumagai beckons to him.) Come—come—come!

Music

"He challenges him with his open fan. He spurs his horse towards him. Their swords flash like waves, once, twice, thrice. They begin grappling and finally fall between their two horses."

Fuji-no-Kata

Then you brought this warrior to the dust——?

Kumagai

I did; and when I saw his face at close quarters, I found his hair was black as coal, and his eyebrows were thin, and fine. His age was the same as our own son. And I realized that he too must have parents. This painful thought was too much for a man with a child of his own. I took him by the belt and lifted him to his feet——

[117]

Music

"—brushing off the dust."

Kumagai

I cannot kill you. Run away! Run away quickly!

Sagami

Then you could not really bring yourself to kill him after all?

Kumagai

Although I urged him to flee, he replied, "Kumagai, behead me. Once I have lost to the enemy, I do not care to live."

Fuji-no-Kata

(Sinking in tears) Can it truly be so? He said, "Behead me?"

Kumagai

When I heard those words my heart filled to overflowing. What if my own son, Kojiro, were to lose to the enemy and for that disgrace wish to forfeit his life? How inhuman is the training of a warrior! I tried—but could not draw my sword.

Music

"Hirayama, who had fled shortly before, calls out in a loud voice from a hill behind."

Kumagai

Kumagai! To spare this man after you have defeated him would show the wickedness of a divided mind, the weakness of a coward!

Music

"Thus he shouted at him!"

Kumagai

Yes, I shall kill him. (To Atsumori) If there is anything you wish to say before, tell me now and I will transmit your words.

Music

"Tears well up within him."

Kumagai

My father has perished in the sea. My mother is very much in my heart. This world is as changing as the passing clouds of yesterday. How my mother fares is the only fear I have. Kumagai, I have but one request— behead me!

Music

"Upon this, Fuji-no-Kata speaks——"

Fuji-no-Kata

—If he had thought so much of his mother, surely he should have listened to the words of his father and remained in Kyoto——

Music

"—instead of going to battle in the valley of Ichi-no-Tani."

Fuji-no-Kata

I was wrong to have permitted him to go to the war cheerfully.

Music

"Though previously prepared to face any misfortune which might befall her son, her heart is broken. Now she is even more deeply grieved on hearing the story of his death."

Sagami

(To Fuji-no-Kata) While all the other warriors of the Taira Clan fled to Yashima, your son remained behind bravely. Would you have been pleased if he had fled before the enemy to save himself and had lived to be mocked and despised as a coward?

Kumagai

True, my wife. Now it is unsafe for Fuji-no-Kata to remain here and attract the attention of her enemies and my subordinates. Take her to some secret place quickly. (He calls his attendant.) Gunji, come here! Gunji!

(N.B. End of the Narration)

Kumagai prepares to take "Atsumori's" head to Yoshitsune for inspection and approval. Fuji-no-Kata prays for her deceased son.

Immediately Yoshitsune arrives in full armor at Kumagai's camp. He has come in order to ensure secrecy in case Kumagai has followed his wishes correctly. The head is to be inspected and identified in the privacy of the camp.

Kumagai takes down the notice-board beside the tree and places it before Yoshitsune. He then removes the deep lid of the head-container, but hastily covers it when Sagami, recognizing her son, cries out. Kumagai struggles with her to prevent her from pressing closer to see the head. He pushes her with the notice-board down the three steps and poses climactically with one leg extended over the top step. Sagami and Fuji-no-Kata weep together and hide their faces in grief.

[119]

Kumagai uncovers the head again, removes it from the box. Staring Yoshitsune in the face,* he thrusts it towards him. Yoshitsune slowly opens his fan and peers at the head through the ribs of the fan. At last he says, "Well done! This is indeed the head of Atsumori."

Kumagai then orders the grief-stricken Sagami to display the head to Fuji-no-Kata. Sagami fondles the head of her son, all the while bravely keeping up the front that it is Atsumori's. Fuji-no-Kata maintains the pretense, although she is beside herself with alternate feelings of joy at knowing that her son is still alive, and yet profoundly sympathetic with the bereft Sagami.

The villain of the play, Kajiwara Kagetake (in actual history, Kaketoki), enters suddenly. He threatens to expose the deception to Yoritomo, the Shogun, who is at best not kindly disposed towards his brilliant younger brother, Yoshitsune. Kagetake stalks across the stage in high dudgeon, poses on the *hanamichi* and runs off. His cry is heard from offstage. Midaroku, a master mason, enters and states that he has thrown a dirk killing Kagetake.

Midaroku is the "deus ex machina" of *Kumagai's Camp*. He disposes of the villain of the play, leaving the heroes unsullied by, in Midaroku's words, "the blood of wicked small fry." Further, he affords the solution to the problem of getting Atsumori, the spared enemy soldier, out of Kumagai's camp and to a haven of safety. His presence assured secrecy of the plan and future security for Atsumori's livelihood.

Aside from Midaroku's theatrical necessity, he also has a part in the lives of the characters in the play. He is an old man and quondam warrior of the Taira Clan. His lord and master, having foreseen the fall of the Taira before the Minamoto, subsidized Midaroku to go around the country giving decent burials to fallen Taira soldiers and erecting memorials to the distinguished. Long ago, he had by chance saved the lives of Yoshitsune, his brother Yoritomo, and their mother once when they were trapped by snowdrifts in the mountains. So the enemy who now reigns in Kamakura owes his life to him. This is the bitterness and sorrow of Midaroku. Yoshitsune orders a large armor box in which Atsumori is hiding to be

---

* For two reasons: 1) he cannot bear to see his own son's face, and 2) he is highly doubtful that he has interpreted the inscription correctly, and wishes to discern Yoshitsune's pleasure or displeasure.

brought forth. Midaroku carries it away, and in this way Yoshitsune repays his debt of gratitude to Midaroku.

It is now time to return to the battlefield as the remaining Taira are staging a last counterattack. Kumagai who has now reappeared in full armor, begs to be excused from further combat. He hands Yoshitsune the braid of hair which marks the warrior's hairdress, removes his armor and helmet and shows himself in priest's costume with shaven head. The shock he has received in complying with the standards of feudal society has made it impossible for him to continue as a warrior. He has renounced not only war, but the world too. He takes his leave, carrying the straw hat and staff of a wandering priest.

Yoshitsune, grieved to lose his ablest general, calls out to him to look at his son's head for the last time. Kumagai is overcome with grief and cries out, "There is nothing left for me now but to plod my way to heaven. Ah, those sixteen years (the span of my child's life) have passed in a moment like a dream, like a dream."

The curtain is drawn, leaving Kumagai alone on the *hanamichi*. He sinks to the ground in grief.

The first half of the 18th century was the height of the puppet theatre. During this time Kabuki incorporated the whole of the puppet repertoire, as well, of course, as enlarging its own repertoire of plays. Kabuki has been labelled eclectic for its adaptations, but the influences of the two theatres were reciprocal. Kabuki from the middle of the 18th century began to surpass and outstrip the puppets in popularity and perfection. So the puppets became more and more imitators of Kabuki. From the beginning the stamp of Kabuki had been on the dolls. Chikamatsu's domestic plays were derived from the soft and warm acting of Sakata Tojuro. From the time Danjuro I first adapted Chikamatsu's *Kokusenya,* the puppeteers had begun to copy his *aragoto* style of acting. They imitated the style of *aragoto* literally, unlike Danjuro's initial borrowing merely of inspiration from the primitive hand-operated *Kimpira joruri* puppets. The *Stopping the Carriage* scene from *The Lustrous Imparting of Sugawara's Calligraphic Secrets* was not originally in the manuscript at all. It was arbitrarily added by Kabuki *aragoto* actors. Now, however, it is faithfully performed by the puppets in Kabuki style as part of the original. Matsuomaru's bizarre make-up and bristling wig were also originally Kabuki ideas of staging. Kabuki owes much to the puppets. In fact, it owes more than half its repertoire; but it is also undeniable that the puppets had generous access to the Kabuki improvements. The continued though precarious existence of the puppets today is largely due to the Kabuki regenerative ideas of staging and acting.

5.

Post-Genroku Kabuki. A second reflowering of Kabuki occurred from 1750 and continued to around 1800. Politically, they were dark years for Japan. The Shogun's Minister, Tanuma Okitsugu and his son, Tanuma Okitoma, the General Secretary, used their positions and power oppressively. But culturally the period was Edo's dawn. The economic rise of Osaka was over, and economic force moved to Edo. As a result, there were great men like Aoki Konyo, Sugita Gempaku, and Otsuki Gentaku who revived the study of the sciences first introduced by the Dutch in the 16th century. There were psychologists like Ishida Baigen and Nakazawa Doji. The classicist of Japan's literature, Motoori Norinaga, appeared. Among color-print artists there were Suzuki Harunobu and Torii Kiyonobu. Edo novels and poetry poured from writers' pens.

With the flourishing of art and trade, the center of theatrical activity also shifted to Edo. There the actors turned inward and improved and polished the art which had developed in the once economically favorable and enlightened atmosphere of Osaka and Kyoto. Edo audiences revived *naga-uta* (long songs), a vibrant type of accompanying music for stage dancing, although it had been banned in 1739 for being too voluptuous. In 1754, Nakamura Sukegoro, a noted actor of villain roles, performed a dance called *The Man at Dojoji Temple* (*Otoko Dojoji*) and thereby broke the tradition that dancing belonged only to players of female roles.

As for playwrights, Edo boasted of the competent Namiki Gohei, Tsuuchi Jihei, and Sakurada Jisuke I. It also had a remarkable group of amateur *joruri* singers who wrote for Edo actors who performed as puppets. Among these were Hiraga Gennai, the first discoverer of asbestos in Japan, and writer of the masterpiece *Yaguchi no Watashi*. There was also the Shogun's private physician Yoyodai, who wrote the brilliant *Mirror Mountain* (*Kagami Yama*), the last of the great revenge plays. It tells the story of three women of the Shogun's palace and is referred to as the "Women's *Chushingura*."

During this period of Edo's flourishing, Osaka had only Chikamatsu Hanji and Suga Sensuke,* the great puppet writers. Because of them, writing for the puppets ended at least with a brilliant swansong. Oddly enough, the name Chikamatsu began and ended the period of great puppet play-writing. Hanji however was probably not a blood descendant of Monzaemon. The name had been passed on to favorites and pupils.

Chikamatsu Hanji's masterpiece was a long play, *Omi Genji Senjin Yakata*. From it only Act VIII remains, the scene of Moritsuna's Camp (*Moritsuna Jinya*), an ancillary plot within a long drama. It was first written for the puppets in 1769. Osaka Kabuki adapted it in 1770. In 1793 it was first performed in Edo.

Background to the story:

The play centers around the historical event of the summer siege of Osaka Castle in 1615 when Hideyori and his generals retreated to make a last but hopeless stand against Tokugawa Ieyasu. With the fall of the castle, Tokugawa Ieyasu usurped full power, and the long reign of the Tokugawa rule was begun. In the drama, because of the sensitivity of the government, the locale is changed from Osaka to Kamakura; the time is changed from the 17th century to the 14th; Tokugawa Ieyasu is called Hojo Tokimasa; Sanada Yukimura is named Takatsuna; Sanada Nobuyuki, his brother, is given the name of Moritsuna.

Moritsuna's Camp is an extraordinary drama from numerous points of

* For a translation of Suga Sensuke's *Gappo and His Daughter Tsuji*, see Appendix.

view. It requires constant thought in order to figure out the motivations of the various characters. The hero's role is one of the most difficult in Japanese theatre, because he must act thoughts often without words to assist in communicating what is passing through his mind. The highly interiorized conception of this hero makes the play one of interpretation rather than one of direct action—although the play certainly does not lack in movement.

Synopsis of the play:

Moritsuna and his brother Takatsuna belonged to two opposing camps. Both were generals. Moritsuna belonged to the Hojo camp in Kamakura; and his brother to the enemy camp in Kyoto. In battle the Hojo camp was repeatedly successful, and all tactics planned by Takatsuna, the strategist for the Kyoto camp, resulted in failure. One day the Kyoto side lost yet another battle, and Koshiro, the son of Takatsuna, was captured by his cousin, Kosaburo, the son of Moritsuna.

The drama begins with Moritsuna's triumphal return to his camp. He is accompanied by his son and the captive nephew, Koshiro. Moritsuna has been charged with the safekeeping of the prisoner. His son has been praised by Hojo Tokimasa, the lord, for capturing the valuable prisoner.

On returning to his camp, Moritsuna tells Mimyo, his mother, the details of his son's gallantry. They are pleased with his exploit.

Suddenly Wada Byoe, a general of the Kyoto camp, is announced. Moritsuna is greatly surprised by his arrival. Wada states that he has come to beg the release of the captive, Koshiro. This extraordinary request leads Moritsuna to think that there is some hidden intention behind it.

Fearing to give an answer before discovering the secret, Moritsuna evades the request. "You surprise me. It's curious that you, an enemy general, have come in person. Why do you urge me so earnestly? It strikes me as strange, very strange indeed," and he laughs at him. Wada is serious, however, and says that he has come even at the sacrifice of his life. Wada's persistence is even more unusual; Moritsuna had not expected the capture to become such an issue.

Then Moritsuna's line of thinking turns. Until then he had wondered at Wada's motives. Now it occurs to him that his brother Takatsuna is seriously anxious for his son. Perhaps love for the son has blinded the father to reasonable action. Thinking of his brother's attitude, Moritsuna becomes irritated.

"Well, I had been confident in my brother Takatsuna, as he is. And now to think of his weak spirit because of his son!"

Wada presses his request. Moritsuna answers, "A youngster like that is of no importance. I might like to release him but . . ." He flatly rejects the request because the boy has been specifically entrusted to him by his lord and thus he says, "I can by no means release him in private." In order to put an end to Wada's insistence in seeking the boy's release, he hastens to add high-handedly, "Try to take him by force, and you will not leave here alive."

Wada's visit has actually been sheer stratagem from the beginning. He has no intention of taking the boy away. So far as he has succeeded in convincing Moritsuna of his brother's anxiety, his aim is attained. He ignores Moritsuna's challenge. He leaves, pretending to go to Hojo Tokimasa's camp to intercede with the lord personally.

Moritsuna, left alone, is lost in meditation. He thinks his brother must have lost his reason out of fear for his son. Why else would he have sent his chief general to recover his son? This overwhelming thought prevents him from suspecting Wada's professed avowal to proceed to Hojo Tokimasa. In reality Wada's scheme was to escape from Moritsuna's camp, the stringent situation, and still to leave the impression that the request had been in earnest.

Moritsuna is at a loss. His most essential obligation is towards his lord. It is against his way to be unfaithful to his lord for the sake of a private affair. To betray the samurai's code was to him to lose all. And yet his brother is about to stray from this very path.

Following this course of reasoning, Moritsuna begins to believe that Hojo Tokimasa has deliberately entrusted him with the captive Koshiro, and intends to use the boy as a means of getting Takatsuna over to his side. If this happens, it will redound to his brother's everlasting dishonor.

Moritsuna is a compassionate and sympathetic man. He is eager to see a noble and brave man in his brother, although they are fighting hard against each other on opposing sides. He well realizes and sympathizes with his brother's paternal love. The more deeply he thinks, the more strongly he fears for Takatsuna.

The boy's existence makes a coward of his brother. Without the boy, his brother would lose the object of his love and would surely fight honorably and to the best of his ability. He resolves to kill the poor child, despite the cruelty of the thought.

But he still has his responsibility towards his lord. This awareness blunts his resolution, for it would betray his master's trust to kill a captive entrusted to his guard, without public cause or upon order. This means he cannot kill the boy with his own hands. Yet Koshiro's death, he feels, is absolutely indispensable at this juncture.

At last he hits upon a solution. He will ask his mother, Mimyo, to persuade the boy to commit harakiri. Should she fail in her persuasion, she is to kill the boy. It would be for his brother's sake, yet he would not be betraying his master. The boy's existence is a trifle to the Hojo camp, while it might turn out to be a grave matter with the Kyoto side. Above all, it might lead to the degradation of his brother. After having reasoned this far, he calls his mother to disclose the intention.

He is seized with pangs of remorse at the inhuman request no matter what the intended good for the brother—to kill a nephew of the same blood and by his mother's hand. He is disturbed; "It would be mercy to beseech to spare his life, and yet to kill him for mercy's sake!" Then the *joruri* recites:

"Woe to a samurai's fate!
Brother and brother,
Nephew and son,
On opposing sides.
Both of a blood,
Fighting with swords,
Blood streaming,
Sounds of battle drums
On the blood-stained fields of war.
The pain in the heart,
Weighs heavy as a huge stone."

Mimyo accedes through her tears, to the request. Moritsuna says, "Well done, my mother. Be good enough to assist him in that moment." The evening bell sounds, and Moritsuna softly intones, "It is already the evening of a short day."

He goes into the inner room. Mimyo, firmly resolved, goes behind the screen at the upper end of the stage. The stage is vacant.

Kagaribi, the boy's mother, disguised as a soldier, appears on the *hanamichi* and shoots an arrow into a tree outside Moritsuna's camp. Attached to the arrow is a piece of paper on which a fragment of an ancient ode has been written ". . . Oh, how I wish I could see him come in secret," in order to suggest to her child to escape. She has managed to enter the camp by mingling with the retainers accompanying Wada Byoe.

The mother's appearance is another part of Takatsuna's stratagem. It is of little consequence whether the boy gets the paper or not. It is enough if it attracts Moritsuna's attention. Wada Byoe came first. Then the boy's mother who suggests a secret escape. Moritsuna, although clever and thoughtful, cannot possibly understand the secret aim. He cannot but think of his brother's fondness for the boy.

Kagaribi stands at the gate of the camp when Hayase, Moritsuna's wife, comes out from within. She picks up the paper and reads the poem and shoots back the arrow with a cryptic reply in poetry, "Whether to go or remain, the barrier at Osaka knows not." Kagaribi interprets this as a sign to wait. Hayase withdraws.

Koshiro, the captive boy, has heard her muttering the poem. He enters on tiptoe. Mimyo follows after him. She tries to make him commit suicide. He will not do so. She starts to kill him, but looking at his face she weakens and breaks into tears.

A battle alarm sounds. Mimyo and her grandson take cover in an inner room. Hayase rushes onto the scene with a halberd under her arm. Kagaribi breaks open the gate and is about to run after her son. Hayase stops her and Moritsuna comes out from within. Kagaribi covers her head with a broad brimmed helmet and hides.

By the alarm, Moritsuna knows that something has happened at Hojo Tokimasa's headquarters. He calls for and sends his son, Kosaburo, to get news.

As the boy leaves, a messenger arrives. He reports that Takatsuna, with only two thousand men under his command, is making an assault on the well-prepared camp where tens of thousands are guarding the Lord Tokimasa. Moritsuna is shocked, and thinks that all is lost. His heart is empty of all thought of the Kyoto or Hojo camps, or of his master Tokimasa. He is full of brotherly love. Death for his brother seems inevitable. "Merciful Buddha! My brother, prudent as he is, is entrapped by a trick— all out of love for his son. Who can survive a single desperate attack against tens of thousands?"

He catches sight of Kagaribi, and turns to his mother, saying: "Now with your maternal mercy say prayers for the repose of his soul." He cries, "Inevitable fortunes of war!" as his tribute of tears to his brother.

A report of victory is brought and Tokimasa arrives bringing Takatsuna's head to be identified by Moritsuna. Moritsuna feels the cruel duty imposed upon him by his lord. The *joruri* speaks for him, "Oh, to have to see the dead brother's head!"

As soon as Moritsuna uncovers the head, Koshiro who had been hiding nearby, jumps down and plunges a dagger into his abdomen. Moritsuna, who has not even seen the head yet, instantly covers it, and queries the reason of the rash act. The boy replies, "I wanted to remain alive until I could see my father again; now that he is dead, I need not live." Moritsuna is confused.

Up to this point the possibility that the head could be a substitute or a mistaken one has been in Moritsuna's mind, but the boy's suicide dispels all suspicion. He is convinced of his brother's death. At the same time he is filled with pity for the son.

"Don't tarry. Be quick and give your witness at once," urges his lord; and Moritsuna resumes the process of identification.

He adheres to the proper formal procedure for traditional head inspections. Finally he stares at the head. He is amazed to find that it is not his brother's.

Recalling the series of the events—Koshiro's capture, Wada Byoe's request for the boy's release, Kagaribi's appearance, and Takatsuna's desperate assault on the camp—Moritsuna begins to realize that all these were concentrated on the single aim of making the head of another person to be taken for Takatsuna's. In believing Takatsuna dead, the Hojo Tokimasa forces will cease their assaults. The boy's death was the strongest evidence for forcing the enemy to think it the real head.

He is astounded at the elaborateness of his brother's plot, and profoundly moved by Koshiro's bravery in sacrificing himself for his father. It has become impossible for Moritsuna to betray the child's spirit in having discharged his grave duty.

Moritsuna announces to Tokimasa, "In spite of the arrow wound on the face, it is without question the head of my brother, Takatsuna."

Tokimasa is pleased and leaves a large armor box as reward for Moritsuna's services.

Moritsuna announces to his family that it was a false head and that his brother is safe. He praises Koshiro for his extreme sacrifice. All weep. He starts to kill himself when Wada Byoe reappears. He pretends to aim his pistol at Moritsuna, but unexpectedly fires into the armor box. Out springs a spy which Tokimasa has left to make sure that Moritsuna has not deceived him. The spy dies. Wada tells Moritsuna it is too early to die yet, "Bide your time until Takatsuna makes his appearance and your loyalty and humanity will be made perfect." Moritsuna bids farewell, and Wada returns to his camp.

During the last half of the 18th century an attempt to reform the Tanumas' political policies was made. The country gradually began to breathe more easily. But no additions were made to the development of the Japanese theatre. The birth and growth of Kabuki were complete. The puppets lingered on without being a vital force. Other arts continued to progress in Japan, but Kabuki remained fixed. The spirit of Genroku embodied in Kabuki, although of no connection with subsequent periods, satisfied a romantic longing after the days of the commoners' rise and the tribulations of the warriors. Kabuki remained what it was—a popular amusement of the people. The people were content with sustaining the great tradition as it was. This content was to remain until the Meiji Era at the end of the 19th century.

IV

Contributions of Historical Kabuki to Present Day Kabuki

The culmination of Kabuki was reached in the middle of the 18th century. But whatever improvements or refinements these subsequent developments may have brought, the kernel of Kabuki remained Genroku in spirit. In substance and technique, Kabuki descends straight from that period. Its chief details of construction, form, and presentation today can be directly traced to their Genroku origins.

1.

Role-types. Before the years of Genroku, Kabuki had already shifted from dance into drama. Fortunately this was accomplished without forfeiting the element of dance in the plays. As for the drama, the initial triangular relationship of male, female, and comedian quickly evolved into eight basic role-types: the hero, villain, woman, comedian or foil, old man, old woman, young man, and child.

Character delineation was restricted to a certain degree by adherence to the stereotyped role classifications, but as the theatre advanced, the number of role-types themselves increased. These new additions are considered subdivisions of the eight basic types; but their individuality and importance make them for all practical purposes independent in their own right. Each role-type is characterized by particular rules of make-up, gesticulation, and voice placement. Each also, to a certain extent, is limited as to its place of relative importance within the drama and as to whether it is a stellar role or one merely played by lessor actors.

These basic classifications and their most important subdivisions fall roughly into the following outline:

1) Hero Roles (*tachi-yaku*)
   a—Supermen (*aragoto-shi*)
   b—Handsome, somewhat effeminate, youthful men of sexual attraction (*wagoto-shi* or *iro-otoko*)
   c—Men of judgement (*sabaki-yaku*)
   d—Men of patient endurance (*shimbo-yaku*)
2) Villain Roles (*kataki-yaku*)
   a—Men of dignity, such as conspirators against the Throne or ruling power (*kuge-aku*)
   b—Men whose villainy is complete and unmitigated (*jitsu-aku*)
   c—Handsome young men, outwardly appearing incapable of villainous action (*iro-aku*)
   d—Minor villains (*ha-gataki*)
   e—Comic and absurd villains (*hando-gataki*)
3) Heroine Roles (*onnagata*)
   a—Courtesans (*keisei*)
   b—Young maidens (*musume-gata*)
   c—Princesses (*o-hime-sama*)
   d—Faithful wives of sincerity (*sewa-nyobo*)
   e—Women who are forced to make extreme sacrifices (*katahazushi no yaku*)
4) Comedians (*doke-yaku*)
5) Old men (*oyaji-kata*)
6) Old women (*kyasha-gata*)
7) Handsome young men (*wakashu-kata*)
8) Children (*ko-yaku*)

Among the male roles, perhaps the most subtle is the "man of judgement." He represents a person of high rank who is entrusted with a grave mission but who exercises his judgement and usually ends up by disobeying his orders. Kumagai and Moritsuna, as seen in the preceding summaries, are two examples of this role.

This type of role developed in Kabuki (and the dolls) for two reasons: the commoners liked to see their superiors confounded; and they liked loyalty—a Confucian tenet and the kernel of *bushido*—presented in such roles as a highly fluid concept which could be subordinated to a higher sense of justice, mercy, love, or respect. If loyalty was followed, the warriors suffered; if it was violated, then it was for reasons closer to the hearts of the commoners witnessing the plays who were not bound by the warrior's code.

The plays with heroes of judgement gave rise to another classification, "plays of divided loyalty." In them the hero either goes over to the enemy side or saves enemy personnel against the dictates of his previously sworn allegiance. The traditional Japanese aphorism, "Yesterday's enemy, today's friend," has many exemplifications in such plays. Their popularity today, since the surrender of Japan and her *volte-face* in allegiance to the side of the Allies, has taken on new significance. Because of the tradition of such plays in Japanese life, undoubtedly a shift in loyalty was easier than it might otherwise have been.

Accompanying these roles of judgement for men are the women, wives, or mothers who are forced into some extremity. These women are called upon to execute tasks of the most painful sort—such as parting from their children, serving their lords or husbands against their wills, or rising to heights of honor at the cost of their human emotions. They are faithful and devoted women placed in positions of suffering. Their ability to bear their cruel fate makes them noble.

The wives in Chikamatsu's domestic plays are commoners and do not fall technically into this classification. But the spirit is the same. The courtesans may have the beauty, but these wives and mothers have the character. Behavior patterns of the Japanese since Genroku have relegated women to an increasingly inferior position. But Kabuki and the puppets have glorified quite as many women as men.

The villain roles of Kabuki are equal in theatrical importance (though not in determining an actor's rank and status) to the hero roles. Kabuki in general revels in villainy, and its monstrous men, the *jitsu-aku*, are made even more monstrous by make-up, wigs, inconceivably evil deeds, and remorselessness. They are grotesque in their actions, and in climactic poses sometimes stick out their tongues, which have been painted blood red, and growl and roar with frightening power.

As the peace of the Tokugawa Era continued and the appetites of the audience grew jaded, more evil and more shocking behavior was added to these villains. The result was, perhaps inadvertently, a remarkable and artistic aspect of the Kabuki art form. By raising the villains to the point of incredibility, a purely esthetic type of character emerged from the plays. His actual villainy became subservient to the grandiose air he presented on the stage. The horrifying aspect of his behavior became lost in the horribleness of his appearance. So gorgeously arrayed and so terrifying in mien are these villains that the relation between them and the evil in the actual world becomes slight and they are divorced from any connection with reality.

Some villains, however, were allowed at the last minute to reform. This reforming is technically called a *modori,* and occurs only after the villain has been mortally wounded. During the *modori,* which is accompanied by the lonely wail of a high pitched flute offstage, the villain explains to his murderer that he has repented shortly before and has just accomplished some heroic action. The man who has killed him regrets his action, and the villain dies at peace with the world.

Fifty per cent of the Kabuki repertoire today contains leading roles of courtesans. In Genroku this proportion was considerably higher, as the organized system of the courtesans was established at that time

THE LAST ACT OF SUGAWARA DENJU TENARAI KAGAMI

Matsuo maru (played by Kikugoro) inspects his child's head while Genzo
(played by Kichiemon) the schoolmaster looks on

THE SMUGGLERS IN CHIKAMATSU PLAY, THE COURTESAN OF
HAKATA AND HER PILLOW OF WAVES

and was a topic of lively interest for the people. The courtesan's position in Genroku was of considerable importance. She was the apex of a social triangle. At the base of the triangle were the commoner and his arch-enemy, the warrior. The courtesan was accessible to either provided he had sufficient money. Her training in the arts, her general education and experience made her greatly sought after and respected by her patrons. To a certain extent, she even exerted a measure of political influence, if her patron was an official of the government. Her power over the feudal lords of the time is evident from the word for courtesans, *keisei,* which literally means the "crumbling of the castle." The appellation arose because of the large number of castles which were sold or mortgaged by lords who competed with the common merchants for the favors of the favorite courtesans.

Since the days of *A Visit to a Courtesan,* few playwrights have resisted the attraction of writing about courtesans. Such roles afford opportunity for two of the basic elements of the Japanese theatre, eroticism and the dance. Her profession is obviously one of love, and her training means that she can be called upon to dance. But her chief appeal to the spectator is her beauty and elaborate accoutrements. The courtesans of Kabuki are dressed in Genroku regalia. They are swathed in layers of inner and outer kimonos, each more highly embroidered than the other. The wigs of thick heavy hair and decorative pins and ornaments sometimes weigh as much as twenty-five pounds. When such a character walks through the streets (the *hanamichi*), it is like a regal procession. She wears wooden clogs 5 inches high. She rests her hand on the shoulder of an attendant at her side who supports her should she stumble. Behind her another attendant carries a large umbrella to protect her from the sun. Around her, several others carry her appurtenances—a long thin brass pipe, the bowl of which is large enough for two or three puffs of tobacco; her purse; tea in case she becomes thirsty, etc.

The public's delight in courtesans' roles has continued and is now a test by which the excellence of an actor of female roles is determined. In 1947 Nakamura Shikan was awarded a prize of money by the Education Ministry for his interpretation of Yatsuhashi, a courtesan who is killed out of jealousy by her pockmarked lover, in Kawatake Mokuami's play, *Kago Tsurube*.

Almost on a level with the courtesans in color and charm are the princess roles, which are treated in a highly formalized and stylized manner. Genroku playwrights and audiences had little conception of what an actual princess was like. Without a model to follow they invented an original and curious stereotype which has persisted down the years. The Princess is always dressed in long-sleeved, red embroidered kimonos. She is devoid of physical strength and many scenes show her struggling to lift her husband's helmet or massaging her legs bruised from even the shortest of walks. When in love, as she always is, the Princess is extremely forward sexually. She always pursues the object of her affections, and only wins out after enduring various hardships. Her life is often endangered but she is saved by devoted retainers. She is also endowed with supernatural powers. Princesses, despite their remoteness from humanity, are always extremely beautiful and sympathetic.

The most celebrated princess roles in Kabuki are traditionally called the "Three Princesses" (*san hime*). The phrase refers to Princess Yaegaki in *Honcho Nijushi Ko,* Princess Yuki in *Kinkakuji,* and Princess Toki in *Kamakura Sandai Ki.* Each has her great scene. Yaegaki is faithful to her lover even after she thinks him dead. He appears and she becomes bewitched by the spirit of a fox and is thereby enabled to steal a helmet from her father for him. Yuki is tied, hands behind her back, to a cherry tree for refusing the advances of a wicked lord. She draws the outline of a rat in the fallen cherry blossom petals at her feet. So expert is her skill that the rat comes to life and gnaws at the rope and she is freed. Toki is in love with her father's enemy. In the action of the play she is forced to perform housewifely duties like a commoner, and is compelled by her lover to kill her own father. Only after all this does she succeed in gaining her lover's consent to marry her.

Roles of old men and women (grouped together as *fuke-yaku*) are relatively few in number, but by no means subsidiary in Kabuki. Chikamatsu Monzaemon was the first playwright to accentuate the part old people play in the lives of his characters. Japan is, of course, a country where filial piety and veneration of the aged are deeply engrained in the minds of the people. It is natural for these roles to assume greater importance than, say, in Western theatre. So great, in fact, are some of these old parts that they are referred to as "pivot points" (*kyogen mawashi*) around which the play moves. Frequently the action of the old characters in the play is the determining factor of the drama. They force the dénouement and control the deeds and destiny of the young hero and heroine as well. In these roles a great deal is made of the ties of age and family devotion. Relations between father and son, or grandmother and granddaughter, for example, are taxed to the utmost, and both sides are strained to the breaking point by the intensity of feeling.

Children's roles (*Ko-yaku*) are used largely for emotional effect. Murders and sacrifice were popular themes, but when the pathos of innocent children was added to them, an even more moving and sensational drama resulted.

The acting of children in Kabuki is highly conventionalized. Weeping is expressed by alternately bringing each sleeve to the eyes; speaking is always in a high shrill falsetto; entreaty is expressed by placing the hands together and shaking the head tearfully. But despite the limits on the acting, the part the child plays is often a very important role. He may be the victim of a sacrifice, or denied the right to be with his parents. Sometimes he is even the avenger of his father's murder.

Genroku's taste for the child and sensitivity to his plight in this world reflected actual possibilities in that day of social changes. There were constant family disruptions, plots against child heirs, and brutal sacrifices of innocent youths by the warriors. Such pathos with its deep rooted connections in the Japanese family system and its sentimental indulgence of the child, has not lost its power to move even today's audiences.

2.

Actors. Actors advanced together with the development of the role-types. Dozens of great actors, each with his specialty of role, arose during Genroku. Villains were always played by actors of villain roles. The player of heroic roles was always the hero. It was thought that a player of women's parts would ruin his acting if he played male parts frequently. It is said that when the Genroku actor of villain's parts, Nakamura Heikuro, once attempted an heroic part, before he could speak his opening lines the audience had already begun to hiss at him. Confinement to one role-type led to constant development and growth within the particular sphere. Only after this development reached a maximum depth, did the actor turn to versatility as a substitute for specialization. This took place in the late 19th century and unfortunately at the expense of some of the finish and polish. Today a number of actors pride themselves on the variety of role-types they can perform.

Actors of the various types of roles trained their own children and adopted students. Actors' families became known for their special role-types. Vestiges of this remain today. The Ichikawa Danjuro family stands for *aragoto* and heroic actors. The Nakamura Utaemon family implies players of female roles, although the actors no longer, as they did in Genroku, live as women even in their daily lives. The Onoe family is famous for its ghost plays. Many of these families hold exclusive rights to the plays which typify their traditionally favored roles.

Another characteristic of Genroku actors and their families which has continued in present day Kabuki circles is the system of family names. This was still another example of the power of the actor in Genroku and the defiant spirit of the commoner in his pursuit of pleasure. At that time it was forbidden by law for any other than the warrior or noble to have more than a first name. Kabuki actors, however, arbitrarily took last names and flagrantly advertised them outside the theatre-houses in defiance of the authorities.

One precaution was taken, however. If the authorities were to object to the two names, the long thin boards on which the names were written could easily be removed and the *yago* substituted. The *yago* (literally, house-name) is an appellation ending in *ya* which identifies the actor as to birthplace, trade, or some other characteristic. *Yago* applied to the specific actor as well as to any other member of the same family. These *yago* have remained in effect until today, although in the 19th century all Japanese (except the Emperor who still has only the one name) were ordered to take two names, and actors were no longer exceeding their right.

In Japan when spectators wish to express enthusiasm for an actor's performance, at his entry or exit, or even in the middle of a climactic scene, instead of applauding, they shout out. Sometimes they call out, "I have waited for that!" (*matte imashita*) or "That's it!" (*soko da yo*), and personal cries of approbation in a mixture of enthusiasm and proper theatre etiquette. It is correct to call out either the *yago* of the actor or the number he is in the generations of actors who have held the same name. In Genroku, spectators called out the *yago* because the double-barreled names of the actors would have been too long to say. In ordinary conversation it is also fashionable to refer to the actors by this name.

The following is a list of the most famous contemporary acting families and their *yago:*

Actor's Name	*Actor's Yago*
Ichikawa Danjuro	*Narita-ya*
Ebizo	Danjuro I was awkward in his

Sansho Danzo	youth and only after praying to the Fudo God at Narita near Tokyo was he able to succeed in the theatre. He was dubbed Narita-ya in commemoration of his successful prayer.
Matsumoto Koshiro Somegoro Kintaro	*Korai-ya* *Korai* was the name for Korea in the Tokugawa Era. The first Koshiro had originally been a storekeeper specializing in goods from Korea.
(Tokyo) Nakamura Kichiemon Tokizo Moshio	*Harima-ya* This branch of the Nakamura family was originally from *Harima,* an obsolete name for an eastern province of Japan.
(Osaka) Nakamura Baigyoku Fukusuke	*Takasago-ya* Takasago originally referred to Formosa. The connection with the Osaka family is unknown.
(Tokyo) Nakamura Utaemon Shikan Fukusuke Kotaro	*Narikoma-ya* Literally means "to become a steed." The connection is now unknown.
Sawamura Sojuro Tanosuke Tossho	*Kinokuni-ya* The Genroku family was originally from the country of Ki, a province of Japan.
Bando Mitsugoro Mitsunosuke	*Yamato-ya* Originally from Yamato, the central province of Japan.
Ichimura Uzaemon	*Tachibana-ya*

Kakitsu	Tachibana is the name of a tree, the leaf of which is the emblem of the Ichimura family crest.
Onoe Baiju	*Otowa-ya*
Kikugoro	Literally "sound-feather": origin
Baiko	unknown.
Shoroku	
Kikunosuke	
Ushinosuke	
Otani Tomoemon	*Akashi-ya*
Hirotaro	Meaning unknown

Actors in Kabuki have several different names, each of which has a special meaning. The stage names on the left hand side of the above list represent degrees of youth and professional advancement. Children of the great actors start out with a minor name. As they progress, their names are changed as a reward for attainment. The change in name is announced during a public ceremony between the acts of an actual performance at the theatre. This ceremony of promotion is called "succession to the name" (*shumei*) and is an occasion of great honor. Each actor's name also has a "hidden name" (*haimyo*). The "hidden name" is of equivalent rank with the regular name, and is given out when two actors of excellence are in the same family. For example: Baiko is the "hidden name" of Kikugoro, and was given to the eldest son of Kikugoro V, while the younger son was given the name Kikugoro. Names can only be passed on after the death of the present bearer of the name. Often long intervals elapse before the name is re-awarded.

The succession of names works according to traditional and established rules. One of the youngest actors on the Kabuki stage today is nine-year-old Ushinosuke, the son of the present Baiko and a member of the Onoe stage family. At the age of five in 1948 he made his stage debut. By the time he reaches adolescence, if he progresses satisfactorily as an actor, he will acquire the next step in rank among his family's names, Kikunosuke. If after this he matures into still greater talent and becomes one of the top ranking actors, he could be given one of three names, Baiko, Kikugoro, and Shoroku, all of which are of approximately equal distinction. However, since his father is Baiko, he will most likely succeed to that name immediately upon his father's death. If he becomes greatest of all members of the Onoe family, he may take the name Baiju, the highest Onoe name in history. If it should happen that no member of an acting family is worthy of the top name in the family, the name may go unused for several generations until a suitable candidate appears.

In the case of bad actors, they either leave the stage entirely or remain with a lesser name until the end of their acting careers. If an actor is an only son in a distinguished acting family, he is usually not permitted to abandon the stage. His father pushes him and forces him to keep on appearing despite his awkwardness and apparent lack of talent. This practice is not as unsuccessful as it sounds. It has often happened that an actor will not reach his full greatness on the stage until very late in his life. A case in point is the late Uzaemon XV who after fifty-five years of mediocre acting suddenly blossomed into one of the most brilliant actors ever to appear, and continued acting at the peak of his fame until his death at the age of seventy-four.

The Japanese are reluctant to predict the greatness of young actors until they are well past maturity. I once asked Koshiro VII whose three sons, all in their thirties, are among the best actors of the younger generation, which of them would be the best eventually. He replied that it would be impossible to know at this time, as an actor's genius emerges when he reaches his middle forties. Then only could be given an answer to my question.

Not all Japanese actors are slow to reach perfection. The present Nakamura Shikan is already acknowledged as one of the greatest of actors of female roles. He was adopted at an early age and was immediately given the name of Kotaro. His talent was such that he was soon named Fukusuke. Later he became Shikan, his present status. He is already assured of becoming Utaemon, the name which carries the highest rank for actors of female roles.

In addition to an actor's personal name (that is, his ordinary family name as a private citizen), his stage name, and his "hidden name," he also has special names which he uses to sign poetry he has written or to sign pictures he has painted. Both the arts of poetry and painting are considered part of the accomplishments of an actor.

Actors' names are further complicated by the use of the generation number (*dai-me*). This is also frequently called out by the spectators when they want to praise a moment in a performance. Since Genroku, each actor's name has been used repeatedly by successive students and children. Each bearer of the name has a generation number appended to the name. For example: one of the oldest names in Kabuki today is Ichikawa Uzaemon. The present holder of the title is the sixteenth in the line.

The name Ichikawa Danjuro has been vacant since 1903, and when revived, will be the tenth since Genroku's Danjuro I. The present Ichikawa Ebizo has already been designated as the next successor. Danjuro is considered the highest name in Kabuki history, not because of its age, but because of the continuous line of distinguished actors who have held it. Many names have lost their rank by a series of poor actors succeeding to the name, and some names have disappeared for lack of children or suitable students to carry on.

In other cases, a young star of promise, but not from a distinguished acting family, may arbitrarily take an entirely original name, and thereby start a new line of names. This is what happened in the case of the present Nakamura Kichiemon I, the doyen of the great remaining Kabuki actors today.

The tight family system of the Kabuki actors established in Genroku sprang from necessity. Their inferior social position forced them to band together for protection among themselves. Actors were called "river bed beggars" (*kawara mono*), and "hut dwellers" (*koya mono*), for many years. Only at the end of the 19th century, during the Meiji Reformation, was their social status elevated, and their profession genuinely respected socially. The Japanese sense of tradition and respect for heredity has sustained the actor's family system to this day. Although lineage, in some quarters of opinion, carries with it certain feudal aspects incompatible within a democratic country, it is unlikely that the system and the distinction accrued to the names through the centuries will disappear before Kabuki itself collapses.

3.

The Stage. Another important contribution of Genroku to present-day Kabuki is the special Kabuki stage and its several related mechanical devices. O-Kuni started in a river bed of Kyoto and progressed from there to lawns, and finally to Noh stages. In Genroku, Kabuki perfected its own unique type of stage. Its principles are still in use today and have even influenced the construction of certain advanced German and Russian theatre-houses, particularly those designed by Reinhardt and Maierhold.

Perhaps the most impressive contribution of the Japanese to theatre craft is the *hanamichi*. A smaller auxiliary passage-way down the opposite side of the theatre to the stage is also used and is called the *kari-hanamichi*. The passage-way through the audience gives the stage an extra dimension to work with. It gives an increased sense of perspective and depth, and is an expression of that vital feature of Kabuki: intimacy and closeness between actor and audience.

The right and left entrances of the Bugaku dancers account for the *hanamichi's* remote origin. The Noh stage which has the bridge passage (*hashigakari*) extending from the right of the stage to the wings made the concept of the passage-way a natural development. It was a simple extension to place it at right angles to the stage. However, the direct origin of establishing the *hanamichi* at 90° to the stage was the rings of Sumo wrestlers. The wrestlers, whose popularity in Genroku was second only to the Kabuki actors and the puppets, borrowed the characteristic drum and flute music used to announce the beginning and end of a Kabuki day at the theatre. In return, it is said, Kabuki borrowed the long and narrow approach to the wrestling arena. As this approach was always lined with flowers, gifts from patrons to their favorite wrestlers, the name flower-path (*hanamichi*) was evolved.

House lights in modern Japanese theatres are not dimmed during performances. Two rows of footlights along both sides of the *hanamichi* are sufficient for full illumination. In Genroku the only lighting came from the ceiling windows over the stage. To light the *hanamichi,* two men (*kurombo*), dressed for invisibility in black, with faces covered, carried long sticks with candles on the end. They were called *sashidashi* and illuminated the actor's face as he advanced to the stage or disappeared through the audience into the small dressing room or entry-box (*agemaku*) at the end of the *hanamichi*. Nowadays these are not actually required. But because of frequent power shortages, light failures, and generally dim lighting throughout Japan, this archaic practice has been revived since World War II. Its esthetic appeal is akin to the closeup in movies, as it focuses the audience's attention on the immediate area of the actor's face.

The Genroku *hanamichi* had a subordinate platform called the "name stand" (*nadai*) which was placed about three-fourths down the *hanamichi* towards the stage. There the leading actor always stopped to declare his name and purpose in the play. This platform subsequently fell into desuetude. It remains in feeling in the form of the *suppon,* an arbitrary point where actors invariably pause, stumble, pose, or declaim their opening or closing lines. In many of the *aragoto* plays of the "18 Favorites," its use remains.

The advantage of the *hanamichi* with its people seemingly rising out of the audience and disappearing into it, is that the dramatic illusion is increased. One does not feel a witness to the program, but a part of it.

Many of the stage settings of the small puppet theatres involved only light back drops. They were insufficient in Kabuki with live actors who required heavy, realistic properties. The joint compositions pouring from the puppet playwrights, with their complicated plots, meant that a rapid shift of scenes became necessary.

The revolving stage invented by the Edo playwright Namiki Shozo in 1729 solved the problem. With the revolving stage as many as four sets could be constructed on the one stage and with a moment's turn could be brought into view. New effects were created to exploit the possibilities of the revolving stage to its fullest. The actor could appear to walk around a house as the stage revolved. He could wander through a forest stalking an enemy, as the turning stage showed different sections of the set. Or, as in *Kezori,* where the actor is tossed off a ship, he could appear to swim around to the opposite side in order to escape the searching eye of the enemy. Naturally much use is made of the *hanamichi.* There, while the scene changes on the stage proper, the action continues and diverts the attention of the audience from the mechanics of scene shifting.

In 1735, Otani Hiroji, pupil of the puppeteer Tachimatsu Hachirobei, invented two of Kabuki's cleverest bits of staging, *seriage* and *hikinuki.* The supernatural element often found in Kabuki particularly required these special types of stagecraft.

Seriage is a large trapdoor in the floor of the stage proper and a smaller one at the *suppon* three-quarters down the *hanamichi* near the stage. Through these holes in the stage floor an actor may mysteriously rise up or disappear downwards.

Effective use of *seriage* is made in the play *Sendai Hagi* where a rat who has been struck on the forehead with an iron fan, runs to the *hanamichi* and disappears through the floor. Immediately from the same trapdoor the villain, a magician (who had assumed the form of a rat in order to accomplish his evil deeds), rises up dressed in rat-grey clothes and bearing a fresh wound on his forehead.

Hikinuki is a process of loosely basting layers of outer clothing together and while the actor continues his actions, an assistant pulls out the threads. At the climactic moment when the character changes his mood or reveals his true identity, the outer layer falls off and the actor appears suddenly in a new costume in startling contrast to the previous one. In *Ogiya Kumagai,* a scene takes place where Atsumori disguised as a girl suddenly throws off his outer clothing and wig, and reveals himself as a man in full armor.

Until Genroku the curtain was not widely used in Japan's theatres. The actors proceeded to the stage and then took up their roles. Genroku audiences demanded a greater sense of surprise and an increase in illusion. A wide cloth curtain of alternative black, green, and terra cotta stripes (*johiki-maku*) was devised. This curtain is pulled to either side of the stage, rather than being raised. If the play is of pure Kabuki origin the curtain is pushed to the left side of the stage. If it is adapted from the puppets, which means that musicians are at the right of the stage in full view, the curtain is pulled to the right side of the stage.

Even this curtain was not enough to satisfy Genroku audiences' desire for suspense and surprise. After the front curtain is drawn, sometimes another curtain is revealed. If it is black, it represents night. If it is blue, it represents daylight or mystery. On occasion to represent an aerial scene, the curtain shows painted clouds. After a suitable musical introduction, this inner curtain is dropped to the floor, revealing a galaxy of brilliant stars in position. Then the action of the play begins.

4.

Plots. Although few plays performed today are preserved in their exact original form, the majority, at least, of plot skeletons derive from Genroku. The basic plots established then were drawn from several sources: legends, story-telling, *joruri* songs, historical and contemporary events.

No additional plots were made in any number until Kawatake Mokuami began his prolific writing in the latter half of the 19th century. Plays in the meantime were little more than revisions and adaptations of traditional plots. Playwrights polished and refined the old plays, but added little new substance to the plots.

The paucity of basic plots does not mean that Kabuki stood still. Kabuki advanced, but in different ways from the West and peculiar to itself. Kabuki concentrated primarily on actors and standardizing acting styles (*kata*). Plot became less and less important as the quality of acting improved. By the time of Kabuki's second flowering in the middle of the 18th century, the plays themselves were scarcely more than a springboard for an actor's skill.

The playwright's duties gradually changed into mere hackwork and rewriting. The playwright lost his creativity. Although there were some excellent craftsmen among them, their position was humiliating. The playwright was expected to submit texts to actors for approval. He copied each actor's part, because actors in Kabuki even today memorize their lines from handwritten texts which give only their own roles (similar to the parts of a score given to the musicians of a symphony orchestra). He also beat the clappers which warn the actors and audience of the approaching opening of the curtain, and he also announces the end of the scene and subsequent closing of the curtain. During the performances the playwright was a prompter. He dressed in black with his face covered and squatted behind the actor on the stage ready to read needed cues and lines.

Plays were constantly revised and altered and the result was that the majority of plays were little more than superimpositions on an already familiar basic plot. Much of this was due to the custom that the playwright must establish a "world" (*sekai*). "World" meant that all plots in a day's performance were about, or at least related to, one famous historical character or incident. In the Japanese theatre this setting of a "world" was an effort to attain unity and yet retain contrast. The "world" was established by mutual agreement between the actor and playwright. Then plots were arranged and revised to fit into the agreed "world." The custom also partly arose from necessity. If the play's "world" was placed in far distant history, the censors were unable to interfere. Even dramas which dealt with contemporary events to which the government was hypersensitive, were set in a historical "world" as a disguise.

The "worlds" were not numerous. The major ones are those whose plays deal with the Soga Brothers' revenge which was plotted in 1170 and was finally consummated in 1192; the stories of the struggles between the Taira and Minamoto Clans, called the Taiheiki "world" or incidents (dating around 1300); the cycle of plays with Yoshitsune as hero; and plays dealing with Toyotomi Hideyoshi or Oda Nobunaga (16th-17th century) called the Taiko "world" or cycle.

Among the most interesting of these "worlds" are the plays involving the Soga Brothers and their revenge. The first full-fledged Kabuki play about the Soga Brothers was written in 1655 by Danjuro I. For three hundred years since then, some version of the story has opened the New Year annually. Before the Kabuki version, the story had long been sung in ballad and had already caught the public fancy as a story. This handy and available material was not only rich in variety, but the government was also lenient with regard to it because its history was so far in the past. In addition, the story lent itself to *aragoto* style of acting, because of the ardor and bravery of the brothers, and as a play it appealed to popular tastes.

The people of Genroku who loved surprises and new tricks of staging in their theatre, paradoxically wanted these in the framework of familiarity, tradition, and customary procedure. These "worlds" satisfied the desire for convention and at the same time offered ample opportunity for new twists and turns. Year after year the spectators watched for the changes in the plays of the Soga "world." They delighted in the familiarity of the play and the conventional styles of the actors in it, and at the same time were pleased with the slight differences made each year for variety.

Plays from the Soga "world" at New Year's time became as familiar to the people as New Year decorations themselves. The actors' ranks and positions within the troupe were even determined by the roles they performed in the Soga "world." In this way these plays served as a guide to the performance, something of the nature of newspaper reviews which state an artist's ability.

The tradition of the "world" in general had its abuses as well as its charms. Often completely unrelated plays would arbitrarily be connected to certain "worlds." Sometimes a play did not suffer. *Sukeroku* written in 1713, about a popular "chivalrous commoner" of the day, was squeezed into the Soga "world" in 1716, thus turning the hero into one of the avenging brothers. *Sukeroku* however remains a great play and is a fortunate example of this forcing of plays into the "worlds." However, many other plays have been unreasonably overlaid. Their original plots were forced into the Genroku basic plots or set "worlds." The result was that it is often impossible to follow the story logically. The liberty taken by playwrights in making sudden revelations that his characters are actually not what they have appeared but really belong in a "world" after all is often unjustifiable.

Basic plots which could be forced at will into a "world" were further restricted by being confined to set dramatic situations. Originality, which dominated the attention of playwrights in the West with regard to plots, took the form in Japan of original treatment of certain unvarying situations deemed to be characteristically dramatic. The fact that Chikamatsu Monzaemon never tired of lovers' double suicides, or that Izumo, Senryu, and Shoraku arbitrarily chose the set convention of "flesh and blood separation," etc., to handle in their various individual ways, is typical of the Genroku playwright's approach. When these set dramatic situations first appeared on the stage in Genroku, they were quickly formalized and soon became standard. Their appeal has waned little since their inception. This perhaps indicates that audiences have changed as little as the plays, and that the problems of humanity underlying the set situations are still moving, although their immediate urgency or pertinence to the present times no longer exists.

Disregard for plot and complete submission to the arbitrariness of set situations do not disturb a Japanese audience. The spectator both in Genroku and today is more interested in seeing an already familiar and prescribed situation and what an actor does under the circumstances, than in following the unfolding of a plot.

Out of the variety of situations with which playwrights and actors dealt, appeared a list of basic scenes which became the kernel of the plays and the chief center of interest. These basic scenes which commanded the importance that in other theatres is taken by plot, are called "scenes of emphasis" (*shonenba*), and vaguely correspond to the Western idea of climaxes. These scenes of emphasis are the keynote to Genroku Kabuki, and through them we see the heart of Kabuki today and the quintessence of Genroku times.

5.

The Major "Scenes of Emphasis": 1) Scenes of torture or pressure (*semeba*). This constitutes any scene where the hero or heroine is surrounded by the enemy and is pressed to reveal information or disclose his identity.

Akoya, written in 1732 by Bunkodo, contains a striking example of this type of "scene of emphasis."

Akoya, a courtesan, is suspected of knowing the whereabouts of her lover who is in hiding. Two enemy officers come to interrogate her. (There is a curious counterpoint throughout the scene. Akoya plays her part as a realistic, glamorous, and naturalistic courtesan of the period. The second of the two investigating officers performs as a puppet. All his actions imitate a puppet as if moved by invisible manipulations. The main investigating officer plays his role with great reserve and dignity, neither artificially nor realistically.)

Instruments of torture are called in order to threaten Akoya. The various tortures of the period are brought on stage by various actors who simulate the clown-like actions of comic puppets. The club, the rack, the finger pincers, etc., are personified semi-realistically by this chorus of comedians. The investigating officer dismisses them and they leave the stage. He commands Akoya to play successively the three musical instruments for which she has gained fame—the *koto* (like a flat harp), the *kokyu* (a sort of small violin played like a 'cello) and the *samisen*. He states that if she is innocent of knowledge of her lover's whereabouts, her performance will be as "clear and unclouded as her mind." The entire hour-long scene consists merely of the actor performing on the three instruments. The climax within this already climactic "scene of emphasis" comes at the point when she forgets to play and raising her head slowly, looks vacantly into the distance, thinking of her lover. As the enemy leans forward to observe her closely, they exchange a quick glance and she resumes the melody. Although he suspects from this lapse that she knows her lover's place of hiding, she has played so exquisitely, he declares that he is satisfied that she is innocent of all knowledge of her lover.

The chivalry accorded the courtesan in Genroku is shown first in the enemy dismissing torture as a means of investigating the truth, and, secondly, in his magnanimity in feigning satisfaction out of deference to Akoya's beauty and artistic skill.

In August 1947 in Osaka while watching 71-year-old Baigyoku's first performance of the courtesan in Akoya in forty-five years, Shirai, the multi-millionaire theatrical producer who mysteriously evaded the 1948 purge of Japan's Zaibatsu, leaned over to me and said, "You see, the fact that a nation that could torture artistically instead of physically, and sacrifice truth for art, proves that we Japanese are not really barbarians, despite what your War Crimes Trials try to prove."

2) Selling of human life (*Mi-uri*): Usually this means the selling of a woman into prostitution. However, this situation has two main variations: the woman may voluntarily sell herself for the sake of her parents or husband; or the sale may be consummated without her knowledge. Although "selling of human life" was popular on the stage in Genroku and remains so today, audience reaction is somewhat different. A scene of selling a woman into prostitution today is one of unmitigated pathos and solicits tears. In Genroku no life was more glamorous and luxurious than that in the gay center. The

more talented girls among the courtesans were accorded every respect and ranked as *tayu,* a class of fifth order in the Japanese social
hierarchy. They could choose their own clients. For the girls whose
beauty or talents did not allow them to reach the status of courtesan,
life was nevertheless comfortable. As for buying or selling men, such
objects of traffic were from the peasant class and the Genroku
merchants had little sympathy for them. Today the sale of a man is
as moving as that of a woman.

3) Substitution of one person for another (*Mi-gawari*): There are
three kinds of substitution:

A—Religious: Where Buddha stands as a substitute for a pious person.
In *Amida no Munewari* a pious girl who wished to atone for her parents'
sins, is saved from her death by Buddha making the sacrifice for her. In
Shusse Kagekiyo, the hero is miraculously saved in battle under similar
circumstances. In *Domyoji Temple,* Sugawara is saved from death by a
statue.

B—Amorous: Many of Chikamatsu's heroines substitute themselves for
their lovers who are thereby saved from death. In Act III of Namiki Sosuke's *The Battle Chronicles of the Two Leaves at the Valley of Ichi-no-
Tani,* two girls in love with the enemy poet, Tadanori, die at the hands of
Rokuyata, a villain, in order to save their lover.

C—Ethical: Where the servant or retainer dies for the lord. In 1689
Chikamatsu in, *Tale of the Loyal Retainer's Self-Sacrifice* (*Chushin Mi-
gawari Monogatari*) wrote the first play with this type of substitution. It
has served as a model for subsequent plays of ethical substitution of one
person for another. Later it became insufficient for a retainer to sacrifice
himself for a lord. The situations were arranged so that he sacrificed an
innocent loved one, usually a child, to increase the pathos. In cases where
the retainer has sacrificed himself, this is always dramatically recalled
later in the play by a relative or loved one in sorrow.
Example: The "Narration" (*monogatari*) in the dance interlude of *Yoshitsune and the Thousand Cherry Trees* where Tadanobu recalls the
sacrifice of his brother.

The religious type of substitution disappeared for the most part

during Genroku because the religious implications were not appealing to materialistic commoners who discounted miracles. Another
aspect of the Genroku commoner's attitude towards religion is found
in the fact that in most Kabuki plays the priest is ridiculed and is
played as a comic character. Immediately after Genroku, dramatists
used these other types of substitution as climaxes for particularly the
third and fourth acts of their historical plays (*jidaimono*).

A substitution shows the conflict of duty, or necessity, against humanity and may be effected with or without the knowledge of the
person whose life is to be sacrificed. As the practice of substitution
had only begun to pass away with the peacefulness of Genroku times,
the problem was not as remote from actual life then as it now seems.
Every warrior of power had several doubles. Such warriors literally
bought the lives of farmers, persons of low station, or those in
straitened circumstances. In time of emergency one of these doubles
was substituted for the warrior in order to make the enemy think
him dead. This led to the custom of branding the doubles when they
were captured alive and when their true identity was discovered. In
Kamakura Sandai Ki, the hero Takatsuna is once clever enough to
have deceived his captors into branding him as a double for himself.
This situation obviously leads to a number of complications in the
plot.

4) Head-inspection (*Kubi-Jikken*): The practice of persons sub-
stituting themselves for others necessitated head-inspections. The dissevered head of an enemy was brought before an inspecting officer,
who because of his previous knowledge of the person supposed to be
killed, was required to identify the head. Dramatically, head-inspections afford a maximum opportunity for mixed emotions on the part
of the identifying officer. A parent is called upon to inspect his own
child's head and must pretend it is the head of someone else. There
is the agony of the parent confronting his child's dead face, coupled
with the necessity for showing no grief which would reveal the secret

substitution to the witnessing agent. Or the inspector, fearing he is to come face to face with a loved one's dissevered head, finds that an unknown substitute has been killed instead. Now the necessity is to display as much false emotion as possible.

Head-inspections of great warriors of high position were conducted according to strictest etiquette, almost as a ritual. Although the practice has been completely done away with now, the traditional rigid procedure for a formal head-inspection in all its conventionality, may be seen today in *Moritsuna's Camp*. Uzaemon XV required fifteen minutes to perform this head-inspection. The scene is complex and involved. The actor, without moving from his sitting position before the head, must register in his face a series of seven distinct emotions and reactions: 1) grief at the grotesque duty of identifying his dead brother; 2) surprise at seeing a false head; 3) perplexity as to the motivation for the elaborate preceding events; 4) joy at the knowledge that his brother is alive; 5) confusion about his course of action with regard to his lord who is watching him; 6) the conflict between brotherly love and his bounden duty to his lord; and 7) resolution finally to deceive his lord and sacrifice his own life if need be as punishment.

5) Slapping with footwear (*Zori-uchi*): The Japanese, who are queasy about street dirt brought in by footwear, are exceedingly sensitive about being touched or struck with a sandal or slipper. This constitutes the grossest of insults.

Mirror Mountain (*Kagamiyama*), written by Yo Yodai in 1782, is a masterpiece of the revenge type of play and contains a famous scene of slapping with footwear. Yo Yodai, being court physician to the Shogun, was among the few playwrights to write authoritatively of life, manners, and scandals within the palace. Three court ladies, Iwafuji (the villain), Onoe (the innocent victim), O-Hatsu (the avenger), are involved in an intrigue of jealousy and ambition. Onoe, a merchant's daughter who by merit has risen high, is beaten with her own slipper by Iwafuji, her superior. From this, the story of revenge develops. The play is based on an actual scandal which took place within the Shogun's court in Edo.

6) Pulling of the obi (*Obi-hiki*): The undoing of the *obi* or long belt which both men and women wear is closely associated with eroticism in the Japanese mind. Overeager men in struggling with resisting women manage to seize the *obi* which becomes untied. By holding to it at one end, the man prevents the flight of the woman. Such struggles are part of Kabuki's color and afford opportunities for dramatic poses with the long strip of embroidered belt linking the two opposing characters.

Iwakura Sogen by Chikamatsu Hanjii contains such a scene in which a depraved priest insistently struggles with a princess who is, of course, saved by her retainer who appears in the nick of time.

7) *Hara-kiri* or *seppuku:** This form of suicide is too familiar to require detailed attention here. *Seppuku* was considered an honorable death, an act of the highest bravery, and was a recognized form of legal punishment. In contrast to Christianity, there is no tenet in Buddhism rejecting suicide as a means of escape from the travails of this world. In Kabuki, *seppuku* is committed for several reasons:

1) As apology to atone for sin or error, or as the highest manifestation of sincerity.

2) In compliance with a command, whereby the superior issues to his inferior an order for him to commit suicide.

3) As entreaty, where the taking of one's life is the only means to prove the earnestness of a plea.

4) In error, where after it is too late the dying man realizes he has been too hasty.

5) In the spirit of bravado, where a commoner shows himself equal to the warrior in bravery and honor.

Seppuku is committed as a result of a conjuncture of tragic cir-

* *Seppuku* is the correct pronunciation today of the ideographs which may also be read *hara-kiri*. The words literally mean "stomach cut."

cumstances. The victim's life becomes so painful to him that death at worst seems better.

Aside from the fact that *seppuku* was condoned at the time of Kabuki's origins, its rationale in Kabuki is simple. A man's life is his only real possession. When the situation becomes such that this possession becomes unbearable, the voluntary forfeit of it becomes man's highest act of courage. At the same time man's loss of his one possession is his greatest tragedy. For the spectator, *seppuku* affords a fourfold emotional reaction: an admiration at self-evident courage; a horror at the tragic spectacle; sorrow at the destruction of a human life, likewise the spectator's only real possession; and relief that the problems producing this tragedy do not confront the common spectator in his life.

8) Murder (*Hito-Koroshi*): Genroku began a succession of plays dealing with murder and killing. Murder is even more characteristic of Kabuki than death by violence is of Shakespeare's tragedies. With the stage eagerly waiting for events to serve as material for new plays, the peace of Tokugawa found murder an exciting and theatrical theme. Aside from the fact that death is the most understandable and stirring subject to a life-loving people, the social structure itself in Genroku was such that murder, on the stage or off, constituted an outlet for the nation's impulses. Civil wars had just ended; killing was still in the people's minds. The warriors had the legal right to strike down commoners, and the government countenanced no redress. The rise of the commoners meant boldness on their part, and despite the threat of fearful punishments, commoners, and in particular the "chivalrous commoners," murdered the warriors. The redlight district, the only place where commoners and warriors alike mingled without social distinction, was an uncontrollable source of quarrels which frequently ended in murder. Revenge itself, forbidden by law in Genroku but tacitly approved by the tenets of *bushido*, begins in murder and ends in murder.

Variations on the theme of murder are numerous, in Kabuki. Aside from revenge where murder is ultimately the cleansing of conscience and destruction of evil, the most common variant was the murder of a kinsman, either unknowingly or after prolonged provocation. In Genroku, punishment for murder was carefully gradated, particularly with regard to kinsmen. In *Summer Festival* (*Natsu Matsuri*), written by Namiki Senryu (Sosuke) in 1745, a "chivalrous commoner" is driven to murder his stepfather. In a long scene, the stepfather goads his murderer by taunting him with a description of the degrees of punishment he will suffer according to the length of each cut inflicted.

In contrast to the Western code of censorship where murderers must be apprehended before the spectator's eyes, it is curious to note that the concept of ultimate justice in Kabuki is followed no further than the flight of the murderer. In a country where Buddhism had gained so strong a hold, as Noh shows so clearly, considerably more conscience in the ethics of murder and punishment might have been expected in Kabuki. That murder is legally punishable and that killing a person is painful for the killer as well as the killed comprise the extent of Kabuki's ethics. The murder situation itself is of more interest than the plot's conclusion. What becomes of the murderer or the portrayal of the resultant justice is considered an insufficiently dramatic situation in Kabuki. The spectators then as now thrilled at the action and ignored any argumentation necessary to a conclusion. The Westerner, accustomed to censorship's regulation that the criminal always be given his just deserts, feels a vague sense of incompleteness at Kabuki's numerous murders and absence of punishments. In the late 19th century the Department of Public Morals insisted that murderers and thieves must be apprehended on the stage. This demand, however, was satisfied by the traditional sword-dance between criminal and arresting police, an inconclusive battle at best.

Even if the legal aspect of crime is inadequately expressed, there still is a moral sense in Kabuki murder. The murder must be either justifiable or the result of the inevitable action. If it is justifiable, no suffering for the perpetration is necessary. If inevitable, the murderer must suffer emotionally. The Japanese theatre, by leaving punishment in the hands of God and considering the killer's mental or physical unhappiness a sufficient temporal punishment, shows in a way a deep consciousness of man's inability to mete out absolute justice. Audiences in Japan do not demand to see the wheels of man-made laws grind before their eyes.

Murder falls into six categories:

1) The provoked murder where the hero kills the villain and thereby satisfies the aroused desire of the spectators. In revenge plays this is a willing act. In others, the hero, provoked beyond human control by the villain, is driven to kill despite himself.

2) The accidental murder where the victim is mortally wounded during a struggle or at night through no direct fault of either party.

3) The murder by mistake, where the wrong person is killed. (In *Yaguchi no Watashi,* Tombi kills his daughter instead of his enemy; in *Taikoki,* Mitsuhide, the traitor, kills his mother instead of the enemy general.) Mistaken murder is usually the deed of an evil person, and is regarded as a punishment from heaven. In order to make an evil person's crime more heinous, the Kabuki playwright sometimes portrays him as remorseless, with no emotion of regret at his deed.

4) The murder in error, where after killing it turns out that the murdered one is innocent of the cause for killing.

5) The duty murder, where a beloved one must be sacrificed for a higher cause. This is the most pathetic of all murder scenes, where the innocent must be sacrificed on the altar of adherence-to-duty.

6) The wanton murder, where in self-defense the hero kills in order to escape punishment for some unrelated crime, or where subordinates are killed in numbers to show the hero's strength or to give lively action to the stage.

Kabuki is however, not as gory to see as it sounds. Blood is rarely used on the stage, and then only as an effective pattern or color design. For example: Sadakuro in Act V of *Chushingura* is dressed in a scant black kimono with face, chest, arms, and legs painted dead white. Offstage two shots are fired. Sadakuro stands motionless facing the audience, then suddenly deep red blood trickles out of his mouth and spatters his trembling knee. The suggestiveness and extreme stylization of Kabuki in general prevent the visual bloodiness which the bare plots might suggest. The sword rarely touches an actor, and a beheading, if performed at all on stage, is comically formalized. The victim covers his head with a red cloth and a round ball of cotton on which a face has been crudely painted is thrown on the stage.

The swordfight (*tachimawari*) is a feature of Kabuki which theoretically comes under the classification of murder. It is a clear example of Kabuki's stylization. Swordfighting in Kabuki is a rhythmic dance, symbolic of a hero struggling with numerous opponents. The opponents, usually arresting police, are colorfully dressed in red and white thin cotton kimonos. They are armed with flowering branches, umbrellas, or billy clubs, rather than swords. Only the hero brandishes a sword. When an enemy is killed he does an acrobatic flip in the air and leaves the stage. In the event of a shortage of actors, as often happens in Kabuki, he resumes fighting again. Swordfights in Kabuki are largely tumbling exhibitions and serve to preserve the tradition of the intimacy of acrobatics and the stage. Swordfights, like all Kabuki scenes, end in a tableau in which the actors strike an elaborate pose which they rigidly hold until the curtain is drawn.

A Kabuki swordfight, to the Western eye, is inconclusive. Those struck down are not clearly put out of action. The final tableau destroys whatever illusion the fight may have created as to who is victor and who is vanquished, since all the actors strike a standing, upright pose. Characteristic lack of interest on the part of the Japanese in the conclusion of the plot requires no more a concise ending than the swordfight. But to the Japanese who have had centuries of knowing that right always triumphs on its stage, it is crystal-clear that the hero has won. The colorful fighting dance is actually designed by the playwright to give the spectators a mental refreshment after the intense strain of the preceding plot situation.

6.

Types of Drama Forms. Since Genroku, Kabuki repertoire has passed through the hands of many succeeding playwrights and willful actors. Each has seen fit to alter his predecessors' work. But regardless of changes of details, the basic plot situations and the general classifications of Kabuki dramas have remained substantially the same.

Since Chikamatsu's time Kabuki repertoire has been composed of three broad groupings:

1) Historical plays or period pieces (*Jidai mono*)
2) Plays centering around events in daily life or domestic scenes (*Sewa mono*)
3) Dances (*Shosa goto*)

Each group comprises approximately a third of the existing Kabuki repertoire (an aggregate of about 350 pieces in all) still regularly performed today. This overall proportion between types of plays has remained the same since Genroku. Edo created a preponderance of historical plays while Osaka and Kyoto balanced the number with domestic plays. Both places gave equal attention to the dance. Alterations, losses of scripts, and the creation of new plays through the centuries have not affected to any great degree the numerical balance between the three types of plays.

1) *Historical plays:* Without doubt the greatest number of masterpieces in Kabuki literature as a whole are to be found among the historical plays. They are plays of warriors, lords, and superiors. Historical plays largely take their material from the war chronicles of the Minamoto and Taira Clans; the Hojo and Ashikaga Shoguns, and vassals; and the valiant warriors, Oda Nobunaga and Toyotomi

Hideyoshi. These plays invariably contain dense and heavy tragedy. Their depiction of historical events, however, is usually inaccurate and somewhat fanciful; but the spirit of the Tokugawa times is realistically portrayed.

Included under the classification of historical plays are two major types of dramas: the Dynasty pieces (*O-cho mono*); and Scandal pieces, plays dealing with scandals and disturbances in the great households of the Tokugawa Era (*O-ie sodo mono*). Dynasty pieces are based on the affairs of the Imperial household or incidents involving nobles of the Imperial court during the period from the 8th to 10th centuries. Of this type of play, the three foremost are *The Lustrous Imparting of Sukawara's Calligraphic Secrets, Ono-no-Tofu,* and *Imoseyama.* They are the chief examples of drama included in textbooks for literature classes in Japan.

A typical Dynasty piece is *Ono-no-Tofu,* written by Takeda Izumo in 1717. It is a Japanese counterpart of the story of King Robert Bruce and the spider. Ono-no-Tofu was an actual historical character who lived in the 10th century and rose from the lowly position of village carpenter to that of a court noble.

Synopsis of the play: Ono-no-Tofu is strongly urged by the leader of a wicked faction at court to join in the overthrow of the Emperor and his government. Ono does not take the plot seriously, and dismisses it from his mind. While returning home, later that day, he observes a frog trying to jump up into a branch of a weeping willow tree. The frog tries over and over again, but each time slides down back into the water. Finally, however, he succeeds in clinging to the branch. Ono then realizes that the evil efforts against the government also, if pursued diligently enough, might succeed.

Ono is attacked by a villain. He tosses him into the pond and the frogs devour him.

Ono's brother Michikaza has an affair with a princess at court, the daughter of the chief advisor to the Emperor. Since such alliances at court were severely frowned upon, Ono is held responsible for his brother's conduct. The father of the princess, who is greatly jealous of Ono's influence at court, calls publicly upon Ono to write a pledge of allegiance to the Emperor since his brother's conduct may have been part of a plot to seize power. Ono is greatly embarrassed as he is illiterate. However, a nun who once nursed Ono hears of this and offers prayers of such fervency that on the day Ono is to write the pledge in public, he is miraculously able to form the characters with his writing brush.

Ono exposes the wicked factions at court, and renounces further connection with the court. He chooses to return to his simple position as a carpenter.

More numerous than the Dynasty pieces are the Scandal plays. Due to the stringent censorship of the theatre, events reproduced in the Scandal plays were set back in time from the 17th and 18th centuries to either the 11th or 14th centuries. These were periods in Japanese history remote enough to deceive the authorities and yet similar enough to fit the subject matter of the plays. There were numerous anachronisms. Costumes were always in 17th century style no matter what the designated period. Clocks and guns were used with impunity. The obvious parallels with the actual period and times make one wonder that the plays were permitted at all. Particularly transparent were the names used in Kabuki for the three great historical characters who established the Tokugawa Era; their name permutations were naïve: Okugawa Ujiyasu for Tokugawa Ieyasu; Oda Harunaga for Oda Nobunaga; and Washiba (his real name) Hisayoshi for Toyotomi Hideyoshi. When the events depicted were too recent, the authorities stopped performances; but with the passage of time they were generally allowed.

An excellent example of a Scandal play is *Sendai Hagi* written by Nakawa Kamesuke in 1717. It concerns a disturbance which occurred in 1660, fifty-seven years earlier, in the house of the Lord of Date in Sendai, Northern Japan. The story revolves around the machinations of a group of wicked retainers to take the life of the young and rightful heir of the Date title and estate. In the play the good efforts of the faithful wet nurse and commoner, Masaoka, prevent the triumph of evil.

Genroku, like all of the Tokugawa Era, was a period of many actual scandals and disturbances, not only in the households of the feudal lords, but at the court of the Shogun himself. Once peace had been established, the fruits of idleness and luxury appeared. The lords, nobles, and their attendant warriors plunged themselves into dissipation. Ambitious villains turned traitor. They attempted to turn to their own advantage the vulnerability of their lords now weakened by dissoluteness and financial difficulties. The events of the day were filled with stories of assassination, exile, usurpation of heirdoms, rightful heirs reduced to ruin, and intrigue. These incidents found their way to the stage and during Genroku were dominant as subject matter for the theatre. Remaining today are only those which, devoid of their contemporary interest, remain as masterpieces of drama depicting the forces of good and evil within human beings.

The attraction which Genroku citizens felt towards the scandals of their betters, the great names (*dai-myo*), has a counterpart in the Elizabethan Era with Shakespeare and his tales of kings and queens. A quarrel between kings is more vital to the state than a tavern brawl, and the people whose lives are affected on a mass scale by a king's quarrel are concerned with it in the theatre.

In a society where the family, clan, group, and community spirit was as highly developed as it was in Japan's feudal times, what happened to the head of a fief affected a vast number of subordinates. By virtue of numbers concerned alone, the subject was a popular one.

In addition Kabuki was the common man's theatre where the problems of his superiors were exposed to view. The warrior always suffered, and this released the commoner's pent-up resentment. In Genroku the commoner felt not a little supercilious delight in seeing his superiors suffer. Although spectators liked to see themselves and their neighbors depicted on the stage, their more urgent motivation for theatrical enjoyment was to see what they did not know and to feel what they had not experienced. They wanted to feel vicariously what would probably never be their lot in life to suffer or enjoy. The theatre afforded an experience of convincing importance, yet, at the same time, it gave a sense of security. The commoners were not confronted with the terrible problems their superiors were subjected to. In this way Kabuki permitted the escapism which the theatres of all nations provide their people.

Also under the classification of Historical Plays, but independent of them, the "18 Favorite Plays," mentioned before, are included.

2) *Domestic Plays:* Domestic plays are best exemplified by Chikamatsu Monzaemon's stories of love, money, and ordinary life, originally written for the puppets. Not until Kawatake Mokuami in Tokyo during the late 19th century did a great writer of purely Kabuki domestic plays appear. Mokuami's plays faithfully depict life of the common man, the types with which one is familiar but of whose daily life or psychology one is unwitting. His characters are thieves, hair dressers, beggars, firemen, and wrestlers. The settings are prisons, shops, theatres, temples, and wherever people of the 19th century might find themselves.

From Genroku to the present day, audiences have demanded the contrast of the two types—the historical plays, in order to peer into the lives and habits of the great, and the domestic plays, in which the commoners see themselves and persons with whom they are familiar. By the beginning of the 19th century, the order of a day's program required that a historical play begin the day's program and be followed by a domestic play. From this came the current words "first piece" (*ichi ban me mono*) meaning historical plays, and "second piece" (*ni ban me mono*) meaning domestic plays. Many plays in their present form contain alternate acts of historical and domestic scenes. To arrange this, the lords and warriors of the historical plays would, as a part of the plot, flee to a commoner's house or village, or disguise themselves as simple people, or return to their own native villages to be with their parents of humble origin, etc.

3) *Dances:* Although the element of dance is present in all types of Kabuki, the dances (*shosa goto*), the third major type of Kabuki drama, is the dance in pure form. Music accompanies all Kabuki, which fact makes the actors' movements rhythmic and potentially pure dance at any point during the action. In historical and domestic plays, particularly those of puppet origin, the accompanying music is divided between the sound effect orchestra hidden from view to the right of the stage, and the narrator and samisen player in view to the left of the stage. In dances, the orchestra is usually in full view upstage. In the event that three orchestras are needed for larger dances, the three sides of the stage are filled with the different musicians required for the varying types of orchestras. The music for dances is of three types: *O-satsuma* for weird or bold effects; *Kiyomoto,* the most voluptuous and graceful of Japanese music forms; and *Naga-uta,* a brilliant, all-purpose, strong type of music.

Dancing is the life blood of Kabuki. Playwrights choose their characters often not so much for their dramatic possibilities as for their adaptability to dance episodes. For instance: Shizuka, Yoshitsune's concubine, is the heroine of countless plays, largely because her fame as a dancer historically makes it possible to present a refreshing interlude of dancing from time to time without seriously disrupting the plot. Even Benkei, the heroic retainer of Yoshitsune, is made to dance in *The Subscription List* to show his rounded abilities and esthetic accomplishments. *Takatoki* contains two dance episodes within the space of an hour. Even among the last of the Kabuki plays to be written, *Omori Hikoshichi,* by Fukuchi Ochi, written in 1897, the dance element is the climax of the play.

Synopsis of the Play: In order to avenge the death of her father (one of the warriors on the losing side of the Southern Dynasty), Princess Chihaya comes to a mountain in Iyo Province to attend a three-day festival of sacred music and dancing, to which all the great lords supporting the Northern Dynasty are invited. The Princess there hopes to encounter

SUKEROKU'S ENTRY DANCE POSES

KIKUGORO AS SHINBEI,
HE WHITE WINE SELLER,
SUKEROKU'S BROTHER

SOMEGORO WITH HIS 5-YEAR-OLD SON
(KICHIEMON'S GRANDSON) WHO
MADE HIS DEBUT IN SUKEROKU

Omori Hikoshichi, the enemy general who defeated her father in battle and caused his death.

At a mountain stream, she meets Omori Hikoshichi, and putting on a demon's mask to confuse and frighten him, attempts to stab him. He easily defeats her, and she explains why she has made the attempt. Omori Hikoshichi in a "Narration" recounts the circumstances of her father's death. He gives her a precious sword which he had taken from her father and which subsequently was entrusted to Omori Hikoshichi by the Shogun for safekeeping.

At this moment, one of Omori Hikoshichi's colleagues arrives on the scene. In order to dispel any suspicions of sympathy with the enemy side, Omori Hikoshichi tells Princess Chihaya to don the demon's mask and pretend to be the spirit of her father who has come to retrieve the sword. Before the colleague's amazed eyes, Omori Hikoshichi pretends to be bewitched, gives the demon the sword, and dances crazily. He finally mounts his steed and rides down the *hanamichi* passage-way.

Dances are of four basic kinds:

1) Dance interludes in a drama proper;
2) Dance-dramas;
3) Dances which depict a custom or personality type, characteristic of the day;
4) Dance adaptations from the Noh.

The first type of dance was originally a part of historical plays and served as esthetic relief from the intensity of the drama where word is more important than movement or music. They were colorful divertissements to break the monotony and were sandwiched in between acts of plain drama. While these dances did not disrupt the continuity, at least they did not carry the drama into any further plot complexity. The largest number of these are the "journeys of love" (*michi-yuki*). Originally an integral part of the drama, many of them have now become independent and are performed separately while the original play has been forgotten. Basically the "journey of love" is a dance in which two lovers are shown en route to a destination. They stop, recall the past, describe the scenery, or make love, and then proceed on their way. Some of these "journeys" do not involve lovers. Their characters may be a mother and daughter traveling to the bridegroom's house, or a concubine and a loyal retainer proceeding to their master's place of hiding.

The second type, Dance-dramas, are plays with full musical accompaniment to which the actors match their gestures. Without the music they would be complete plays; without the actors' speeches, they would be complete dances. *Kanjincho, Omori Hikoshichi,* and ghost-dances in general come under this classification.

During Genroku the religious element in Japanese mythology descended into a taste for the supernatural, usually of the form of revengeful ghosts, spirits of spiteful lovers, snakes in human form, or women bewitched by foxes. These dances generally tell a story which has complete form and they can equally stand as dramas.

The third type, custom or personality dances (*fuzoku mitate mono*), are an expression in dance of the common people wishing to see themselves on the glamorous stage. They tell no connected story and are usually solo dances where a character such as a depraved priest, a blind beggar, or a young girl in love appear and dance out a mood. These dances depict the manners, customs, and personality types of the times. Many were taken from popular pictures, the *otsu-e,* a Genroku type of drawing which preceded the famous color-prints. Curiously enough, despite the permanence of drawing as opposed to the impermanence of the dance, pieces like *Tobae, Ukare Bozu* and *Wisteria Maiden* (*Fuji-musume*) have long outlived their original prints.

The fourth type, adaptations from Noh, are numerous. Those borrowed in the Genroku period (unlike those more literally adapted later in Kabuki history) underwent such transformations as to be almost unrecognizable when compared to the original. One of the more important of Kabuki dances of this type is *Dojoji,* called in Kabuki *The Maid at Dojoji Temple* (*Musume Dojoji*). It was the chief vehicle of the great dancer Kikugoro VI who, until his death at the age of sixty-five in 1949, performed it annually.

The legendary story and Noh version tells of a beautiful village maiden who fell in love with one of the local priests of Dojoji temple. The priest, having taken vows of celibacy, rejects her advances. The maiden in her venom at being spurned turns into a snake and pursues the priest. Terrified he runs to the huge temple bell which by a miracle of heaven falls down and covers him. The snake coils around the bell and the heat of her fury melts the metal. The priest, snake, and bell dissolve in flames.

The actual dance performed on the Kabuki stage is the ghost-memory and re-enactment of this traditional myth. On a certain day a beautiful maiden asks admittance to Dojoji temple. The priests are shocked by such a brazen request. She explains that she is a temple-dancer traveling from place to place to collect funds for the reconstruction of a nearby temple recently destroyed by fire. They finally admit her to the temple where she performs her sacred dance. During the dance she malevolently casts her eye at the new temple-bell. The priests become alarmed and try to prevent her from dancing further. The bell falls over her. There is a comic dance interlude by the chorus of priests after which the maiden re-emerges in the guise of a fearsome snake-demon. She battles with the priests who fall back in alarm, and climactically mounts the bell in triumph.

Told in words, the dance sounds uninteresting. In actual performance, with all the movements and gestures, it is an exciting experience. Costumes are gorgeous and elaborate with silks of many colors, and heavily embroidered brocades of silver and gold. From the top of the stage hang rows of paper cherry-blossoms. To the right is an enormous papier-mâché bell, suspended by a thick cord of white and red twine which drapes across the stage. The two-hour dance of the young maiden is divided into several sections, requiring altogether nine different changes of costume. These changes are effected on stage during the course of the actual dance. The dancer as part of the dance movement itself removes a few basting threads from the long sleeves and thick hem of the kimono. With the rhythmic changes in the music, a crouching attendant in 18th century ordinary dress assists the dancer to pull off the outer covering and a brilliant new costume change of contrasting colors is revealed. The nine changes in the Dojoji dance symbolize the snake, for in Japanese mythology, the snake and not the cat, is supposed to have so many lives.

In the course of the performance various extraneous properties are used by the dancer: fans, a blue and white cloth handtowel, a tall

The thin hand towel is a characteristic part of Kabuki, and may be used as a head decoration or a property. (L) a style used in the gay quarter (R) a style worn by boatmen

hat of golden paper, tambourines which have tinkling metal discs inside their highly ornamented covering, and small golden drums. The background of the wide stage (in Japan legitimate theatres are the size of American movie-houses, whereas movie-houses are the small intimate size of Broadway's legitimate stages) is decorated with artistically drawn paintings of the temple and its environs. Across the back of the stage, the orchestra of a dozen singers and an equal number of musicians intone the music to accompany the action.

As the dance increases in speed and tempo, its excitement grows. Gradually it becomes more and more apparent that the maiden is a snake in disguise. Finally she appears in her true colors with a visage of painted streaks and a vermillion mane.

Characteristic Genroku spirit and exuberance is revealed particu-

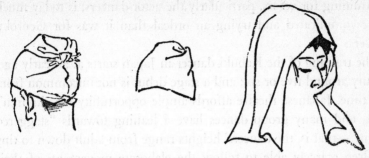

(L) *A securely tied thin hand towel* (Kenugui) *worn by a man ready for action who doesn't want to be bothered by his hair coming loose.* (R) *Thin hand towel worn by women traveling in disguise*

larly clearly in the adaptation of the Noh *Okina*. In Noh, the accent is on Okina, the symbol of long life. In Kabuki, it is on Samba, the comic figure who dances like a doll ringing a Buddhist bell in amusement. In subsequent years a considerable number of the comic plays of Noh (*kyogen*) were also adapted with great success as Kabuki dances.

Kabuki dance today has reached an extraordinary degree of perfection. True to the spirit of the Japanese attention to detail and its inclination for refinement, dance has grown into an extremely subtle art form. Undoubtedly in Genroku, dance was far more casual and less polished than it is today, where centuries of details and additional embellishments have widened and deepened the task of the finished dancer. Dance in Genroku was probably overburdened with its dramatic content, but this has lessened with the years, and today dance in Japan in general is virtually an independent form. Judging from drawings and contemporary accounts, though for the most part they are fragmentary and incapable of telling much of the fleeting movements of dance, one may conclude that the basic postures and movements of Genroku's dance are still embodied in today's Kabuki.

The stage in Genroku was the life of the actors, as it is today. But the training for actors, particularly the actor-dancers, is today much more complicated and trying an ordeal than it was for Genroku dancers.

The training of the Kabuki dancer in Japan starts at an early age, usually around five or six; and a stage debut is not uncommon from this time. Japanese theatre affords ample opportunity for children's roles, and many group dances have a leaning towards "staggered height"—that is, the dancers' heights range from adult down to tiny children scarcely able to follow the elaborate movements of their elders. Audiences are indulgent toward the children in their mistakes, and they carefully watch for signs of promise in them.

Players of women roles are primarily dancers. These students start first to develop a feminine walk. They practice with a sheet of ordinary letter-paper held between their knees. If it falls, then the proper feminine posture has not been correct. This forces the feet to be a little pigeon-toed and to slither across the floor while the body sways slightly. The opening of the kimono which extends down the front of the body to the floor, must not be disturbed by the walking movement. The heavy wigs force the head to move gently from side to

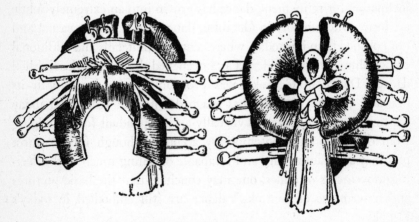

Courtesan Wigs Weighing 20 Pounds

[172]

side balancing the shift in weight with the body motion. Elbows are held at the hips, and even in the more athletic female dances they rarely move from a close proximity to the waist, except of course as in the case of *Dojoji,* where the woman throws off her disguise and appears as a demon. Fingers are always held close together, but sometimes to break the monotony of the hands' flat surface, the fourth and fifth fingers of each hand are slightly crooked and bent to give a characteristically Japanese, asymmetrical contour. The thumb sometimes is curved under and held close to the inner palm—otherwise it is held tightly at the side of the index finger. Occasionally the gesture of pointing (which because of its rudeness is used in the sense of playful teasing rather than in the sense of indicating an object) necessitates a gentle curving of all the fingers, leaving only the index-finger extended.

Players of men's parts (*tachiyaku*) affect the opposite body posi-

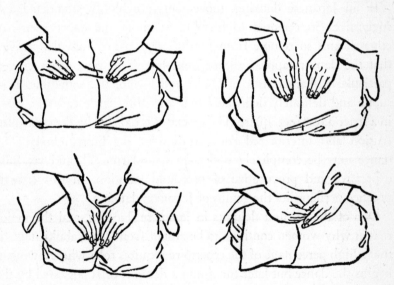

Placement of Hands When Sitting. Above: (L) Samurai: elbows held out (R) Townsman. Below: (L) Man Bent on Pleasure (R) Priests and Aged Persons

tions. Fingers are generally splayed wide apart. Men's knees never touch, and elbows are held away from the body, pointing slightly outwards. The movements are bold.

There is no abstract or psychological dance, and the connection between song-words and dance-movements is inseparable. Japanese dance movements are determined in one of three ways for each dance-section: 1) the gestures of the dance may follow each word and enact it in mime; 2) the dance may describe in general the atmosphere, mood, or meaning of the words without following the poetry literally; or 3) the dance-gesturing may form puns, a kind of plastic paranomasia on each syllable of the words. This latter form of gesticulating is exceedingly complicated and requires not only a mastery of the language and poetry of the song, but an immediate and intimate knowledge of the swift-changing and abbreviated gestures symbolic of the fragmentary sentences.

In all Japanese dancing, movements are highly attenuated and suggestive (as opposed to literal). At times the dance seems so ethereal and so remote from normal, day-to-day muscular activity that the dancers appear almost immobile. This type of dancing is particularly characteristic of Osaka and Kyoto, and sometimes is so subtle and delicately delineated that an entire dance can take place in a space a few feet square. The spectator is dazzled by the controlled tension and interiorized concentration of the human body. The dance may be completely understated, undermoved, and yet fully expressive and provocative of profound emotion. In this esthetic practice perhaps lies the genius of Japanese dancing.

One of the greatest delights in Japanese dancing, and the major reason why women continue to be absent from the Kabuki stage, is that a high percentage of the repertoire requires roles where a woman begins the dance but later turns into a demon; or is possessed by the spirit of a lion, a spider, or some malevolent force. The latter part of these dances requires a physical exertion and virility that the slender and small physique of Japanese women cannot sustain.

Among the most difficult parts of Japanese dancing are the fan tricks (*ogi no sabaki*). The fan is the most significant characteristic of Japanese dancing. All dances, at least for part of their duration, make use of fans. The fan helps the symbology of Japanese dance-gesture language. It may serve as a falling leaf, a tea cup, a letter, a moon rising behind a hill, a flute, a sword, or merely as a decorative adjunct to the dancer's movements. Many of the *ogi no sabaki* require virtuoso handling. The fan is made to whirl or spin to look like ricksha wheels. It is tossed in the air to turn over and return to the hand. Sometimes when the dancer has finished with the fan, he throws it, still spread open, backwards over his shoulder into the hand of a waiting attendant who catches it in mid-air. Often a dancer will use two fans, repeating each trick of twisting and turning with either the right or left hand. The handling of the fan is difficult. Teachers say that "for a real dancer the fan and the hand are one. The fan in use is no more than an extension of the arm." The arm of course is an extension of the body; and the body in dance, to the Japanese, is an extension of the meaning of the song.

In Japan, as in most of Asia, it is impossible to separate the dance from its drama context. Esthetically, the principle is that dance is superior to straight drama, and so in the most deep and intense moments, dance must take over to produce a still higher plane of emotional response in the spectator's sensibilities.

V

The Esthetics of Kabuki

The Kabuki we see today as a crystallized and final art form is an accumulated sum of three hundred years of development and growth. The successive fashions and tastes of various historical periods have affected Kabuki for good as well as for ill. Some of Kabuki's past has disappeared entirely; some has remained exactly as it was originally conceived and initiated on the stage of yesterday; some has been refined and improved, even modernized beyond all recognition. However, the overall appearance of Kabuki today is fundamentally and esthetically the same as it has always been throughout its history.

Kabuki, which has remained Japan's chief theatrical form since it first appeared, is a composite and synthetic drama characterized by being an amalgam of several disparate artistic elements. Kabuki fuses into a single form the arts of music, dance, acting, literature, as well as graphic and plastic arts. No piece of Kabuki repertoire lacks in any of these factors, and although the proportions within a particular play may emphasize one of these aspects more than another, the mood and feeling of a fusion of the arts is never lost. This attitude was the outgrowth of the traditional saying in Japan that "art is the palm of the hand; the arts are the fingers."

Each of the arts within the combined art of Kabuki is responsible for certain effects. Music gives Kabuki its dynamics, its rhythm, and its continuous pace. Dance makes the actors concentrate on grace and determines a large part of Kabuki's special kind of movement and gesticulation. Acting adds the qualities of pantomime, speech, and declamation, and of course provides the important dramatic factor of engendering emotion through plot circumstance and the story of the play. Graphic arts are utilized in the wide variety of scenery, properties, and costumes, which are treated sometimes literally and sometimes abstractly or suggestively. Plastic arts are rivalled in the frequent poses and studied groupings of the actors. Literature, lastly, is in the texts and poetry of the plays themselves bared of action and music.

The idea that drama is a blend of all these elements, and that without them working together as a single unit, drama loses its basic and essential esthetics, has been deeply ingrained into the Kabuki-dominated people of Japan. So widespread in fact is Kabuki influence that it forced Osanai Kaoru, the distinguished pioneer in the field of Japan's modern theatre, when he organized the first theatre group modelled on Western styles of acting, to decorate his studio wall with a maxim for his students: "Cry! Don't sing! Walk! Don't dance!"

Until the rise of modern drama, the concept of theatre as a unification of the arts was at the root of Japan's dramatic theory. From this it is obvious that a special type of dramatic form emerges. It is also apparent that to make this amalgam of various arts a workable and superior product, some type of framework must be found in order to give the several parts free play and to permit the exploitation of their full esthetic power and effect. The Japanese in their Kabuki have taken spectacle as their overall framework. The Japanese sense of spectacle is the sustaining and unifying theory at the back of Kabuki. Spectacle, not in the sense of musical comedy or extravaganza, but as an esthetic foundation for an art primarily, although not exclusively, designed to please the eye. Through appealing to the eye, the dissident art elements within the framework become harmonized and expressive, and fall into proper place.

[178]

Even the invisible arts of music and literature become a matter for sight. Music determines the movement; movement is the expression for the eye of what the ear has heard. Literature is created for the stage as much for its decorative possibilities as for its intellectual appeal. This does not mean, however, that Kabuki is an eye art only. The eye appeal is at the core of its guiding and determining principles, but from this base-point Kabuki proceeds to appeal to other sensory perceptions with music and speech for the ear and incense for the nose. More subtly, Kabuki plays are governed by the seasons. In January, the coldest month of the year in Japan, the repertoire is given over to plays of spring, with the sets abounding in flower blossoms and the actors dressed in spring finery. Even the name for the January program is called The Spring Appearance. It must be remembered that Japanese theatres are unheated, and the warmth of what they see is supposed to penetrate and warm the spectators. Similarly in summer—and Japanese theatres are not air-conditioned —ghost plays are always enacted to "chill" the audience. The inner senses are affected by Kabuki not only by the stories themselves, but by a typical Kabuki trick of creating enormous emotional tension through dense tragedy, then suddenly, and often unrelatedly, releasing the strain, by introducing a moment or character of the lightest frivolity and humor, and even sometimes of complete nonsense. The shaking of this inner sense, if one may call it this, by these rapid and alternate differences in tone, is in effect a purely esthetic reaction and unrelated to any sort of intellectual consideration.

1.

Color. Spectacle, as the Japanese regard it in their theatre, divides itself into two parts, color and motion. Through these two media, the effect and import of drama are interpreted to the audience.

In Japan the feeling for color is almost a lust. Flamboyance among the people at large began in Genroku. The peace of the Tokugawa Era brought wealth; wealth brought luxury; and luxury meant among other things, ornate, elaborate, and colorful costumes. Commoners in Genroku were ordered to wear sombre outer garments, but they lined them with the most expensive cloths. On the stage, open extravagance in dress reached its highest degree. The gaudiness of the costumes was something of an expression of the people's frustrated desires as common citizens. There they could see their actors wearing colors and expensive patterns beyond their wildest hopes in actual life.

Certain colors are always associated with certain favorite characters of Kabuki, and usually the significance of the color has a specific origin. For example, the role of Sukeroku is always connected with a certain color of purple known in Genroku as the "Shogun's purple." Sukeroku always appears with a cloth band around his head (*hachimaki*) and socks (*tabi*) of this color. In order to make this particular color, a red dye (*beni*) procurable exclusively from China is necessary. Before Genroku, only the Shogun of the land was wealthy enough to import this luxury item. Sukeroku, the "chivalrous commoner," by wearing the Shogun's special color not only around his head but on his feet, shows that he rivals the ruler in wealth and publicly flouts him, the highest authority in the country. Sukeroku also appears with an umbrella which is noted for its special color, a curious dull indigo. This color is known as "Between the Mountains" (*yama ai zome*) and is connected with Sukeroku, not for its expensiveness but rather for its expansive associations. Tokyo (then Edo) lies between two mountains, Fuji and Tsukuba. At sunset in summer, in the days when Tokyo was not so built up as a city that the country view was impaired, Fuji looked indigo and Tsukaba looked black. By mixing dyes of these two shades, the color of Sukeroku's umbrella appears.

It is a commonplace to say that the costumes of Japan's Kabuki are the most lavish in the world. The subject matter of the plays alone, without the glamorization of the stage, demands the richest kinds of costuming. The brilliance of the great houses, the gay quarters, and the wealth of the Genroku merchants, are represented in full splendor. Some of the costumes of the courtesans are so bulky and large that the actor can move only with the assistance of one or two attendants. An *aragoto* superman character is usually so heavily garbed in layer upon layer of wide-sleeved and lengthy costuming that he is scarcely able to reach his six-foot long sword through the constricting folds of materials.

The taste for colorful costumes gave rise to the convention that once a Kabuki actor makes an exit, he must reappear wearing a different costume. As noted before, many of the plays have scenes where several costume changes take place before the eyes of the audience and without the actor interrupting the course of his action. A few threads are removed from the hem and sleeves, and suddenly an entirely new costume is revealed underneath (*hikinuki*).

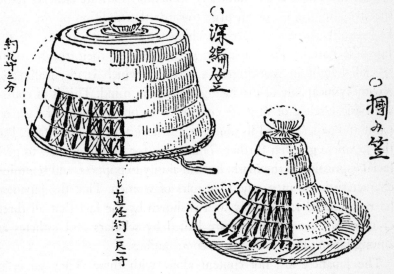

Straw Hats used by Strolling Beggars or Persons Traveling in Disguise

Make-up in Kabuki is also treated as an important part of the color aspect of spectacle. Because of Genroku's primitive lighting, un-

[181]

doubtedly the convention of immediately perceptible make-ups arose. With the establishment of role types, make-ups became standardized and have continued down to today because of their appeal as color. The face of a good, handsome or high-ranking man is painted chalk white. The evil, brave, or low-ranking man is painted varying degrees of red. The shade of red is determined by several factors, such as the degree to which he is wicked, whether he is in a state of high emotion, or whether he has for any reason spent much of his life in the country exposed to the elements. To express inner qualities of a more complex nature, the *kumadori* make-ups of *aragoto* are used.

Kumadori, the most colorful and spectacular Kabuki make-ups, pose an interesting esthetic problem. Historically, they are a normal development from Gigaku masks which covered the entire head, through the delicate Noh masks which barely cover the immediate area of the actor's face. Culturally, *kumadori* indicate either a retrospective clinging to, or an urge towards the tradition of the mask. Esthetically, *kumadori* reveal a characteristic artistic feeling of the Japanese nation. The Japanese, particularly in their theatre, take special delight in working in a medium which is physically and obviously incapable of producing the aim in mind. This is of course the basic essence of any art endeavor—to put a flower or face on paint and paper; a bird in stone; or a historical event on a stage. But the Japanese go even further. They have, for example, tried to give facial expression to the mask, human ability to puppets, and feminine characteristics to men who play roles of women. That the Japanese have succeeded remarkably well is shown by the fact that all three of these last named efforts are hailed by scholars and esthetes as among Japan's most brilliant art contributions.

The Japanese are not content alone with these. They go even further and build art forms on the reverse of their achievements. For example, a large body of Japan's legitimate theatre, as well as among artists of the geisha circles, consists of women who perform exclusively as men. Kabuki actors are required to study the puppets for pointers in their own performance. And even the human face of the Japanese actor is trained to be mask-like.

The contradictory element within the *kumadori* make-up lies in the fact that it differs from the mask in that the Japanese mask is capable of changes in expression. When looking up, the mask seems to smile; and depression appears when the actor inclines his head or casts his glance downwards. *Kumadori,* however, is designed to keep a continuous expression on the actor's face, a function rightfully belonging to the mask. *Kumadori* make-up is fundamentally an expression of anger, the emotion which according to Darwin is the most difficult to sustain over a long period.

Such make-ups are not only colorful but decorative. Their lines are governed broadly by the following principles: for strength, the lines curve upward; for weakness, villainy, or humor, the lines slant downwards.

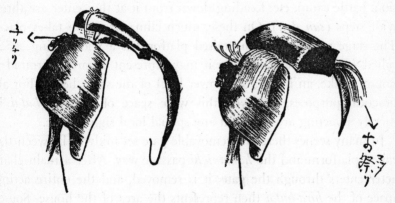

Wigs Used in Kabuki

Kumadori make-ups are also a convenience for the spectator. They reveal the inner nature of the actor to the audience—although the other characters on the stage (usually not made up in *kumadori* style) seem unaware of this open exposure.

[183]

Certain facets of the *kumadori* convention follow a natural and logical law; others violate all concepts of rationality. But the color and spectacle of such make-ups do not offend the instincts and cannot fail to delight an audience of any country regardless of their unfamiliarity and strangeness.

Kabuki settings and decor match the color and splendor of the characters. The great width of Japanese stages and their enormous depth permit the most elaborate of sets. Entire forests, gardens and palace interiors and exteriors are constructed as background to the plays. Certain scenes require literal reconstructions of the facades of famous places of Japan, such as Kiyomizu and Kinkakuji temples of Kyoto, or the Imperial Palace in Tokyo. In certain sets, the action takes place on three levels or stories of the building on the stage.

The most usual set of the Kabuki stage which serves for almost any type of scene, is the raised platform square in the center of the stage (*niju-butai*). This area represents the inside of a house, palace, mansion, battle camp, etc. Leading down from it at the center are three wide steps (*san dan*). On these, much climactic action takes place. The stage area around the raised platform is a wide acting space called *hira-butai*. On occasion it may represent a garden around a house, a lake, an island, or a lower level of the same house. For all practical purposes, however, this wide space of the *hira-butai* is merely an acting area without any special local significance.

In many scenes there is a removable gate set midway between the raised platform and the *hanamichi* passage-way. After a main character enters through the gate, it is removed, and the entire acting space of the *hira-butai* then represents the area of the house. Sometimes a smaller removable gate is placed on the *hanamichi* itself and long scenes, such as clandestine meetings, spying, overhearing, observing the action at the center of the stage, and the laying of villainous plots, are enacted there.

The raised platform, its surrounding area, and the area of the stage nearest the *hanamichi* all afford space for three different groups of actors to perform their joint parts free from interference or distracting proximity. Certain types of acting are performed at each of the three areas. The result is a complex pictorial composition where the same theme is enacted in various ways at the same time at three different levels. The effect is somewhat analogous in music to a contrapuntal fugue. This convention of the separation of the stage into several parts also furnishes the actor with an opportunity to indicate a sense of progression or of movement from one stage to another without a change of scene.

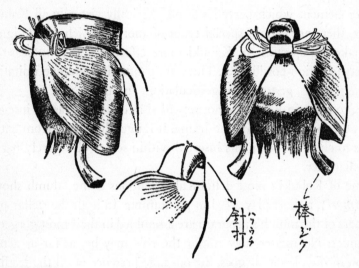

Wigs Used in Kabuki

This type of relatively simple stage setting is augmented by the advantages of the revolving stage which makes possible a series of scenes in rapid succession during the course of each play. Like the colorful variety of costume changes, the sets of Kabuki are also changed with commensurate facility and speed in order to increase the feeling of a constant shift in colors. The Japanese, who are not fettered by the idea of certain colors matching certain other specific and limited colors, freely indulge their lust for riotous and, to our eyes, clashing colors. The brilliantly dressed actors perform against equally elaborately decorated and flamboyantly painted sets. The impression on the spectator is one of overwhelming colorfulness.

2.

Motion. After color, motion is the second aspect of Kabuki's spec-tacle. Motion in its purest form is of course the dance, particularly abstract dance. But Kabuki is essentially a drama form, and its particular types of motion are conditioned by this factor. Aside from the dance element which pervades atmospherically virtually all Kabuki plays, there are certain special types of motion which are designed to make the spectacle of Kabuki more effective and to increase its variety of action-possibilities. These are pantomime, human imitation of the puppets, gesturing or gesticulation, and the pose.

Pantomime in Kabuki is not regarded as dance, but as an integral and necessary part of straight drama. It ranges the gamut from entire plays to climactic segments inserted within scenes of a purely narrative character.

One of Kabuki's most delightful inventions is the "dumb show" (*danmari*), a short play acted in pantomime. In it all the stellar performers of the month's program are assembled in their most gorgeous costumes. No matter how minor the role may be, as far as actual action in the play itself goes, the on-stage presence of all the leading actors is considered necessary because of the prestige this type of play indicates traditionally. In the course of a "dumb show," the actors move around the stage making appropriate and eloquent gestures as the story poem is sung out by the musicians at the side of the stage. The plots are of the most fragmentary nature such as the training of a youth in the art of combat by mysterious creatures of the forest, or a scene at a mountain shrine where various characters, good and bad, appear and gesticulate aimlessly. At the end of the play, the curtain is drawn, leaving the leading male star of the month's performance at the side of the stage before the *hanamichi*. To the accompaniment of drums and flutes played with tremendous ferocity, the actor executes a difficult and complex *roppo* (the "six directions" movements created by Danjuro I), as he makes his exit down the *hanamichi* to the back of the theatre.

These "dumb shows" make little sense other than by the sheer beauty of their motions and movements. The action is dramatically halted periodically and the actors remain stationary in something of the manner of circus tableaux. The appeal lies in the lavish spectacle of the star-studded, beautifully arrayed and gracefully moving cast of characters. A genuine appreciation of this type of Kabuki is considered the mark of a connoisseur. The restless movements and fantastic postures of the actors in the course of the play are referred to as "living pictures," and although their connection with drama as drama may seem to the Westerner somewhat far-fetched, to the Japanese their purpose is important and decorous as a necessary type of theatre embraced by the larger type of Kabuki drama as a whole.

Closely related to the "dumb show," which is set invariably at the dead of night, are the numerous night sequences found in Kabuki plays in general. For these scenes, the backdrop is a plain black curtain to symbolize night. Characters on the stage perform as if in the dark although the lights on the stage and over the audience are glaring. The majority of the night scenes deal with the subject of robbery. Thieves are lying in wait. They hear the voice of an approaching wayfarer. They blow out their paper lanterns. As the innocent wayfarer appears, they knock his lantern out of his hand, and total darkness is assumed by the audience. As they attempt to rob him, he clutches at his purse which accidentally falls to the ground. The group moves around feeling the ground and bumping into one another as they try to find the lost purse. Sometimes an extraneous character arrives and seeing the struggle blows out his lantern. He joins in looking for the purse, finds it, and flees. The curtain is drawn on the frustrated group who are unaware of what has happened and vainly continue their search.

Another type of night pantomime, also derivative from the "dumb show," occurs sometimes during long fighting scenes in which a lone man is pitted against many opponents. The temple bell strikes, and night is assumed. The characters begin to strain their eyes and look as if they are trying to penetrate the darkness. They continue the fight through touch rather than by sight. Needless to add, often the wrong man is killed.

Pantomime is also utilized in Kabuki for climactic scenes. These occur usually after several preceding acts where emphasis has been on speech, in order to lay the foundation of facts for succeeding acts. Pantomime in these instances not only affords relief from wordiness, but allows the actor to carry the intensity of emotion to a climax. During such passages there is silence on the stage, and the actor is required to convey a series of multiple emotions through simple mimetic actions.

An example of this sort of emotional mime appears at the end of the climactic Fourth Act of *Chushingura*. The bereaved Yuranosuke, after the death of his lord, stands in front of the castle which he has surrendered to the governmental authorities. He takes out of his sleeve the dirk with which his lord committed *seppuku* and stares at it. He wipes the still fresh blood off on to the palm of his hand, and brings it to his mouth as a bitter pledge to avenge the unfair death of his lord. The evening bell strikes and calls him back to himself. For fear that he might have been seen making this secret pledge to himself, he quickly hides the dirk next to his heart and prepares to leave. As he blindly starts on his way in the dark, he stumbles on a small paper lantern with the crest of his beloved lord. He removes only the paper lining with the crest. He replaces the rest of the lantern on the steps of the castle; so that no one can say that anything was stolen from the castle at the time it was surrendered. Then pulling himself together, he starts towards the *hanamichi*. The entire set and backdrop representing the castle is slowly pulled to the furthermost wall at the back of the stage. On the *hanamichi* he takes one last look at the castle as it recedes in the distance before his eyes. For the first time since the death of his lord, he gives way to his tears and staggers from the scene grief-stricken.

More subtle and histrionically difficult examples of pantomime also occur in Kabuki. Some of these "scenes of silence" require a complicated sequence of emotions to be conveyed to the audience without the actor's moving. Head-inspections are usually of this nature. Another kind of this sort of "interiorized" pantomime appears in the play *Izayoi Seishin*, an adaptation by Kawatake Mokuami of an older play. Seishin, a priest, has fallen in love with a young courtesan. Because he has violated his religious vows, he attempts double suicide with her. He fails in his attempt to die and at last pulls himself onto the bank of the river. That same night he encounters a youth who carelessly reveals that he is carrying a large sum of money. In attempting to steal the money, Seishin accidentally kills the youth. In the silence and solitude of the darkness, Seishin reflects on his past. He realizes that he has by now accumulated such a number of degraded acts on his soul that he resolves to enter upon a life of evil and completely abandon himself to wickedness. As he slowly lifts up his face the audience sees his expression has changed from innocence and sorrow to one of utter depravity. There is no verbal harangue or soliloquy discussing his decision. Through expression alone, the actor shows Seishin's conviction.

A similar example of pantomimic gesturing and facial expression is the moment when Benten Kozo, in a play of the same name also by Kawatake Mokuami, is found out; he is a notorious thief disguised as a woman. While still completely garbed as a woman he must show merely by crossing his legs and by his facial expression, the relinquishing of his female disguise. His face changes from feminine to masculine without the removal of make-up or wig.

In addition to pantomime, puppet-like actions also comprise a considerable part of Kabuki's spectacle of motion. The large proportion alone of plays borrowed from the puppets implies that a large amount of basic action of the actors must be influenced by puppet styles of movement. In these plays, since there is always the accompanying music and song of the *joruri,* the actor is far freer to move, act, dance, or pantomime in a variety of ways than he would normally be when he is responsible for the speeches as well as the story of the play.

The Kabuki actor is given full scope for incorporating puppet action into his performance in scenes which require "narrations" (*monogatari*). In many of the puppet dramas borrowed by Kabuki, there is at some point a dramatic moment when the leading actor recounts some event which took place in the past or in a preceding act. The "Narration" begins with the actor announcing, "I shall now tell you the story . . ." or some similar phrase to inform the performers as well as the audience that a "narration" will ensue. The actor then describes the event in puppet-like gestures and poses, using only a fan and a sword as properties.

In some "Narrations," such as the famous *Toyata Monogatari,* Toyata, when he begins to tell his story, drops all semblance of human actions and performs precisely as a puppet in faithful obedience to its irregular and jerky movements. To accentuate the effect, another actor dressed in black like an old-fashioned puppeteer, appears on the stage and goes through the simulated motions of manipulating the human "puppet."

The esthetic purpose of these interludes of puppet-like actions is not only for variety, in that differing styles of acting contrast with one another simultaneously on the stage, but also it is to enhance the idea of several characters with their individual emotions and natures impinging on one another in various ways.

Gesturing or gesticulation and the pose are also indispensable in the Kabuki concept of motion. Acting as a whole in Kabuki is noteworthy for its series of exaggerated, dance-like, expansive, and carefully measured gestures and movements. The continuative movement of the actor's actions is punctuated with poses.

The pose is as necessary a part of Kabuki as phrasing is in music. At intervals the actors momentarily pause in position and all motion on the stage is arrested. The tableau which results must be a proportioned arrangement of the main characters involved at the specific moment of the play. The pose is a kind of exclamation point interjected at given intervals to signify the end of a sequence of movements or to call the audience's attention to the importance of the specific moment.

The principle of movement in Kabuki is that if at any moment it were photographed, the result would be a charming and pleasing picture. The pose is the best of these theoretically photographic moments. The color prints of Genroku, and later years, are not merely portraits of the actors, but of the actors in these poses, and as such have been acting guides to Kabuki actors of subsequent centuries.

Kabuki literally moves from pose to pose, or in other words, from tension to tension. Time between poses is fluid. In effect, the pose serves the purpose of the spot light, a form of lighting unknown in Japan's classical theatre. Actors not required immediately in the foreground efface themselves by turning their backs to the audience, leaving the main actor or actors with the full focus of the audience's attention. For the conclusion of all plays, however, there is a grand tableau or super-pose in which the widest assembly of characters possible within the story of the drama is employed.

An indispensable part of the main poses is *mie*. To "cut" a *mie* means, while striking a grandiose pose, to open the eyes wide and cross one eye. The eye to be crossed is determined by whether the attention of the performer is directed to the characters to his left or to his right. In other words, if the villain is standing to the right of the hero who is striking the pose, then the hero will cross his left eye to the right, while the right eye is kept staring ahead. If the pose requires both the villain and the hero to strike a pose simultaneously, then each crosses an eye in the direction of the other. As the actor prepares to "cut" a *mie,* a stage attendant (in the old days, the playwright) rapidly beats two wooden clappers on a small floor board of resonant wood at the side of the stage. As the actor completes the pose and crosses his eye, two resounding whacks of the clappers signify that the motion is completed and the pose over. The clappers intensify the emotion and drama, and alert the audience to the importance of the moment. The crossing of the eye is regarded as a movement to show the maximum tension of an actor's emotional agitation.

Women, instead of "cutting" a *mie,* employ a device known as *kimari.* For their climactic poses they tighten their facial muscles, tense their bodies in whatever attitude required, and remain motionless for a few seconds. In both the *mie* and *kimari,* while the clappers are beaten, the head is rolled to form a specified diagram.

Motion in Kabuki with its punctuating poses demands rhythm. Music in some form or other, whether in dance or drama, underlies Kabuki as a whole and sustains its rhythm. Even in silent pantomimes where music is relatively unimportant, or may even be absent briefly, a fundamental beat courses throughout. With truly great artists like the late Nakamura Baigyoku, rhythm was all important. For each of his roles, he set a basic regularity of pulse, and with almost metronomical precision maintained it by his acting and movements. Kabuki's speech also follows the rhythm of the plays. Although the declamation sometimes bears similarities to song, it never exceeds being more than a type of extremely stylized and florid speech.

3.

Reality versus Unreality. Kabuki's several inner art forms are smoothly blended by their unifying common denominator—spectacle. This however is in the nature of a mechanical or technical

THE ESTHETICS OF KABUKI

solution to Kabuki's problems as an art production. There is a deeper esthetic problem within the content of Kabuki not so easily solved. This is the question of reality or unreality, and the extent to which either may dominate the stage. To this day a complete and satisfactory answer has not been found either by the actors or scholars. The spectator now eschews the problem by justifying any mode of acting as "Kabuki," and so saying a sort of wavering compromise between truth and fiction is automatically accepted.

Chikamatsu Monzaemon once wrote, in defining his esthetic theory of drama, that art lies somewhere in the shadowy frontiers between reality and illusion. In Kabuki these frontiers are defined in a peculiarly Japanese way. There are moments on the stage of complete and literal representation of reality, followed by such fancy as to border on the nonsensical. Sometimes through the vast art resources available to Kabuki, a perfect illusion is created, independent either of reality or of methods of creating fiction. Often this illusion is deliberately broken by the insertion of passages which of necessity force the spectator back into an awareness of himself and remind him that what he has been seeing is merely a stage performance. For example, often actors will refer to themselves or to other actors in the course of the play by their names. The late Uzaemon, who was considered one of the most beautiful actors of the Japanese stage, sometimes in the course of a play when called upon to refer to one of the characters as handsome, would gratuitously insert a line, such as: "as beautiful as Uzaemon himself." Another example of this type of wilful interjection of reality into plays occurs in the entry-dance of Sukeroku. It has always been a tradition for various merchants, each of whom was responsible for various articles of clothing, to send gratis to the actor the complete costume of Sukeroku. Although this practice has been discontinued, the music accompanying Sukeroku's entry-dance still contains a reference to the receipt of these clothes and Sukeroku in the course of his dance bows in acknowledgement towards the audience among whom these merchants formerly sat.

The whole question of reality and unreality is to the Japanese mind a different problem from what it is to the Westerner. The Japanese approach it from a point of view which seems unrealistic to a mind unaccustomed to Kabuki. An amusing story which shows the attitude towards the question was told me by the late Koshiro VII. In the 1920's when Japan's theatre was at a height of awareness of the Western theatre, the Ministry of Education undertook to consider the problem of women appearing in Kabuki. The head of the committee studying the problem went to the three greatest actors of the time to solicit their opinions on which they could base their recommendations to the government. They first asked Utaemon, the greatest of the *onnagata* man-actresses. He replied, "Why should women appear when I am here? There is no woman in all Japan who can act as femininely on the stage as I." They next asked the progressive and somewhat heretical Kabuki actor Sadanji II, who replied, "Of course, by all means let women come on the stage in Kabuki. The stage needs the authoritative realism of women." Lastly Koshiro gave his opinion. He said, "It is too late for women now to appear in Kabuki. A type of woman has been created and has become familiar in Kabuki. To change this would mean that Kabuki would lose its flavor. If women had appeared a hundred years ago they could have created their own kind of woman for the stage; now all they could do would be to imitate what men have created for them."

Perhaps this last answer solves the problem. Kabuki has attained its own blend of reality and unreality. It has created its own flavor which derives from hovering in its own way between the two poles. It now remains only a matter for the spectator to draw delight from the result.

Historically, the problem has tormented the Kabuki actor and playwright. But there have been numerous factors inherent within the situation to complicate and obscure various possible solutions.

If one takes Uzume's dance before the Sun-Goddess as the beginning of all Japan's theatre arts, Kabuki's remote origin lies in the artifice of dance designed to express the erotic. O-Kuni's Kabuki, the direct progenitor of Kabuki, as we know it today, did little to oppose this combination of dance and eroticism. Such origins naturally tend to the creation of suggestive rather than realistic art. Dance by its stylization of movement, and eroticism by its indication rather than graphic portrayal, both oppose reality and literalness. As a drama form Kabuki was also indebted to its predecessor in the field, Noh, whose attenuation places the symbol above direct representation. Still later, at the time Kabuki incorporated the characteristics of its competitor, the puppets, it was further constrained to move away from realism. Puppets, no matter how skillfully operated, remain stiff, unreal imitations of human beings. Kabuki by borrowing from the puppets developed a style of acting which is an imitation of an imitation, and the actor in action is in a way a human being twice removed from his own humanity.

At the root of all Kabuki's determinants is what is known as the Kabuki spirit itself. This spirit is defined in the original sense of the word *kabuku* which means ultimately a desire for an unusual flavor, for a kind of disporting through dance and playlets, for an outlet and sublimation of wild, irrational emotions deep within. In the beginning of Kabuki as now, there is still delight in the odd, in a particular kind of disassociation from reality in the theatre. And because of this specialized taste, common to all people but expressed to its most extreme degree in the Japanese, Kabuki evolved and maintained its unique atmosphere and rarefied esthetic air.

This underlying spirit of Kabuki, determined by the tastes of the public, resulted in the patterns and forms on the stage assuming a validity in their own right, of equal importance (and sometimes more) with the emotions which subtend drama in its normal sense. Sometimes the artistic achievement is at the expense of intellectual justification, but the art stands on its own merits as such. Because of the strength of the Kabuki spirit, Kabuki did not develop into a logical theatre form; it remained attuned to itself, and to its audiences.

In the midst of these factors preventing Kabuki from drifting into realism, there was also the natural urge of the people towards a theatre which approximated the reasonable. Kabuki was a people's theatre and as such was expressive of the problems peculiar to its day. The increase in intellectual awareness on the part of the rising commoners found arbitrary convention harder and harder to accept either mentally or emotionally. As the compulsion towards reality grew, Chikamatsu appeared with his domestic plays where commoners saw themselves accurately glamorized and victimized on the stage. For a time these domestic plays satisfied the desire for realism. At the same time the historical plays and *aragoto* preserved the Kabuki spirit which negated realism. In addition, the pure estheticism inherent within the artistic Japanese as a nation was supported by the dances. But the issues soon became clouded. Domestic plays became artificial—a natural enough occurrence considering their origin in the puppets. Naturalness and realistic accuracy were introduced into the historical plays. Dances became more and more dramatic and their stylized gestures gradually became more explicit. The ultimate result was a mixture of elements in each.

The Japanese explain the contradictory pulls toward reality and unreality as the struggle between *shajitsu* and *shai*. *Shajitsu* means "realism" or literally "to reflect reality." *Shai* is "emotionalism" or literally "to reflect the import of an action." An example of these two contrasts can be seen in the play *"Wait a Moment"* (*Shibaraku*). There is a moment when the superman hero lops off the heads of eight people when he merely touches his sword. Realism or *shajitsu* would demand at least that he draw his sword. *Shai* however is content with the import of his action, and for the Kabuki audience it is sufficient to make the suggestion in order to be completely convincing.

The problem has been mooted since the beginning of Kabuki. One story of how actors regarded the question has been handed down since the time of Danjuro II. It tells of a role in which it was required of the actor to stand at the corner of a house and lift it up from its foundation. Danjuro II used one hand to accomplish the feat. Sawamura Sojuro another actor of the same era said, "No one can lift a house with one hand; it would be better to use both hands." Danjuro replied, "It would be impossible for the strongest man in the world to lift a house. The lifting can only be deception. But the point of the deception is to *show* strength. Lifting the house with one hand *shows* greater strength than if done with two hands."

The problem of *shajitsu* and *shai,* that is, whether Kabuki should strive to be realistic or should be content with its characteristic fancy, reached a climax in the Meiji Era with the two great actors Danjuro IX and Kikugoro V. They both at times tried to instill rationality and realism into Kabuki. On one occasion Kikugoro V was fastidious to the extent that for the dance *Modori-bashi,* he sent a stagehand to Kyoto to determine the exact number of boards in the actual bridge where the dance is supposed to take place. Danjuro IX for a time deleted all *mie* eye-crossings from his performance. He also prophesied, incorrectly, that by the time of his death the extravagant make-ups of *kumadori* would be considered ridiculous and discarded. But despite their efforts there was so strong an urge within Kabuki, and so profound an esthetic justification for its irrationalities, that Kabuki continued in its old way, if somewhat modified by their momentary innovations.

Today the struggle continues in a less virulent form. Kikugoro VI was a proponent of realism. His desire for natural simplicity in acting led him to adjust his acting and that of his pupils to a form midway between pure Kabuki and modern drama. Sometimes the result fell short. But to a large extent this was a matter of opinion, and a large following approved his innovations. For example, one of Kikugoro VI's greatest dances was *Yasuna*. It tells the story of a man who has lost his mind after the death of his lover. He wanders through the spring fields carrying his lover's kimono. In the course of the dance he talks to himself and thinks that he sees his lover. The mood alternates between the demented lover amusing himself chasing butterflies, picking flowers, etc., and sadly recalling that there is this great emptiness in his heart—a sorrow which he cannot quite formulate in his clouded mind. The traditional end of the dance requires that Yasuna strike a rigid pose of holding the kimono outstretched and crossing his eye in a *mie*. Kikugoro VI in order to give the dance a pathos of realism, and incidentally after having seen Pavlova's "The Swan," made Yasuna cover his head with the kimono and sink to the ground in grief. To the Kabuki expert, however, this sort of sentimentality is a violation of the spirit of Kabuki.

The greatest of the Kabuki actors living today and the doyen of the stage is Kichiemon who has always opposed Kikugoro's novelties. It is largely due to Kichiemon that today's Kabuki has not become more perverted towards realism. He makes a specialty of roles origi-

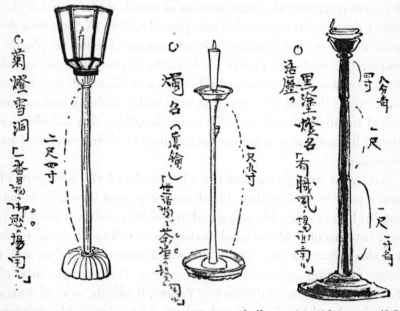

Three Types of Candle-Sticks. (L) *Height, 2′ 4″—used in* jidaimono. (M) *Height, 1′ 9″—originally used as timekeeper for time spent with a courtesan.* (R) *Height, 2′ 5″—used in realistic historical plays.*

nally written for puppets, and his mastery of this intricate form of acting is probably among the finest ever known on Japan's stage.

It is a difficult problem to decide the extent to which realism can be introduced into the art of Kabuki. The pulls are apparently too great for any major break away from its origin. Kabuki texts were written years ago. Upon them a succession of actors have built an accumulation of distinguished traditions. According to the contemporary tastes of each ensuing era, certain forms of acting styles became ironclad, and to violate them would indicate ignorance rather than originality to the Japanese mind. There is in general much which prevents an actor from achieving realism within Kabuki. There are too many basic and traditional inconsistencies. If they were resolved, Kabuki would end up as a plain modern theatre performed on a hopelessly incongruous base, and all its deep esthetic delight would vanish.

Once the conventions of Kabuki are accepted, the spectator is free to be indulged in an emotional experience which exceeds the limitations of human reality. He begins to function in a higher realm of emotional intensity. Kabuki is in this way a threefold experience. It consists of the meaning, the sensory perception, and the emotional impact. There is a word (or song) which explains the meaning, then follows the sound of the accompanying music, and lastly there is the sight of the interpretative gesture. The intensity and largeness of the gesture carry the impact and enable the spectator to be moved emotionally not by a realistic actuality, but esthetically by an emotional essence above and beyond reality. Kabuki in this way is an intense abstraction from reality, yet at the same time, a deeply moving experience firmly rooted in universal humanity.

VI

Meiji Era Theatre

Comparable in breadth and scope to the extraordinary social and economic changes of Genroku are the reforms initiated during the Meiji Era in the latter half of the 19th century. Both periods in Japan's history are characterized and reflected in their contemporary theatres—Genroku by Kabuki, and the Meiji Era by the rise of a modern theatre, the first break away from Kabuki.

The Meiji Era refers to the long rule of Emperor Mutsuhito (posthumously named Meiji, literally "shining rule") from 1868 to 1911. During this reign, three staggering events took place that shook the entire Japanese nation:

1) The dissolution of Japan's feudal social structure;

2) The return of the Emperor to power and the end of the shogun system of military control (hence the alternative designation of the era as the "Restoration");

3) The influx and impact of Western civilization on the heretofore isolated country of Japan.

These three factors had great and far-reaching consequences on every aspect of Japanese life. Not least among them were the facts that the people at large were awakened and the nation as a whole was spurred into a frenzy of activity.

Until Japan's recent defeat in war, the "shining rule" of Meiji was generally considered one of the world's brilliant examples of a national change towards enlightened government. We have since seen, however, much of the period discredited. What once appeared as good reforms, now in the light of the sweeping changes made at the insistence of the Occupation Army, seem most suspect. Japan's shift from an anachronistic feudal state into a full-fledged modern power was apparently only superficial, and motivated by equivocal aims.

Meiji in theory freed the masses and offered all men equal opportunity; but the government retained a state symbol, the Emperor, who was so shrouded in superstition that the symbol was capable of being used to unite the country for any end, nefarious or not. Education was declared the right of the people but in practice it was little more than propaganda. The instruments and inventions of science were used to ensure the dissemination and effectiveness of government aims over the country at large. The welcoming of the best of the West turned out to be a study of the methods of physical power. Freedom was tolerated but only in so far as the protests of the people did not disturb public tranquillity or undermine the morality of the warriors, by now called soldiers. Underlying Meiji reforms, as we look at them in retrospect from the ashes of a defeated Japan, was a spiritual power speciously called "Japanese psychology." This power was the emotional residue of the nation's history and the inner energy of the people. But Meiji fanned it into a flame whose fanaticism ultimately expressed itself in expansionism and national suicide.

The confusion and viciousness of the Meiji Era had immediate effect on the stage in a variety of ways.

Kagura, an early dance form, was reconstructed and its content made to extol the Emperor's mythological origins. The new *Kagura* emphasized the powerful unity of church and state personified in the Emperor. The authorities hoped that these dances performed in temples and shrines would, while giving entertainment and amusement, imbue the people with a responsiveness which could be later turned into obedience to serve the ends of power.

Noh because of its associations with former shoguns and the foreign religion, Buddhism, disappeared until it was ascertained that it was not in serious conflict with the new times. Kabuki profited by this absence and began to adapt a large number of Noh plays into its repertoire. For the first time the warriors were unable to withhold their Noh from the commoners. Esthetically some claimed, and still do today, that Kabuki vulgarized Noh by over-simplification of texts and over-elaboration of action and accompanying music. But regardless of the criticism, the antiquated plays were given new life and the people at large for the first time could understand and delight in them.

Kabuki, whose origins had been democratic, should have been welcomed by the Meiji government which carefully maintained a semblance of the people's importance in the new social structure. But the innovations of Meiji, at first sight, appeared to have left no room for Kabuki. The influence of the West made the Japanese aware of the fact that a broader field of drama than Kabuki was possible. Since Genroku, it had not occurred to the people and intellectuals of Japan that drama could mean anything wider in scope than their traditional Kabuki. Kabuki was also attacked because it was anachronistic in a 19th century world, that it was grotesquely traditional, and that it was unsuitable and unworthy for a modern nation to have as its main theatrical fare such archaic drama.

In 1886 the elite of Meiji society, under the guidance of Suematsu Kensho, who had just returned from a tour of the Occident, organized the "Theatrical Reform Group." They proposed a complete reformation of Kabuki to make it compatible with the changes which had been effected in the government. They insisted in their policy platform that:

"1) New plays be staged, written by learned men and based on historical facts which will inspire popular confidence instead of Kabuki plays which are full of absurdity and nonsense, obscenity, and vulgarity.

"2) Actresses be employed on the stage instead of men whose performances are unavoidably unnatural.

"3) European-style management of theatres be adopted."

Kabuki would have succumbed to the opposition against it had it not been for a triumvirate of outstanding artists: the actors Danjuro IX and Kikugoro V and the playwright Kawatake Mokuami. These three, dominated by the implacable will of Danjuro IX, are responsible for holding Kabuki together during its most troubled time since the Edo government's persecutions in the early 17th century. For this they of course deserve the highest praise. But at that time, because of the spirit of the times, they too fell victim to some of the regrettable aspects of the Meiji Era.

In the light of contemporary events, it is difficult to regard these men fairly, because much that they did now seems damaging to Kabuki. It is also undeniable that they injected into Kabuki a vitality which was its last spurt of energy and culminated in its final peak of development. Both Danjuro IX and Kikugoro V were doubtless among the greatest actors Japan has ever produced. Kawatake Mokuami, who divided his playwriting, editing, and setting down in writing of traditional plays between the two actors, was certainly a writer of a magnitude second only to Chikamatsu Monzaemon—and if versatility and variety are taken into consideration, he far exceeded him.

Both Danjuro IX and Kikugoro V continued the onerous traditions bequeathed them by the long line of their actor-ancestors. They also lifted the art out of the casualness to which it, as a people's popular drama performed before uncritical audiences, had eventually degenerated. Aware of the influences from the outside world, they sought an intellectual satisfaction in Kabuki. Traditional forms and styles of acting (*kata*) were not enough for them. They tried to find a rationality within these forms and styles, and either created entirely new forms or filled the old with fresh intensity and a closer approximation to reasonableness. They selected less gaudy costumes and less fantastic make-ups to match their more human and normal standards of acting.

At the same time, as much as their intellectuality led them to disapprove of the irrationality of Kabuki, their emotions led them to respond to the nationalistic attitudes of the Meiji Era. They supported the expansionistic temper of the government with its aggressive intent toward China, Formosa, Okinawa, and Korea, and with it they condoned the concomitant revival of the concept of the warrior's code of loyalty to the master (now the Emperor). Danjuro IX, in particular, eschewed plays with heroes possessing *futa-gokoro* or "double-heartedness," a word synonymous with treachery. Among these were many of the best plays of Kabuki repertoire, such as: *Sanemori,* where a warrior saves an enemy child and goes over to the opposing side; *Ishikiri Kajiwara,* where the hero recalls how when he had once tried to kill the enemy general his hand had become numb, and he now feels the enemy side to be the side of righteousness; *Moritsuna's Camp,* where a warrior betrays his own lord; and *Adachi ga Hara,* where the heroine is married to, and in love with, a traitor.

Kumagai's Camp, however, in which a warrior terminates his service to his lord, presented less of a problem to Danjuro IX. To end the play he created a special *makusoto* (an emotional postlude performed by the star actor on the *hanamichi* after the curtain has been drawn and the main story of the play concluded). There Kumagai, after saying, "Ah, those sixteen years have passed like a dream, like a dream," sinks to the ground in tears. Danjuro's interpretation called for the sound of battle drums whereupon Kumagai stands up, reaches automatically and instinctively for his sword. Then he remembers that he has renounced warriorhood, and again sinks in tears over his lost profession of arms. In this way he makes his exit down the *hanamichi*.

Danjuro's patriotism and response to Meiji thought did not stop with his choice of roles. He also altered lines at will. For example, in *The Village School* where Genzo the village school teacher realizes that at last he is to be forced to sacrifice one of his innocent students in order to protect the life of his lord's son, the original version contains an emotional outburst of protest against this tragedy. Genzo and his wife say tearfully in unison, "How painful it is to be asked to serve a lord" (*semajiki mono wa omiyazukai*). Danjuro IX, however, gave this line to the wife and he (Genzo) then defiantly interrupts with "It is only now that we *can* truly serve our lord!" (*omiyazukai wa koko ja wa i na*)

Danjuro's training since childhood and his true talent were naturally in the field of pure Kabuki. But his personal convictions and the pressure of this unfortunate period in history militated against him. Finally in 1878, together with Kawatake Mokuami as his playwright, he openly rebelled against the inconsistencies of plot, language, and costume of Kabuki, and performed the first of a series of dramas which became known as "Plays of Living History" (*katsureki geki*). These plays were enactments of historical incidents performed in every detail with all the accuracy that extensive research could reveal. Their popularity was moderate, and only Danjuro's brilliant acting sustained them. The spirit behind these plays was too studied and too motivated by propaganda to endure for long, and with Danjuro's death in 1903 "Plays of Living History" were forgotten. Shortly after the China Incident, the Board of Information, Japan's scandalous propaganda agency, urged Kabuki actors to revive some of these "Plays of Living History" as a morale factor for the home front. But their lack of genuine artistic validity as drama defeated the purpose. The drop in theatre attendance when such plays were performed made their value as a propaganda medium negligible.

BAIGYOKU AS COURTESAN AND KIKUGORO AS HER LOVER
IN A SCENE FROM YUGIRI IZAEMON

SOMEGORO AS UMEOMARU
IN KURUMABIKI

Kikugoro V, Danjuro's friendly rival, was less absorbed by Meiji's militaristic tendencies. History held less interest for him than the present. In Kabuki forms he excelled in Domestic Plays and in Mokuami's Living Domestic Plays (*ki-zewamono*), plays of ordinary people of the era acted in traditional classical style. Not to be outdone creatively by Danjuro IX, Kikugoro V in 1879 appeared with the first of "Cropped Hair Plays" (*zangiri mono*). The designation, "cropped hair," refers to the fact that in the Meiji Era with the abolition of certain social distinctions, hair-styles also changed. Until Meiji a man's station in life was indicated by his hairdo, i.e., the way the scalp was shaved and the length of hair and method of tying it. With the levelling of all ranks of men, ordinary close-cropped hair (*zangiri*) became the fashion for all classes high and low. Kikugoro's "Cropped Hair Plays" were so-called because the characters appeared with the characteristic haircut and costume of the Meiji Era. These plays were the second step in the development of a modern theatre in Japan, and the first time since Genroku that Japan had even the semblance of a contemporary theatre.

The first of these "Cropped Hair Plays" was also the first Western play ever performed in Japan. Kawatake Mokuami adapted into Japanese style a translation of the plot of Lytton's *Money*. Like the "Plays of Living History," the "Cropped Hair Plays" were moderately successful, but lasted only during the lifetime of their creator. All these plays have long been absent from the boards of Japan's theatres.

Danjuro, Kikugoro, and Mokuami, despite numerous failures and frequent political band-waggoning, left an overall effect on Kabuki which was actually a much needed improvement—only, however, because of their genius and not because of their political convictions which were the product of the Meiji Era. They dressed up shabby texts. Language which had been confined to the court or high stations was used on the stage accurately. For the first time many Kabuki plays were put into permanent written form after centuries of having been transmitted orally. Even costuming, in so far as consistent with Kabuki's demand for splendor, was made to follow more closely the correct historical patterns. Their scholarship clarified the past, and they moulded tradition into an artistic standard which surpassed much previous attainment. Even today their memories are a strong force. With Japan's defeat in the war, many of their innovations have been dropped and the spirit of Kabuki has swung back toward Genroku. But no actor today dares defy certain of the acting traditions and stylistic improvements introduced by Danjuro and Kikugoro. And most Kabuki programs today end with one of Mokuami's "Living Domestic Plays."

As crowning achievement for their labors, they were rewarded by being the first Kabuki troupe to be seen by an Emperor—except for the perhaps apochryphal appearance of O-Kuni. In 1887, Emperor Meiji commanded a performance of *The Subscription List* (*Kanjincho*) to be held within the Palace grounds. From this date the social status of actors in Japan was assured. It is interesting to note that no subsequent Emperor has seen Kabuki. The present Empress saw the first performance of *Chushingura* since World War II, and the present Emperor attended a performance of the Bunraku Puppet Theatre in Osaka, also since the war. These three times are the total theatrical experiences of Japan's rulers.

Despite the dual quality of negative and positive achievements of Kabuki in the Meiji Era, it is impossible not to regard the period as the third and undoubtedly last flowering of Kabuki since Genroku. Curiously, the Kabuki actors themselves were responsible for giving incentive to the modern theatre of Japan, the force destined to be Kabuki's most dangerous enemy.

1.

"Political Drama." The Kabuki actors Danjuro IX and Kikugoro V were fragmentary parts of a larger movement towards a modern theatre which evolved out of the Meiji Era. Their efforts were pro-

gressive steps, but never constituted a real break with Kabuki styles, and therefore never truly became realistic enough to be counted as "modern."

The direct forerunner of present-day modern theatre in Japan was the result of the political parties which arose during the Meiji Era. One of the most important things to emerge from Meiji was the promise to the people for the first time in Japanese history of a Constitution. In 1881 it was publicly announced that by 1890 the Constitution would be completed and put into effect. In order to prepare the people for representative government, various political parties were formed shortly after this announcement. One of these, the Liberal Group (*Jiyu Dantai*), may be credited with having started the modern theatre movement of Japan.

In 1888 Sudo Sadanori (1866–1909), a member of the Liberal Group, wrote and produced a short play which had as its hero, Itagaki, a leading statesman and chief formulator of the Meiji Constitution. This new type of drama was dubbed "Political Drama" or *soshi geki*. The term *soshi* applied to men who belonged to the newly formed political groups. Other political parties followed suit and used "Political Dramas" as a serious means of conveying to the illiterate population the aims and desires of the party platforms.

Out of this politico-dramatic ferment appeared a curious figure, Kawakami Otojiro (1864–1911). He wrote and starred in a large number of "Political Dramas." His plays and style of acting were considered so realistic by the people used to Kabuki's extravagant affectations, that audiences literally did not know whether the characters were actual or actors. His performances must have been riotous occasions. There are stories of the day to the effect that on one occasion a member of the audience leapt onto the stage and murdered one of the villains. Audiences also frequently shouted out warnings to the actors if a villain approached or if their actions were going to lead them to destruction.

As part of Kawakami Otojiro's realism on the stage, he used

women as actresses. Not since the 17th century had the Japanese seen a real woman on the stage as a serious actress, although in 1890 shortly before Kawakami Otojiro's plays, a vaudeville troupe in the Asakusa entertainment quarter of Tokyo had staged some dances with both men and women participating.

Audiences at first attended these "Political Dramas" out of curiosity. The political content was actually of interest only to the party members, and the plays in themselves were not really important. But there developed among the people at large a desire to see this new type of acting and drama which was so different from their familiar Kabuki. Catering to this, Kawakami Otojiro turned the "Political Dramas" into what was called "New School Theatre" (*Shimpa*). In 1891 he drained the plays of political significance and expanded their subject matter, but unfortunately the result was the worst sort of melodrama.

In the course of Kawakami Otojiro's theatrical activity, he married the most gifted of the actresses in his troupe, Saddo Yakko. Together they toured not only Japan, but also Europe and America, and by so doing did Japan's theatre a great disservice. Saddo Yakko was undoubtedly talented in acting which is more than could be said of her husband; but the vehicles at her disposal were shocking bits of melodrama and silliness concocted by Kawakami Otojiro. Europeans and Americans who saw their unfortunate performances immediately assumed that they had seen the best of Japanese theatre and condemned it as insignificant. This impression continued in Western drama circles for some years.

Kawakami Otojiro was not content with the damage he had done abroad. In 1902 after returning to Japan he performed the first plays Japan was to see in "Western" style. He displayed tragic misunderstanding of Western theatre and a complete intoxication with a culture that he had not even begun to assimilate. To mention only one example, Kawakami Otojiro's Hamlet came down the *hanamichi* on a bicycle.

Although Kawakami Otojiro was the father of modern drama in Japan, he was basically nothing more than a sensational charlatan. None of his plays or dramatic theories have survived. His innovations, however, paved the way for the emergence of a serious theatre.

2.

Shinsei Shimpa. During the 1890's in the midst of the theatrical confusion of the Meiji Era, several noteworthy groups of actors appeared. Their style of drama was called *Shinsei Shimpa* (literally New Life New School). The designation, *Shimpa* referred to Kawakami Otojiro's theatre, and was taken over by the *Shinsei Shimpa* troupes because there were basic similarities between the two.

Shinsei Shimpa troupes as a theatrical form developed from the "Political Drama" and from Kawakami Otojiro's "New School Theatre." But they avoided certain pitfalls. They ignored political content, avoided imitation of Western plays, and toned down the rank and sensational melodrama which Kawakami Otojiro had spread over the theatre.

Shinsei Shimpa, then as now, consisted largely of plays in typical Meiji costumes, concerned with Meiji problems. The plots are stock situations, familiar in Kabuki as the "duty-versus-humanity" conflict. A good number of them deal with success stories, and some are merely mood pieces where atmosphere substitutes for plot sequence. *Shinsei Shimpa* is not quite a modern theatre because it is completely caught in the aroma of the Meiji Era and has today therefore become anachronistic. A certain lack of full-fledged artistic merit prevents it from taking a place as a classical theatre hallowed by great and glorious traditions.

Shinsei Shimpa was the first theatrical form differing from Kabuki to become firmly established and to maintain its position even to the present. As a theatrical form it represents a large step away from Japan's Kabuki-dominated stage. *Joruri* reciting is not used.

Sound effects are all realistic. The musical side-orchestra (*geza*) of Kabuki where varying drum beats and sounds of samisen are used to represent wind, waves, snow, etc., is dispensed with. The acting is simple and not exaggerated. Except for the rather melodramatic conventions inherent within the plots themselves, the actors represent pretty much how ordinary people of the Meiji Era would have acted in normal life. The characters in the plays are invariably middle-class.

Another of the main differences between Kabuki and *Shinsei Shimpa* was that both women and men were allowed to appear in women's roles. The actresses for the *Shinsei Shimpa* plays came from all walks of life. Some were former geishas, some were daughters of professional actors, and many were ordinary girls who simply wanted to act despite the stigma of the stage and the opposition of their parents. The curious phenomenon of both men and women appearing at the same time on the stage in female roles produced a sort of compromise characterization of women on the stage. The men became more feminine, and the women performed with a somewhat stylized air. The success of the experiment is shown by the fact that in *Shinsei Shimpa* plays today, it is impossible for a person unfamiliar with the actors themselves to differentiate between the actual women and the women impersonators.

Shinsei Shimpa, regardless of whatever criticism may be levelled at it today, was of great significance in the growth of the modern theatre in Japan. It served as a bridge between the classical Kabuki and the completely modern theatre.

3.

Growth of Modern Theatre. A major step to improve the standard of theatre in Japan and to establish a truly modern theatre of exemplary quality, was taken in 1906 by Dr. Tsubouchi Shoyo who founded the Literary and Art Association (*Bungei Kyokai*). The distinguished Dr. Tsubouchi Shoyo was a pioneer in many respects.

As early as 1884 he translated Shakespeare's *Julius Caesar* into Japanese, and provided thereby Japan's first acquaintance with a masterpiece of Western drama. He was also responsible for the first research into the history of Japan's theatre. In 1893 his *History of the Japanese Theatre* appeared, and was until recently the standard textbook of the theatre.

The Literary and Art Association was composed of a group of intellectuals and artists who wanted to see in Japan a contemporary theatre of social importance and artistic beauty. Since many of them had studied in the West, they naturally inclined to adopt aspects of Western theatre. They produced the best translations of Shakespeare and Ibsen ever to appear in Japanese, some of which are still used in modern-day performances. They also wrote a considerable number of creative plays, all in naturalistic, everyday style. Among the best of the playwrights who wrote these first modern dramas of Japan were Iwano Home, Mayama Seka, and Sano Tensei. After a long period of study and training, the Literary and Art Association produced its first public performance in 1911. Two years later the Association was dissolved, but the fruit of their labors had by then spread throughout Japan and continued to develop among other groups of intellectuals.

Shortly after the inception of the Literary and Art Association, another important theatre group was founded. In 1909, the brilliant playwright and actor-director, Osanai Kaoru, organized the Free Theatre (*Jiyu Gekijo*). Unlike the Literary and Art Association which concentrated on the literary and intellectual aspects of the modern theatre, Osanai Kaoru's Free Theatre was primarily interested in the actual production of the plays and the training of actors to perform. This group probed into every detail of acting, staging, lighting, settings, and general production, and the polish and finish of their performances attracted widest attention.

Some of the great Kabuki actors who had heretofore looked down on attempts at a theatre apart from Kabuki became interested in the possibilities of the modern theatre. Chief among them was Ichikawa Sadanji II, who worked with Osanai Kaoru in his Free Theatre. Sadanji was perhaps the most progressive and energetic of Kabuki actors since Danjuro IX. He made a study of theatre in Russia in 1908, and brought back a considerable amount of new ideas and practices which were adopted by the Free Theatre Group. Sadanji, while never abandoning Kabuki altogether, performed many modern plays completely divorced from tinges of Kabuki styles.

The popularity of modern theatre in Japan increased considerably. Troupes sprang up all over the country, each with their own particular ideas as to details of performance and subject matter of the plays; but common to them all was the hope of making the modern theatre a part of Japanese life, and of using it as an expression of social problems.

In the early 1920's a new force entered the Japanese modern theatre, and quickly began to dominate all theatrical activity. This was the emergence of the left-wing theatre groups whose aim was to make the theatre a more vital factor in effecting socialistic reforms in the government. Chief among these were the brilliant Tsukiji Little Theatre Group and the Vanguard Troupe. Their members had become disillusioned with the turn of events rising out of the Meiji reforms, and profiting by the richness of talent and public appreciation of the modern theatre which Meiji had made possible, they whipped the theatre into a sharply critical organ for social reform. Other troupes who wanted the theatre treated purely as an instrument of propaganda followed. One of these was the Japan Proletarian Theatre League whose membership was composed of four acting companies in Tokyo alone, and a dozen others in various major cities. In Tokyo and Nagoya there was a Korean Proletarian Theatre Group which did much to ease the tense relations between the Korean and Japanese populations of those cities. In 1931 the International Arbeiter Theatre Bund was organized, and represented the first union of professional actors with amateurs. The actors provided assistance and theatrical guidance to the workers of factories and various unions, and in turn the workers were of course of use to the politics of these left-wingers.

Nineteen hundred and thirty-seven saw the outbreak of the China Incident, and all left-wing activity was immediately suppressed by the government. The theatre as an outlet for social criticism in general was banned. The left-wing troupes, instead of suspending activities, reorganized themselves and began to direct their attention to productions of art for art's sake, and foreign dramas. Two of these groups, the New Cooperative Troupe, headed by Murayama Tomoyoshi, and the New Tsukiji Troupe, headed by Hijikata Yoshi, attained a high degree of technical skill. While the majority of non-left-wing troupes became paralyzed by the propaganda demands of the government and the restrictions placed on them, the left-wing troupes increased their artistic stature.

Finally in 1940, the increasingly interfering and carping military government of Japan ordered all but the most reactionary of troupes to dissolve. The leaders of the more blatant of the troupes were incarcerated on the grounds that they were spreading Communism and not contributing to the war effort. In this way, Hijikata, Murayama, and Senda Koreya, Japan's most capable actor-directors and foremost proponents of the modern theatre, were removed from the scene. In 1945 after Japan's defeat in war, they, together with all other political prisoners, were released.

In the course of the various strivings of Japan towards a modern theatre, the hold of her classical theatre was never lost. As the motion picture was comparatively unknown, the theatre represented the only entertainment of the people, and there was room for tremendous theatrical activity in Japan. The seeming modernization of Japan in the Meiji Era with its various social and political changes certainly dealt some severe blows to the Japanese instinct for preserving their traditions. Many thought that the dominance of the classical theatre would be broken merely by showing what types of drama lay outside their own islands, and by indirectly stimulating the Japanese towards individualistic discovery and creativity in their arts. But because of the fact that Japan's new energy in the Meiji Era became a political factor, successive governments quickly suppressed it, and with it, all liberal thought which is, as they well knew, the only soil that nurtures a progressive theatre.

The Japanese were thus made to hark back to their traditions for spiritual and artistic sustenance. This factor alone prevented the free theatrical activity which plays havoc with classical theatre. Until 1945, at least, Japan remained caught in the hold of her ancient drama, in spite of a tremendously healthy and progressive beginning towards a modern theatre.

VII

The Theatre Today

Japan's defeat in the Pacific War has had and will continue to have more bearing on her theatre than has any other event throughout her entire history. Before the war no country had proportionately as many professional troupes roaming its countryside as Japan. No country had as many legitimate theatre-houses. Few other countries had so large a population dependent on theatre as its main source of entertainment.

The economic chaos resulting from the war caused the number of Japan's troupes to sink to a third of the pre-war level. Because of war damage, the number of theatres was cut in half. The reduction in the average Japanese's standard of living and the tragedies of post-war inflation have meant that Japan can no longer sustain so large a number of live actors. The movie industry is rapidly taking the place of the theatre. The motion picture asks no food, no traveling expenses, and only the simplest of stages. In Japan the average time for making a movie is less than four months, and once made, it costs little for the exhibitor or for the audience. It is highly doubtful if the theatre can withstand the economic hardships and the movies for long.

The theatre of any nation usually springs from the people, and by the time it reaches a high degree of perfection, it is taken over by the classes capable of sustaining the luxury of art. When these groups become incapable of supporting the art, it is likely to disappear.

Today the only two classes who seriously want to support Japan's classical theatre are economically impotent: the older generation which was formerly wealthy and is now in greatly reduced circumstances; and a large body of young students who feel that Japan's future lies only in commerce or culture, and having little taste for commerce, they have chosen culture in the form of the classical theatre. There is little likelihood that their financial position will be altered.

1.

The State of Classical Theatres. Bugaku dances have for the last thousand years been supported by the Emperor. With the Occupation-sponsored reduction in Imperial Household grants, the Emperor can no longer afford to continue his patronage. A group, the "Music Friend's Society," has been formed by scholars to solicit contributions from the public and present *Bugaku* dances in ordinary theatres with tickets available to the general public. With this support, it is hoped that the 30-odd remaining dancers and musicians will be able to eke out their livelihood in post-war inflationary Japan. Whether or not assistance from the "Music Friend's Society" and the income derived from popular recitals will prove constant enough to continue for any length of time is problematical.

The difficulties confronting Noh are somewhat similar. For centuries the warrior classes maintained it. Since the late 19th century its continued existence is due exclusively to the private support of the wealthy. With the pressing problems of a defeated Japan and the dissolution of large concentrations of wealth, Noh's support grows more tenuous. Noh today is performed in Tokyo on an average of ten times a month before small audiences of three hundred persons in the three remaining Noh theatres not destroyed by air raids. In all there are perhaps ten thousand regular spectators of Noh in Tokyo. It is slightly more popular in the Osaka area.

Another problem is the dearth of Noh performers. For example, at present there are only six performers in Tokyo of the hand tabor (*tsuzumi*), a difficult and important instrument of Noh music. There is only one student to carry on when these six cease to perform. The postwar amusement tax and the extremely limited audience for Noh preclude salary raises which would make employment more attractive for the musicians. The government has recently lowered the amusement tax for Noh plays which makes it possible for more of the student public to attend performances.

The Bunraku Puppet Theatre today plays only in Osaka in one small theatre seating around seven hundred persons. There are only thirty doll manipulators and twenty *joruri* singers left. When compared with the past, this number shows an alarming loss of performers. But Bunraku has become an international institution and were it to collapse economically, public opinion, both national and international, would force the Japanese government to subsidize it adequately to support its remaining artists.

Kabuki plays to packed houses (100,000 persons monthly, twelve months a year, on the average), at the largest undamaged theatre in Tokyo, the *Tokyo Gekijo,* and at the newly repaired Kabuki-Za. But these audiences are in the main composed of war profiteers or black-marketeers who want to spend their ill-gotten gains and get a veneer of culture at the same time. Sometimes they are country folk who are unable to see their favorite traditional Kabuki in the provinces, and having capitalized on the illegal sale of foodstuffs, have the money to buy tickets. Tickets for Kabuki cost 200–300 yen (before the war the best seats cost 8 yen), including the government's 150% amusement tax, and are now prohibitive for the average Japanese.

Kabuki has become tiring and difficult for audiences now, and is regarded in somewhat the same way as opera is in the West—greatly appreciated by the connoisseur, but too onerous for the average person's comprehension. This is borne out by the fact that in the 1930's, ninety per cent of Japan's metropolitan theatres were devoted to Kabuki, while today only thirty or forty per cent feature it. The

[219]

balance of theatricals today are devoted to vaudeville, musicals, stage shows, and the modern theatre.

Kabuki is the most recent of Japan's classic drama forms, and is still capable of supporting itself by the people. So far it has felt the urgency for protection less than other classic forms. But critics and scholars with an eye to the future are clamoring for government subsidization for Kabuki as well as for Noh, Bunraku, and Bugaku. For without outside support the tradition of the Japanese theatre of necessity will disappear with the changing tastes of the modern Japanese public.

Shinsei Shimpa has lingered on since the Meiji Era. Although it invariably runs today at a serious financial loss, it is protected and maintained by the aged heads, Shirai and Otani, of Japan's largest producing company, Shochiku Co., Inc. These two men (whose rise from peanut sellers in the Kabuki theatres to czars of the theatrical world is one of Japan's most fantastic success stories) feel a deep sense of obligation and allegiance to the Meiji Era. They turn over a certain proportion of profits made from their various theatrical enterprises each year to cover the annual losses of *Shinsei Shimpa* performances. By this they are doing a service to the handful of great *Shinsei Shimpa* artists who are still living.

Although *Shinsei Shimpa* is by no means popular, some of the leading actors have considerable standing in the theatre world. Mizutani Yaeko is one of the leading actresses of today and is equally at home in straight modern drama. Kitamura Rokuro is, aside from the top Kabuki actors, the greatest actor of Japan. He plays female roles exclusively. Almost on a par with him is Hanayagi Shotaro, another actor of *Shinsei Shimpa* who specializes in roles of geisha and coarse women. During the 1920's Shotaro's popularity was such that when he appeared in certain patterns of kimono, they became the rage of Tokyo's more daring society. His popularity has waned considerably with the decline of this type of theatre.

In January 1947, an attempt was made to revive *Shinsei Shimpa*

[220]

and Shotaro's box-office appeal, by persuading the great Kabuki actor Kikugoro VI to appear together in a *Shinsei Shimpa* play with Shotaro. This was the first time in history that a Kabuki actor had performed with a *Shinsei Shimpa* actor. The honor to Shotaro, since Kabuki actors rank highest in the strictly graded theatrical hierarchy of Japan, and the novelty of the joint appearance were supposed to attract large audiences. But the choice of play defeated the purpose. The critics did not object to the novelty of the combination, but they exploded in high dudgeon because the play was erotic, particularly with regard to the month of the year. The play, *Emmei-in Nitto,* is the simple story of a forward woman who tries to seduce a priest. She knows that he has once murdered a man and threatens to expose him if he won't succumb to her charms. January is the month in which the Japanese family as a group goes to the theatre, and critics attacked the play and performance for its bad effect on children. A later attempt to wed *Shinsei Shimpa* and Kabuki also failed, and their separate fates remain unchanged.

The plays of *Shinsei Shimpa* are ephemeral. Few have lasted from the Meiji Era to the present. Only a handful are given repeat performances, and those only because they are clever vehicles for some leading actor. The writing of *Shinsei Shimpa* plays each year is done by a group of hack writers who are paid by the producing company according to the number of words actually used. They write, as Kabuki writers originally did, on the basis of what actors are available and what personal accomplishments they wish to exploit. There is also a group of independent writers recognized in their own right who compose pieces for *Shinsei Shimpa* upon request. Among these Kubota Mantaro, Hasegawa Shin, and Kawaguchi Masutaro are perhaps most widely known. So steeped in the atmosphere of the Meiji Era are *Shinsei Shimpa* and its writers that the theatre as a vehicle of contemporary expression is literally unknown to them.

An example of this occurred in May 1947. A program to commemorate the promulgation of the Occupation-sponsored New Constitution was planned. All leading artists were to participate in the festival. Kabuki's most brilliant dances were scheduled. "Freedom Symphonies" and "Constitution Choruses" were written. *Shinsei Shimpa* was to be represented, and Kawaguchi Masutaro was asked to write a play celebrating the new constitution. The result was a play called "Lingering Snow" (*Zan Setsu*), which dealt with the subject of some political prisoners who were freed in the Meiji Era and who celebrate the promulgation of the first Constitution of 1899. Occupation officials were forced to point out that it was the 1947 Constitution to be celebrated; so in two weeks Kawaguchi rewrote the play. The final version consisted of the political prisoners taking the Meiji Constitution apart point by point and deploring the absence of a positive guarantee of human rights and freedom for the individual.

Shinsei Shimpa today is a fairly recent but already obsolescent drama form, out of step with the times and lacking in sufficient intrinsic value to justify its continued place in Japan's theatre of today. When the fairly aged stars of today die, the end of *Shinsei Shimpa* will certainly have come.

2.

The State of Modern Theatre. The vaudeville, variety, and girlie-show are the most popular of live-talent entertainments in Japan today. They meet the tastes and pocketbook capacities of the vast majority of post-war Japanese. Although in the rural areas, even when sandwiched between movies, only the personal appearance of a top-flight movie star can draw sufficient spectators to meet the enormous inflationary expenses of a vaudeville troupe.

The Osaka area is dominated by a variety show deluxe, the Takarazuka All-Girl Troupe. The Takarazuka has hundreds of girls who perform everything from imitation classical dancing to rockette-like routines and musical comedies. But aside from the froth of the

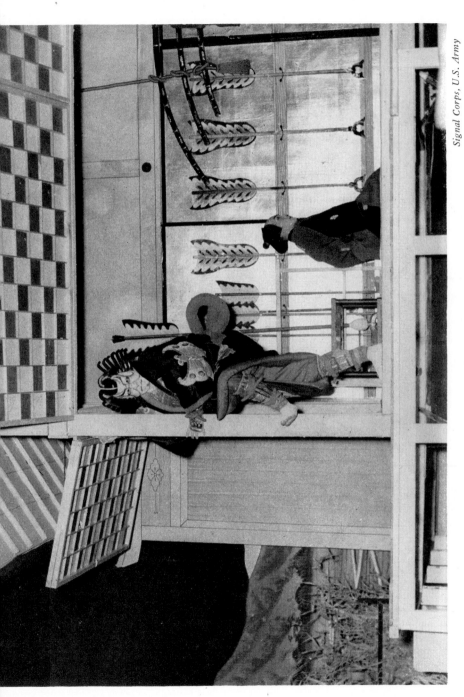

A CLIMACTIC POSE IN YANONE (ARROWHEAD)

vaudeville, there is an active modern legitimate theatre in Japan today. At present it is dominated by three controlling factors: 1) Eroticism; 2) The sword theatre (*kengeki*); and 3) The left-wing theatre.

Eroticism: Censorship of Kabuki has been in effect off and on since the end of the 17th century. Eroticism has always been first on the list of censorable material. The introduction of gas lighting in the 19th century with the resultant performances late into the night precipitated even more severe restrictions. Persons of the audience were not only forbidden to visit the actors in the rooms backstage, but were not even allowed to spend the night in tea houses near the theatres. Despite efforts to keep the number of theatres to four (the number fixed for Tokyo in the Genroku Era), the Department of Public Morals (*Kyobu Sho*) in conjunction with the Metropolitan Police grudgingly allowed the number of theatres to be increased to ten in 1872. But there was a move at the same time to place the theatres outside the city limits which would have been tantamount to complete curtailment of attendance.

Censorship consisted not only of controlling suggestive action on the stage, but included analysis of questionable lines, and in cases of *double entendre* the passages were summarily deleted. This mania for protecting the morals of the people was designed to keep the military class and the entire population of potential warriors incorrupt. In 1941 it reached the point that the leading samisen player of Kiyomoto music was called into the police station and required to play various tones while policemen passed on whether or not the sound was too voluptuous. Until the end of the war, plays which contained erotic business, dealt with moral corruption, or presented a passionate love story in too favorable a light, were forbidden. With the freedom guaranteed the Japanese by their defeat in war and capitulation to the democracies, the classic theatre has returned somewhat to its lusty origins. Ichikawa Ennosuke, a second-rate Kabuki actor noted for his experiments, even put a kiss into Kabuki. Before the war kisses were not only banned in Japanese theatres and movies, but were deleted from all imported films.

The present wave of eroticism actually touches only the second-rate theatres to any great degree. In an effort to combat the country-wide decline in theatre response, suffering owners of small theatres have staged a series of erotic displays with alluring titles, such as *Festival of Breasts, The Abortionist,* and *Dance of Nakedness.* Even the fairly reputable Moulin Rouge Theatre in Tokyo capitalizes on the erotic. In their play, *River of Life (Seikatsu no Kawa),* the anti-communist theme is livened up by an attempted rape of a married woman and the undressing of another woman who lies down to offer herself as a substitute for the married woman—a postwar Kabukiesque "substitution" (*migawari*). The play was a popular success not for its theme, standard of acting, or excellence of plot, but for its scenes of sex.

Sex killers invariably find themselves depicted on the stage since the war. The noted Kodaira who seduced and murdered ten girls in 1947 was apprehended, and within six months at least thirty plays had been written and produced, each graphically depicting his heinous crimes.

The most sensational play staged since the war has been *Gates of Flesh (Nikutal no Mon).* It tells the story of a band of prostitutes who have approached their profession in a businesslike spirit, and who have solemnly pledged that their affairs will be conducted in a purely financial and dispassionate manner. The play develops on the theme that one of the girls falls in love, does not accept money after rendering her services, and is discovered by the others. The prostitutes punish her by stripping her clothes from her and whipping her in turns. The success of this play has been remarkable, with repeated runs in metropolitan areas and dozens of plagiarized versions by amateurs springing up over the country.

Gates of Flesh affords a peculiar insight into Japanese nature. Audiences go to see the naked girl and the passionate love scenes. This symbolizes freedom from police interference and is exceedingly novel for the Japanese who is having his first experience with democracy in the theatre. The fact that the characters are prostitutes, however, does not strike the Japanese as erotic. Prostitution in Japan has only been banned since the defeat, whereupon the girls promptly moved to the streets. Kabuki, born at a time when the gay quarters were at their most colorful and represented the only truly democratic areas in Japan, has inured the Japanese to the feeling of evil or nastiness in prostitution itself.

In *Gates of Flesh* the girls strike a chord of understanding deep in the Japanese mind. They become admirable because they function according to a code. And this code is foisted upon them by necessity. They function obediently and a violation is punished. This is in effect a modern version of the essence of the feudal system when by birth, sometimes by choice, oftener by the dictates of parents, one is placed in a group and is to serve according to the tenets of the "gang." Disobedience is punishable. In the classic theatre, the punishment is hara-kiri or death; in the postwar theatre, in, for example, *Gates of Flesh,* the punishment is an erotic flagellation.

The surge of sex plays and erotic displays created a problem for SCAP's Civil Information and Education Section as well as for the Censorship Detachment. The Japanese actually have attempted nothing as sexy as what one sees nightly at Kearney's in San Francisco. But SCAP officials discouraged producers from performing any such plays. They informed the Japanese police that they had the right to hold producers and theatre-owners responsible for violations of the Japanese Penal Code regarding immorality on the stage. This may easily be the first step toward wrecking the democratization of the Japanese theatre so far achieved. By invoking a pre-war law and by returning to the police the former right to interfere in theatricals, the Occupation has paved the way for full scale censorship after the Occupation ends. The return of police censorship has been further assisted by the need for safety precautions. Already the old pre-war police boxes in all theatres have been reinstalled—this time on the pretext of checking whether the theatres are overcrowded or patrons are violating smoking rules. At present, since the Occupation is still in power, the police have exercised no direct censorship.

Sword Theatre (Kengeki) : Much Japanese drama, as is its national civilization, is linked with the sword. *Kengeki* literally means sword theatre, and is a somewhat heavy word for the colloquial expression, *chambara* (swordfighting). The classic swordfights (*tachimawari*) of Kabuki, which are the origin of the Sword Theatre, are esthetic and so closely akin to dancing that they cannot be criticized. But the hold that realistic swordfights have over modern audiences in Japan is astounding. The popularity of such plays is perhaps analagous to the grip class B Western movies with their gunfights have on parts of America.

The plots for sword plays are usually focused on some famous gang leader (*Oyabun*). He is invariably a Robin Hood of great sword ability, generous, helpful to the weak, merciless to the strong, moral to the degree of continence, studious, and accompanied by absolute devotion from his followers (*kobun*). It is obvious that this relation is identical to the samurai's allegiance to his lord and of the people en masse to their Emperor. The way the leader draws his followers to him is usually in one of two ways. His personal excellence and great power attracts adherents who, after proving their devotion, belong to him. Or they become involved in the *is-shoku ippan* dilemma. *Isshoku ippan* means "a meal and a night's lodging," and the recipient of such favors, even though accidentally incurred, implies the deepest kind of debt of gratitude.

One of Japan's most popular subjects for sword plays is the story of Kunisada Chuji, a leader who after giving Asataro "a meal and a night's lodging" demands that he go out and kill a certain man. The man to be killed turns out to be Asataro's uncle. (Here we have the duty-versus-human nature conflict which moves the audience to tears). But in obedience to his duty towards Kunisada Chuji, Asataro precipitates a swordfight and chops off the man's head. (Here we admire the man because adherence to duty is noble). It all turns out to have been a misunderstanding, so Kunisada Chuji and Asataro go off on an "aimless journey." (Here is a carry-over from Kabuki's lack of conscience and inconclusive resolution of plot.)

In sword plays the focal point is not the plot, but the climactic swordfight. In most of these plays, the merest thread of a story is sufficient to attract an audience, provided the star performer is a famous sword artist. Shortly after the Occupation of Japan began, due to the pressure of Allied censorship, sword plays decreased, and the artists were forced to tour the countryside far from the eyes of censorship, in order to earn their living. In the major cities eroticism was the one answer to the vacuum created by their absence.

It had been thought that with the confiscation of swords by the Occupation, and the long series of punishments for beheadings of prisoners of war by the minor war crimes trials in Yokohama, that the Japanese had begun to forget the so-called cult of the sword. This was found not to be the case. Two and a half years after the Occupation, in February 1948, the New Country Troupe, in an effort to recuperate from a long series of disastrous financial losses, pulled out of its repertoire a play called *Miyamoto Musashi*. Miyamoto Musashi was a hero of the Meiji Era who became a masterful swordfighter. After innumerable victories, he reverted to religion, abandoned the sword, and became one of Japan's greatest painters. This was the historical man, and is a worthy subject for a "democratic" as opposed to a "feudalistic" plot.

The play version performed by the New Country Troupe shows Miyamoto Musashi's religious instruction (he was suspended from a tree for three days by the priest), his study of books, his repeated refusals to accept challenges, his renouncing of a woman who is in love with him, and finally, for the climax of the play, he is forced to accept a challenge and kills ten men. Throughout the entire play, enemies lurk around and spring upon him with drawn swords at various intervals. He defends himself with flower branches and adroit parryings. Finally at the climactic match when he draws his sword, it glistens and all are afraid. At two points in the play the house rings with applause and calls of "We have waited for this," first when he embraces the girl before sending her away, and second when he draws his sword for the match.

It is surprising that such a play could have been one of the biggest successes since the war. It has the sketchiest of plots, no real end; it was acted on the lowest of artistic levels, and has not the slightest connection with postwar Japan. However, this does not mean that Japan's theatre will not eventually progress out of sword plays and melodrama. It does mean that Japan is at the moment still steeped in a lot of out-dated theatrical claptrap, and that despite her postwar individual thought and collective changes, she remains emotionally caught in certain aspects of the militaristic spirit fostered since the Meiji Era.

Left Wing Theatre: Japan is in a curious position with regard to the future of her theatre. Her classics will undoubtedly fade away with the times, as the concepts from which they originally sprang, disappear. Their only hope will be government subsidy which means the destruction of their connection with the people and the loss of their vitality as art. The alternative is complete extinction. Defeat in war has brought with it an increasing awareness on the part of increasingly concentrated audiences in the metropolitan areas. Such audiences and such awareness cannot sustain for long either an erotic theatre or the sword theatre. Japan's erotic theatre is largely the result of the excitement of a postwar, released as it were, Japan. The sword plays are a fascist lingering, but remain popular because of their familiarity and the aura of forbidden fruit which Occupation censorship cast over them by striking them, for a time, from the boards of Japan.

[228]

Japan's modern theatre is an open field, and any competition against it today appears to be only temporary. Japan is on the verge of losing her past theatre which obviously paves the way for the emergence of a vital modern theatre. Such an opportunity is unique in the annals of history. Unfortunately years of conventionality, government interference, and censorship pressure have killed most freedom of expression among Japan's playwrights. It is now hardly likely that overnight Japan will start producing literary dramas of significance. But the fact remains that what plays the Japanese now create certainly should determine the future course of her theatre. In other words, where her theatrical inspiration comes from today will undoubtedly determine to a large extent the destiny of her dramatic art. At present the only genuine inspiration seems to be from Japan's left wing theatre.

It has been seen that Japan's fundamental concept of modern theatre, beginning with the Meiji Era, was as a political instrument. In Japan's subsequent history, the power of the theatre as a means of stimulating social reform has never been forgotten. The persecution of the 1930's now appears to have been a boon to the left wing theatrical groups. When they were forced to abandon their political activities they concentrated on the artistic improvement of the stage. During this period, the distinguished actor-director Hijikata Yoshi abandoned his title and went to Russia for study at the Moscow Art Theatre for six years. Now the results of his and others' serious study of art can be placed to serve the ends of either political convictions or of artistic attainment. The fact is only too evident today that Japan's leading directors and actors of the modern theatre are leftist. Hijikata Yoshi, Murayama Tomoyoshi, and Senda Koreya are openly members of the Communist Party, and have made consciously or unconsciously Japan's modern theatre and left-wing movement identical.

This phenomenon is inherent within the nature of the problem. In the arts the ideology of the left urges reform and of necessity insists on activity. The right usually contents itself with the status quo. In Japan the theatrical status quo is so tradition-bound and caught in the past that it cannot continue as a force, despite any efforts of its scholars or remaining fascists. In addition, the right seems to regard the theatre as a world of fantasy and not really a part of political activity. The left, on the other hand, respects the theatre as an important organ of propaganda. Within a year after the Occupation of Japan, a Communist School of the theatre was established. And wisely so, for their ends, if one considers the majority of people in Japan, for how better can they be reached than through the visual representation afforded by the theatre? The country people and farmers will not read or listen to involved speeches, but they will readily go to the theatre and lose themselves in the dream world of play-acting. And despite a rapidly shifting status since the War, at present no other major country in the world is less dominated by the motion picture, and is still so much in the clutches of the legitimate theatre as Japan.

Labor unions have been the leftists' most fertile soil. Unionism which despite government suppression was powerful in Meiji Japan, and historically familiar to the Japanese, is fermenting with activity. The group spirit of the union is more natural to the Japanese temperament than in, say, individualistic America. And theatricals are a vital part of union activity today. They afford opportunities to raise money, to offer diversion, to work together, and to satisfy the vague cultural urges inherent within all people. Every union in Japan has a theatrical department, and agencies like the Japan Cultural League (*Bunren*), supply scripts for the amateurs to perform. The Japan Cultural League has subsidiaries such as the New Theatre People's Association (*Shin Engeki Jin Kyokai*) who encourage amateurs and unions to engage in theatricals. Contests are held, directors and instructors are dispatched. In general, the most energetic amateur activity in Japan today is found in leftist-dominated union theatricals.

See pg. 236

SHOROKU IN A *MIE* AS THE SPIDER IN THE MONSTROUS SPIDER

Beginning with 1948 in line with Japan's Communists' long-range planning, attention was turned to the children's theatre. Here charming little plays express understandable concepts which, while being innocuous, are the basic platform from which either democracy or communism can be preached. Such plays, as the following, are typical.

The Feast of the Fox (Kitsune No Gochiso): A hungry fox is looking for food. He is refused by the other animals. He is advised by a donkey that everyone must work to live. So the fox reforms himself and grows wheat. After the harvest he makes bread and distributes it to the other animals.

The Gathering of Insects (Mushi No Tsudoi): An insect is caught by a spider, but is rescued by the combined efforts of his fellow insects.

Children of a Village (Mura No Kodomo): Rokuro attempts to organize a children's organization, but his plans are disrupted by other bad children. He is discouraged, but another group which has succeeded in getting organized encourages him to continue his efforts.

The Story of Rubbish (Gomitame no Monogatari) written by Murayama Tomoyoshi's son, Ato:
In a refuse heap near a doghouse, unusable articles are talking with each other. There are ashes, a cracked vase, a broken straw hat, a newspaper, and an empty can of peanuts. The ashes are taking shelter from the rain in the doghouse, but are soon driven out. A toothbrush, the only one who is employed, comes back from work saying that the rain ruins the shoe polish business. All wish to start a new life, but helplessly resign themselves. The empty can despises labor and boasts of his high knowledge. An orange peel appears with a sodden face; she has been in a bathtub to make the water smooth and fragrant.

The toothbrush tells his companions the story of a miserable war orphan who stared at candy in a shop window until the owner drove him away. All want to do their best to rehabilitate the country, so that there will be no vagabonds or street urchins. They rack their brains trying to think how to be useful. The dog advises the straw hat to become a lamp shade. The vase finds in the newspaper an advertisement of a hospital for chinaware and determines to go for treatment. The orange peel thinks of the fact that ashes make good fertilizer. Even the crumpled newspaper is found to be useful as material for finger dolls used in puppet shows. All rejoice at their future, and the empty can apologizes for his haughty attitude. He becomes ashamed of himself and makes up his mind to form a set of horse hoof coverings (shoes) together with other cans of a neighboring refuse heap.

The children's theatre of Japan is becoming a political springboard. The fairy-tales, and the heavy moral teaching implicit in them, are being supplanted by the thoughtful, well written and understandable socially conscious children's theatre of the left-wingers.

In the professional modern theatre, the revival of leftist activity has been as gentle as any movement could have been. It began with plays like *Setting Sun* (*Rakujitsu*) in which two drunks argue, equally persuasively; one is for the Emperor, the other for Communism. This was the first time in twenty years that the word, Communism, had been heard on Japan's stage. Then there are plays in which active union members are accused of Communism, and the punch line becomes, "If our aims and Communism are identical, it is only coincidence." Then appeared plays which glorify the death of Communist martyrs under Japan's Fascist government, or which glorify the Chinese Communist "anti-war" movement during the China Incident.

As the average Japanese's antipathy to the word "communist" or "left-wing" decreased, the modern drama grew bolder. With this boldness has come the nearest approach to good plays which postwar Japan has so far made. The new plays, *Arms and Freedom* (*Buki to Jiyu*) and *Ruins* (*Haikyo*), are filled with social significance, and present a sincere grappling with the problems of postwar Japan. They are lengthy, intellectual, well-written, and in the last analysis are the only signs of genuinely creative life in the Japanese theatre today. Even the best performances of foreign plays, such as Simonov's *Under the Chestnut Trees of Prague*, Chekov's *Cherry Orchard*, and Tolstoi's *Resurrection* (in the Moscow Art Theatre version), have been performed and directed by leftists. Shakespeare's *Midsummer Night's Dream* owed its recent artistic and financial success solely to its Communist director, Hijikata Yoshi. In 1950 the best and most famous of the non-Communist troupes, Zenshin-Za, openly announced that all of its members and leaders had joined the Communist party.

Whether the drama of Japan will ever be powerful enough to bear strongly on the politics of the country is a difficult question. But the fact remains that Japan's most active modern theatre is inspired by the left. Her finest artists are leftist. Her most ardent amateurs are leftist labor unions and the children's theatres. The soil in which the seeds of these efforts are sown is a people as yet more inclined to listen to the theatre than to speeches or books.

APPENDIX

Three Translations of
Kabuki Plays

Faubion Bowers

The Monstrous Spider (*Tsuchigumo*)
A dance-drama adapted from the Noh, and included in the Onoe
Family's collection of plays, "Ten Favorite Plays, New and Old."

Gappo and His Daughter Tsuji (*Sesshu Gappo ga Tsuji*)
Adapted from a Bunraku Puppet Theatre domestic play.

Sukeroku (*Sukeroku Yukari Edo Zakura*)
An original Edo Kabuki play in *aragoto* style, and included in the
Ichikawa Family's collection of "Eighteen Favorites."

Notes on the Translations
The charm of Kabuki is essentially in its atmosphere. The language is beautiful in Japanese and is filled with poetic allusions and
plays on words which are impossible to translate. The word is actually an excuse for music, and music in turn is an excuse for acting or
dance-like movement. In this way the text is seen to be only a third

[235]

part of Kabuki. In translation, unfortunately, it becomes even less significant. However, some of the mood, it is hoped, shines through.

The titles of Kabuki are selected for the beauty of the ideographs, and are uneven in number. They are usually meaningless, and are designed to express the atmosphere of the drama. Plays are rarely spoken of by their original titles which are too difficult even for the actors to remember. They are referred to, for convenience' sake, by the names of the leading characters or the main scene.

I

THE MONSTROUS SPIDER
(*Tsuchigumo*)

Notes:

In ancient Japan it was believed that a race known as *tsuchigumo* (ground spiders), had formerly inhabited the land. Etymologically the word comes from *tsuchi gomori* (living in caves). Since legendary time a tale called *Tsurugi no maki* was widely popular and is considered the prototype of all subsequent spider stories in Japanese literature. *Tsurugi no maki* is substantially the same as the present version of *The Monstrous Spider,* except that Raiko's sword is named *Hizamaru* which after successfully killing a spider "four feet high and living in a huge mound," is renamed *Kumo kiri maru.* Raiko is the stage name of the actual historical man known as Minamoto Yorimitsu who lived from 994 to 1021 A.D.

The story appears in Noh under the title *Tsuchigumo;* in *joruri* storytelling as *Tsuchigumo Taiji,* written by Inoue Harima-no-jo; in a puppet play as *Kanhasshu Tsunagi Uma,* written by Chikamatsu Monzaemon in 1724. In the puppet version, the spider is treated as a demoniac form of a Taira maiden named Kocho. The only Kabuki version known today is the present adaptation from Noh.

In 1881, Onoe Kikugoro V was pressed for a new play in order to commemorate the thirty-third anniversary of the death of Onoe Baiju (Kikugoro III). A patron suggested that since Kikugoro V's grandfather, Onoe Shoroku I, had played a form of *Tsuchigumo* in 1804, and also the late Baiju had played a role of a ghost spider in 1845, both with great success, a play on a similar theme would be appropriate. Kawatake Mokuami's help was enlisted. The selection of *Tsuchigumo* from the Noh was partly an effort to find a match for *The Subscription List* (*Kanjincho*), an early Noh adaptation and already long a success with the rival Ichikawa family. Subsequently the government had reinvoked the traditional law forbidding Kabuki players from borrowing from Noh. After considerable pressure from a high official, a patron of Noh and of Kikugoro V, the author and actor, were finally allowed to introduce the text into Kabuki. Critics assailed it as impure, since it was seven parts Noh and three parts Kabuki. But after repeated performances, it was successful and became one of the "10 Favorite Plays, Old and New, of the Onoe Family" (*Shin Ko Engeki Ju Shu*). *The Monstrous Spider* was the first adaptation from the Noh during the Meiji Era, and started the spate of adaptations which followed.

In Noh as well as in their adaptations in Kabuki, "demon plays" of which *The Monstrous Spider* is typical, follow a characteristic form: a) the demon in disguise (winning over his opponent); b) a comic interlude (performed by extraneous characters); c) the demon in his true colors (vanquished by his opponent).

The dance-drama is performed to the accompaniment of *Naga uta* (long song) music. The setting is a painted background showing a single pine tree, characteristic of Noh plays, and at the side, stalks of bamboo.

Synopsis

The Monstrous Spider is the story of Raiko who is suffering from a mysterious ailment. He has asked the prelates of various Buddhist temples to pray for his recovery. At midnight the "Monstrous Spider" assumes the disguise of a priest and tries to kill him by his sorcery. Raiko cuts him with his sword, and by following the blood tracks his retainers, the four loyal paladins are able to pursue the spider to his lair. The spider is killed and Raiko recovers from his ailment.

Characters

The priest Chichu (in reality the Monstrous Spider)
Raiko
Yasumasa (Raiko's attendant)
Watanabe no Tsuna (Raiko's retainer)

Sakata no Kintoki (Raiko's retainer)
Urabe no Suetake (Raiko's retainer)
Usui no Sadamitsu (Raiko's Retainer)
Kocho (a lady attendant)

(Yasumasa enters)

Yasumasa: I am Hirai Yasumasa, an attendant of Lord Raiko, and the bravest warrior of the Minamoto clan. My lord, having been sick in bed for some time, had the apothecary prepare medicines for him. As they had no effect on him, he asked the prelates of various temples to hold Buddhist services for his recovery. To my great joy, I hear that he is better, and I have come to inquire after his condition.

(Seats himself)

Music:

"Drifting, drifting with the wind,
Clouds float in the sky.
There appears Lord Raiko
Long suffering from his illness,
Wishing to breathe the freshness of the evening air."

(Raiko enters)

Yasumasa: How do you feel, my lord?

Raiko: The apothecary has done well and, thanks to his ministrations, I am much improved of late. Look at the chrysanthemums here in the garden.

Yasumasa: Chrysanthemums are flowers of good fortune. It is said that their fragrance has the virtue of prolonging life. I hope you will completely recover before long, my lord.

Raiko: At the end of August, I went to Ichijo——

Music:

"When the long autumn night
Turned to dawn at last,
We, the lady and I,
Parted from each other
With much regret.

[238]

And as I came back in the cool breeze——"

Raiko: I felt cold and then fell ill.

Yasumasa: Your attendants did all they could.

Music:
>"His Majesty the Emperor
>Deigned to send the head apothecary
>To prepare medicines for him."

Yasumasa: And I hear, much to my joy, that you are better.

Raiko: Go and rest yourself.

Yasumasa: Thank you, my lord.

Music:
>"Thus saying,
>Yasumasa retires to the anteroom."

(Yasumasa leaves)

>"As the moon begins
>To hide behind the clouds,
>Quietly and gracefully.
>Kocho, the lady attendant,
>Approaches Lord Raiko."

(Kocho enters)

Kocho: Is anyone here?

Page: Who is there?

Kocho: I, Kocho, a woman in attendance.

Page: My lord has been long waiting for you. Come in, please.

Kocho: Thank you.
   (Kneels before Raiko)
   I have brought you medicine from the apothecary. How do you feel, my lord?

Raiko: Much better these few days. I will soon be restored.

Kocho: I am most glad to hear it, my lord.

Raiko: The hills must be aflame with autumnal tints now.

[239]

Kocho: Oh, they are like burning fire.

Raiko: Come and describe them to divert my mind.

Kocho: With pleasure, my lord.

(She begins to dance)

Music:
"Takao mountain is famous for its maple trees
With their autumnal tints.
The summit of Ogura mountain is lit
With the splendour of the setting sun.
The yellow leaves of Arashiyama,
Tremble in the storms.
The river Oi
Flows, flows with floating
Yellow and red leaves."
(Kocho concludes her dance and sits down)

Raiko: Thank you for your description. You may go now.

Kocho: Yes, my lord.

(She leaves)

(Raiko is attacked by a fit of trembling. The page puts a heavy cloth around his shoulders)

Music:
"Clouds and mist hide the moon.
The lamp once so bright darkens.
Suddenly there stands a priest with a rosary in his hand."

Chichu: How do you feel, Lord Raiko?

Music: "Raiko looks up as if in a dream."

Raiko: How strange! Where have you come from, your Reverence?

Chichu: I am the priest Chichu, who lives on Mt. Hiei.

Raiko: Why have you come? It is the dead of night.

Chichu: I hear that you, seriously ill, have asked the prelates to pray for you. I too have come to hold a service for your recovery.

Raiko: You are quite welcome, your Reverence. In your ascetic practices, you must have traveled far and wide.

Chichu: I was born in a family of respectable warriors, and for the salvation of my father's soul, I became a priest. . .

Music:

> "To wander about this world
> Clad in black religious robes.
> One day I walk along the beaches of the northern seas,
> And on the next I visit the far distant shores of Kyushu."

Chichu: People praise the flowers in spring and the clear moon in Autumn. . .

Music:

> "But for me, having renounced this world,
> Nothing interests me, nothing attracts my attention.
> I have practiced many austerities,
> Have waded rough streams and crossed wild stretches."

Raiko: I am much pleased to have so virtuous a priest hold services for me.

Chichu: I shall now pray to the Five Buddhas for your recovery.

Music:

> "Approaching Lord Raiko
> The figure of the priest
> With a rosary in his hand
> Looks suspicious.
> The page challenges him."

Page: Take heed, my lord.

Raiko: What do you mean?

Page: The priest looks strange indeed, my lord.

Music:

> "Raiko, surprised at the word, turns.
> The light goes out."

Raiko: It must be by the power of some monster that the light went out. There is no wind tonight.

Chichu: You notice it now for the first time?

Raiko: Your figure is like a spider!

[241]

Music:

> "And the monstrous figure
> Like a huge spider
> Approaches Raiko
> And weaves its web around his body.
> Raiko takes up his sword
> And slashes the monster.
> The spider now quite desperate
> Runs to escape and disappears."

(Yasumasa hurriedly enters)

Yasumasa: I have come here, my lord, surprised at your voice.

Music:

> "Yasumasa, exhorted by his lord,
> Runs off in full spirit.
> Lord Raiko goes into the inner room
> Accompanied by his young page."

(At this point there is a comic interlude-dance of no meaning, after which a green cloth-covered frame is brought on the stage.)

> "Here deep in the mountains
> Where pines and oaks grow thick
> It is dark. In the dead of night
> No one passes
> On the solitary road overgrown with grass.
> There stands an old tomb,
> Deserted and crumbling,
> Thickly covered with moss.
> In comes Yasumasa
> Followed by Tsuna, Kintoki, Sadamitsu and Suetake.
> With pine-torches in hand
> They have reached the old tomb
> Following the spider's tracks of blood."

Yasumasa: We have followed the tracks of the old spider that forced his way into my lord's mansion and tried to kill him.

Tsuna: Is it that the monster inhabits the wood there?

Kintoki: There sounds in the grass-overgrown tomb a groan like that of a man.

Sadamitsu: It must be the spider suffering from his wound.

Suetake: Let us slay it with all our might.

Yasumasa: Follow me.

The Four: Yes, sir.

Music: "The four announce in loud voices. . ."

> This is Hirai Yasumasa,
> The bravest warrior under the command of Lord Raiko!

Tsuna: I am Watanabe no Tsuna, one of the Four Retainers of Lord Raiko.

Kintoki: And I am Sakata no Kintoki.

Sadamitsu: Usui no Sadamitsu.

Suetake: And Urabe no Suetake.

Yasumasa: Come, let us destroy the tomb. You are to die, monster. No matter how divine your power may be.

The Four: Let us attack!

Music:

> "They take to destroying the tomb,
> But draw back, affected by the poisonous air.
> The earth shakes and quakes
> And a flame blazes up
> And a gush of water
> Breaks forth from the web.
> Not at all dismayed by the horrible scene,
> They break the tomb.
> There appears the monstrous spider
> Wonderfully huge and full of horror."

Yasumasa: You monster!

The Four: What are you?

Music:

> "I am the spirit of the old spider
> Long inhabiting Mt. Katsuragi.

I intended to turn the country
Into an infernal region reigned by me
I planned to do harm to Raiko first of all.
My plan has failed
You wish to kill me? Let us fight!"

Tsuna: Your nefarious plan,

Kintoki: Has brought this punishment upon you.

Sadamitsu: You have suffered a wound,

Suetake: And now you are to die.

Yasumasa: Slay the monster, at once.

Spider: How impertinent! You shall be unable to move, bound by my web.

Yasumasa: However devilish your power may be, I will kill you.

Spider: I will take your life instead.

Music:

"The spider weaves and weaves
His web of silver white
And the five warriors
Strong as they are
Can hardly move.
Like butterflies and dragonflies
They are trapped in the web.
But without losing courage
They struggle and strike at the monster.
At last he loses power.
Yasumasa gives the spider a deathly blow."

(The ensemble strikes a pose)

"And the story of this distinguished exploit
Has been told from generation to generation."

II

GAPPO AND HIS DAUGHTER TSUJI
(Sesshu Gappo Ga Tsuji)

[244]

Notes:

Gappo and His Daughter Tsuji, written in 1773 by Suga Sensuke, has a tenuous connection with the Noh play called *Yoroboshi.* In the Noh, the character Shuntoku maru is "for a certain reason" driven from his house by his father. He becomes blind. At a Buddhist temple, the son and father meet again, and they are reconciled.

In 1937 *Gappo and His Daughter Tsuji* was banned by the Japanese Government for depicting the illicit love of a mother for a stepson. There are, however, two interpretations of the play: One is that Tamate, the mother, does not love her stepson really but pretends to in order to save him from her other stepson's attempt to usurp the power of the house (this is the interpretation used by the older actors under the influence of Danjuro IX). The other is that she is really in love, but despite this affection, fulfills her duty as a mother. The play was revived with tremendous success after the war in 1947 by Baigyoku and Kichiemon.

Characters

Gappo
O-Tsuji (Tamate Gozen), his daughter
O-Toku, his wife
Shuntokumaru, Tamate Gozen's stepson
Princess Asaka, Shuntokumaru's fiancée
Irihei, Tamate Gozen's footman

Gappo ga Tsuji tells the story of Gappo who renounced his samurai life, became a priest, and retired to the country with his wife, O-Toku. Their only daughter, O-Tsuji, married one of the ruling lords of the country, and her name became Tamate Gozen, Her Ladyship Tamate. As she was only nineteen, she apparently fell in love with the younger of her two handsome stepsons—partly due to her youth, and partly due to her lack of attraction towards her aged husband. In feudal Japan, the difference between a stepson and a true son was not recognized; thus Tamate's love was technically incestuous.

Jiromaru (the older stepson) wished to usurp the power of the house by killing his brother, Shuntokumaru (Tamate's beloved). To save him

[245]

from death, Tamate gave him a strange potion made from a poisonous abalone. Disfigured and leprous, he flees the house with his sweetheart, the Princess Asaka, and goes to Gappo's retreat in the country.

As the play opens, Gappo and his wife are seen offering services for their daughter, who after the scandal of making love to her stepson is considered dead.

Music: "O-Toku offers a cup of water before the family altar. She prays for their daughter's repose in the other world. She keeps back her tears. The toll of the evening bell comes within hearing.

"Lady Tamate easily finds her way along the road in the night and in the path of love. She seeks Shuntokumaru. Disguised, with her face hidden, she stands at the familiar gate of her parent's home.

"A small voice is heard from outside the gate."

Tamate: Mother! Mother!

Music: "Gappo is certain he has heard his daughter's voice."

Gappo: Is my daughter not dead? Has she not yet been killed for her sin?

Music: "Chanting, 'Save us, merciful Buddha,' he rises to his feet; but remembering his wife, he looks back. She has not heard their daughter's voice. He then feigns ignorance."

Tamate: Open the gate, please. Mother! Mother!

(She kneels at the gate and waits.)

Music: "O-Toku at last hears the voice."

Toku: Gappo, did you speak?

Gappo: No, I have said nothing.

Toku: But I was certain. . .

Gappo: You are mistaken!

Toku: I may have misheard, but I thought I heard our daughter's voice.

Music: "Tamate wonders and rises as she hears her mother's voice."

Tamate: If that is my mother's voice, then please open the gate. Mother, Tsuji, your daughter, has come home.

Toku: Our daughter has come back! Could I be dreaming? I am coming— wait a moment.

Music: "She rushes to the gate when Gappo takes her by the sleeve and holds her."

Gappo: Don't speak of our daughter. I don't know whether she actually gave herself to her stepson or not, but at best she misconducted herself and left her husband's house. Takayasu, her husband, ought to have killed such an evil woman. I wonder how she has lived out until today. Why has she come here? Although we prohibited our daughter from telling her husband of our straitened circumstances, he has helped us in every way. For that reason we have been able to survive up to now. We two owe him a great debt. However, our daughter deceived him and made illicit love to his son. Even if she has returned, I'll not let her cross our threshold nor let her touch the gate. She must be dead! Surely she has been killed! Do you think it's our real daughter that has spoken now? It is a fox or a badger in human form. Were it our daughter, then it must be her ghost. The dead having a close tie with one is a fearsome thing. You must not unbolt the gate. I say now, you must not.

Toku: Even were it a fox, a badger or a ghost, I should like to see our daughter's face once again. Even if it is a terrible thing and I were to swoon in fright, I will be happy only if I see her face once more.

Music: "The mother would rather see her daughter again than live."

Toku: I should like to glance at her, for one moment, please.

Music: "She thrusts Gappo away and goes toward the door, but he again stops her."

Gappo: You heard me. Don't you understand? If it were really our daughter, I should have to kill her. Out of my paternal love and my obligation to Takayasu, I should have to punish her for her sin. Although I am now a priest, I cannot permit so vile a creature to live.

Toku: Oh, for God's mercy.

Gappo: Now, I must stop you. I hate doing so, but you must not open the gate.

Music: "Gappo does not shed tears, but his daughter and wife understand his mind. Unable to see her parents, Tamate weeps. She brushes her tears away and puts her mouth to the gate."

Tamate: It is natural for you to be angry, Father. I have a reason for it, but I must not let others hear my explanation. Open the gate, please.

Music: "She asks them to open the gate in a tearful voice when her mother speaks."

Toku: Have you heard, Gappo? She has a reason. Please listen to her. If you regard her as a ghost, not as our daughter, we can let her in without reservation. Please do as I say.

Music: "As she speaks, Gappo relents."

Gappo: Very well. Since it is merely her departed soul, we need not hesitate because of a code.

Toku: Shall we call it in?

Gappo: Call the ghost in and offer it rice and tea.—I mean—place the food upon the altar for the dead.

Toku: I am glad you are persuaded. I will open the gate.

Music: "She loses no time in going to the gate."

Tamate: Mother.

Toku: My precious daughter.

Music: "She touches her daughter to make sure that she is really alive."

Toku: I can hardly believe my eyes. It is neither a fox, badger, nor a ghost. How fortunate that you are alive. Not knowing, I have spent my days and nights in tears. How strange that you returned this very night, while we were offering a million prayers to you. I wonder if it is all a dream. If it is, I hope I will never be awakened.

Music: "The mother embraces her daughter repeatedly and sheds tears of joy. Gappo wants to see his daughter, but from his deep sense of obligation he faces the other way."

Toku: I have so much to say and hear. Rumor has it that you fell in love with Shuntokumaru and fled from the mansion. People speak ill of you, as if you had committed adultery. However, I, your mother, am certain that you have not done such a thing. I know it is a false report. It is a lie, isn't it? Isn't it a lie?

Music: "Touched by her mother's kindness in regarding it as false report, Lady Tamate is embarrassed."

[248]

Tamate: Thank you for your kind words, Mother, but as fate would have it, I have such a feeling for him.

Music: "Even when I am asleep, Shuntoku does not leave my mind. I long for him so strongly that I am forced to confess my heart openly. The colder his answer to me, the more do I love him. I hope you will aid me in finding him. Let me marry as man and wife legally. Think of your mother's love for me. I place my hands together and plead with you to comply with my request.
"She places her hands together as if in prayer and urges her mother to comply.
"Her mother is revolted by her words, and can only stare at her. Meanwhile, her father angrily brings a sword from the inner room."

Gappo: You insect! Fie on you. Now listen. I will tell you of my father, Aoto Saemon Fujitsuna, who was a favorite with Lord Saimyoji Tokiyori at Kamakura, and called the model of men. Thanks to him, I rose high in the world. I was admitted to the rank of lord and worked assiduously. But when the present Lord Saganyudo succeeded his father, I was slandered by his sycophants. I renounced his service and became without employment. More than twenty years have passed since I retired from the world and became a priest. However, I have kept my integrity just as my father would have done. How could I have had such an immoral and beastly woman as you for a child? Think of your indebtedness to Takayasu. You were a lady's maid, but after the death of his wife, he kindly took interest in you and allowed you to become his second wife. Although he must have wanted to kill you, he has suppressed his emotion and intentionally saved your life because of his feeling towards us, your parents. If you appreciate his kindness and have even a spark of shame, you should be able to give up your love—no matter how deeply you may desire. I heard you say you want to become Shuntoku's wife and asked your mother's permission. How could you dare say such a thing? Your husband has spared your life because of his obligations, but I shall have to kill you out of my obligation to him. Be prepared for death! I will kill you!

Music: "He loosens his sword but his wife clings to him."

Toku: Here, here, Gappo! Wait, you are mistaken.

Gappo: Why am I mistaken?

Toku: He has spared our daughter for mercy's sake. Even if you kill her, you will not repay your obligation to him, will you?

Gappo: Yes and no.

Toku: Well, now our duty is to dissuade her from becoming Shunto-kumaru's wife and let her become a nun instead. Thus, she will be exonerated, no matter how grave her crime may have been.

Gappo: But . . .

Toku: If she retires from the worldly life, she'll be as good as dead; and we will have fulfilled our duty towards her husband, our benefactor.

Music: "She soothes her husband, and draws near to her daughter."

Toku: My dear daughter, as you heard just now, your love will never succeed. Resign yourself and become a nun.

Music: "You are beautiful and young. It is hard for me as your mother to urge you to cut your hair and take the vows, but I only want to save your life.

"She clings to her daughter and weeps that things have come to such a pass. Her daughter jumps back and changes color."

Tamate: Oh, don't talk nonsense, mother. I hate the thought of becoming a nun. Why should I cut such fine black hair and renounce the world?

Music: "Now I'll change my coiffure into the style worn in the gay quarters. When I meet Shuntokumaru again, then he'll love me. Hearing this, her father loses patience."

Gappo: You see, there is no good in her. Now, I can restrain myself no longer.

Music: "The father holds himself ready to kill her. Her mother frantically looks to find a way to save her."

Toku: It is no wonder that you are angry with her. Let me talk to her for a while. I will try to make her change her mind and give him up.

Gappo: Well, then, are you going to persuade her?

Tamate: Oh, no. I can't be persuaded. I won't give him up.

Gappo: What a thing you say, you fool!

Toku: Gappo, we've long been in matrimonial harmony and this is my earnest request of you.

Gappo: I don't want to save her life, but since you are her mother, I shall have to comply.

Music: "At his wife's insistence, he goes to the inner room without casting a backward glance at them. The mother pulls her stubborn daughter's hand and forcibly takes her daughter to the dressing-room."

(Irihei, the footman, loyal to his young mistress Tamate, appears, looking for her. He finds her sandal outside the door and she is inside. He hides himself and waits to see if he will be needed.)

"The blind Shuntokumaru, with Princess Asaka holding his hand is led into the room."

Shuntoku: Asaka, if my stepmother sees me in this condition, blind and disfigured, then she will lose her love for me. Lead me to her.

Music: "Just then Lady Tamate rushes out of the dressing-room."

Tamate: Oh, it has been so long since I saw you last, dear Shuntoku. I am happy you are here.

Shuntoku: I recognize your voice, Mother. Why have you come here?

Tamate: I have taken so much trouble to see you again.

Music: "She clings to him. He disengages himself from her grasp."

Shuntoku: Don't Mother. As I told you in the mansion, it is forbidden for a man of virtue to marry a girl who even has the same surname as his. It is absurd for you to make love to me. You are my stepmother. To make matters worse, I have lost my eyesight and have become disfigured by leprosy. Don't you see my miserable condition? Are you not revolted by my face? Shame on you, Mother!

Music: "He sheds tears and reproaches his stepmother."

Tamate: Don't say such a silly thing. I could never feel other than love for you. It is because of me you are suffering from such a dreadful disease.

Music: "She wants him to love her. How desperate is her love for him. From the Bay of Ashi as far as Naniwa she has pursued him. 'Please love me.'

"She clings to his sleeve, but Shuntokumaru again thrusts her away."

Shuntoku: Tell me, mother! Why was my accursed disease caused by you?

Music: "He wants to hear the reason."

Tamate: Last November I secretly gave you poisoned rice-wine.

All: What?

Tamate: It had the miraculous power of causing a leprous disfiguration. There were two bottles, I drank the ordinary, but poured the poisoned one into your cup. I wanted to disfigure your face so that Princess Asaka would no longer love you. To that extent I have tried to succeed in my love for you.

Shuntoku: I am sorry to hear such a terrible thing.

Tamate: You thought it was caused by some sin in a previous existence; so you left the mansion. Since then I have sought everywhere for you.

Music: "She always keeps the abalone shell from which he drank the poison."

Tamate: I love you from the bottom of my heart, though I'm afraid I am not worthy of being your stepmother. Please give in to me!

Music: "She prostrates herself beside him and asks for his sympathy. Shuntokumaru is horrified, but since she is his stepmother, he endures the mortification. Asaka loses her temper."

Asaka: How cruel you are! Why have you disfigured his noble face? It's horrible that you should fall in love with your stepson. Now you must restore him to health. How cruel you are!

(Irihei rushes in)

Irihei: Don't be silly, madam! How can you do such a thing? Even if you did not give birth to Shuntokumaru, you are still his stepmother. It is against the laws of nature to make love to one's son. Such a thing could be done only by animals. He has a fiancée, named Asaka. You have driven him from the house by your advances. Fie, for shame! I beg you to give up this insane love.

Music: "Paying no attention to his warning, Tamate rises to her feet."

Tamate: Now that I am so deeply in love with him, no one can reason with me. Now I will take Shuntoku with me anywhere. I will succeed in my love for him, even if I die. If anyone interferes he will regret it.

Music: "She leaps on Shuntoku and takes him by the hand. Gappo over-hearing this is beside himself in rage. He rushes and stabs his daughter."

Gappo: I who have not even killed a fly in twenty years, have killed my own flesh and blood, vile daughter! Now die!

Toku: Merciful heaven! Oh, my beloved daughter!

Tamate: It is no wonder you are angry with me and hate me, but I've a deep reason behind my actions. Before I die, let me tell you the story.

Music: "Her breathing is painful to her."

Tamate: Jiromaru, my husband's son by his concubine, did not want to let the legitimate but younger son, Shuntoku, succeed to the family fortune, so he plotted with Tsuboi Heima and attempted to kill the rightful heir. Knowing Shuntoku would be killed, I made love to him and poisoned him to drive him away from the mansion. All only to save his life.

All: Truthfully?

Tamate: I have this abalone cup, which will prove my innocence. I am afraid my husband regards me as an immoral woman and an adulteress. I regret that he will not know the truth before I die.

Music: "She laments, but her father still questions her closely."

Gappo: If you knew so much about Jiromaru's evil doings, why didn't you tell Takayasu? If you had done so, Shuntoku would not have suf-fered from the accursed disease and you would not have needed to make illicit love to him. Even if you reply cleverly, I will not be fooled by a trumped-up excuse.

Tamate: If I had told such to him, he would have forced Jiromaru to commit harakiri, or would have killed him by his own hand even. Though he is a wicked man, he too is still my stepson.

Music: "I have wanted to save both my stepsons at the risk of my life. I am their mother."

Gappo: If you truly accepted your responsibilities as a mother, why did you run after Shuntoku after he fled from the mansion?

Tamate: If I had not seen him again, throughout all his life he could not be cured of his affliction.

[253]

Music: "Hearing her words, Irihei comes forward."

Irihei: Do you mean to say that he cannot be restored to health unless you are with him?

Tamate: I confessed the circumstances to the druggist when I asked him to make the poisoned rice-wine. I also asked him to tell me in detail of the antidotes. Hereditary leprosy is hopeless, but the disease caused by poison can be cured if the afflicted drinks the life-blood of the liver of a woman who has been born at the hour, on the day and in the month of the year of the Tiger. But it must be drunk from the vessel in which the poison has been put. So I have carried this abalone shell about looking for him. Now I have spoken my mind. Are your doubts about me dispelled?

Music: "Gappo draws close to her."

Tamate: Are your doubts dispelled, Father?

Gappo: Yes, yes, yes! Oh, my daughter, forgive me. Not only have I cursed you but have taken your life by my own hand. This done by your very father. Pardon me! Forgive me!

Music: "Asking for her forgiveness, he prostrates himself and sheds tears of regret. Shuntokumaru blindly gropes his way towards her.

Shuntoku: I cannot thank you enough for your kindness.

Music: "He bows low to her. Asaka approaches her."

Asaka: I have not up to now understood you. I have looked down on you and hated you. Please forgive me.

Irihei: Although you ought to be called the model of womanhood, I'm sorry you've been falsely charged and now have to die.

All: Poor Tamate!

Tamate: Now, now, Father, take the life-blood of my liver and give it to him with this shell. Act quickly, before I die.

Gappo: At first I hated her so I could stab her, but now I feel such pity for her that I cannot touch the sword to her. Irihei, you are young, please take my place.

Irihei: I cannot take the blood of one who has so cared for my master. Please excuse me. I will do anything but this.

Tamate: Then I will do it myself.

[254]

Music: "She grasps her dagger with the point downward."

Gappo: Wait a moment, my dear daughter. This is your last moment. I will offer prayers a million times and surround you with the protection of a rosary. Then you will breathe your last peacefully. Let me say a service for you.

Music: "So saying, he counts his beads. Tamate holds herself ready to die. She draws Shuntokumaru near to her and with the dagger in her right hand and the cup in her left hand draws blood from her liver. Thereupon her father frantically beats the bells of salvation. Her mother bursts into tears. Shuntokumaru respectfully drinks the blood. He drains his cup. Suddenly his eyes open and the disfiguration disappears. He looks at them. All are overjoyed that he has been restored."

Asaka: Oh, at last he has recovered from the disease.

Irihei: The remedy worked.

All: Yes, indeed!

Music: "They are filled with wonderment."

Tamate: I am glad I have cleared myself of the dishonor. Now I can die without regret.

Music: "Tamate is a model of womanhood and her mind is as clear as the moon reflected on the inlet. Indeed she is pure."

Tamate: Tomorrow, I shall see the moon from the lotus flowers of heaven.

(She dies and all are weeping as the curtain is slowly drawn.)

III
SUKEROKU
(Sukeroku Yukari no Edo Zakura)

Synopsis

Sukeroku is a three-themed play. It deals with the love between Sukeroku, the handsome commoner, and Agemaki, the most beautiful courtesan of Yoshiwara; Sukeroku's search for his stolen sword, without which he cannot avenge his father's death; and the insulting of the warrior, the wicked Ikyu, by the commoners.

The Bearded Ikyu has come to Yoshiwara to see Agemaki. They quarrel over her lover, Sukeroku, and she leaves. Sukeroku appears. He is searching for his stolen sword. Knowing that people of all types come to Yoshi-wara, he quarrels with everyone, forcing them to draw their swords, all in order to find the thief. He tries to make Ikyu draw his sword, but Ikyu, who has stolen it, refuses.

Sukeroku's older brother, Shinbei, appears and pleads with Sukeroku to mend his quarrelsome ways. After learning that he is searching for the sword in order to avenge his father's murder, Shinbei is pacified. Suke-roku's mother appears, cautions him and leaves with Shinbei. Ikyu re-enters looking for Agemaki. He finds Sukeroku and tries to draw him into a plot against the Shogun. Inadvertently he draws the stolen sword and Sukeroku starts to fight. Agemaki stops them and Sukeroku leaves planning to return to kill Ikyu that night and retrieve the sword.

Characters

Sukeroku (In reality Soga Tokimune)
Shinbei, Sukeroku's brother (in reality Soga Sukenari)
Soga Manko, Sukeroku's mother
The Bearded Ikyu (in reality Heinai Saemon Nagamori)
Kanpera Monbei, Ikyu's follower
Senbei, Ikyu's follower
Fukuyama, a seller of noodles
Agemaki, a courtesan (Sukeroku's lover)
Shiratama, a courtesan (Agemaki's trusted friend)
Various courtesans and minor attendants

The scene takes place one evening early in the 18th century outside Miuraya's, a residence of courtesans, in Naka-no-cho, the heart of Yoshi-wara.

(Agemaki is walking down the *hanamichi* with her attendants. The courtesans are lined up across the stage outside Miuraya's, awaiting her return.)

Yaeginu: Look everyone, Agemaki is like a boat being tossed by the waves.
Aizome: Agemaki, where have you been——
Everyone: To have drunk so much!

(Agemaki looks at the courtesans.)

Agemaki: Indeed! Indeed! O illustrious assembly! I am grateful that you have awaited my return. And where do you think that I have been that I should have drunk so much? It embarrasses me to say it, but I was called into house after house along Naka-no-cho where they offered me countless cups of wine. At Matsuya's one disagreeable warrior brought me his cup and forced me to drink three. More than this, an old drunk tried to get me completely under; but I foxed him and rewarded him by making him drink them. I left him snoring away! No matter how much the drunkard a man may be, when he sees me, he excuses himself and flees! (Agemaki laughs.) Perhaps it is vainglorious to say, but I, Agemaki, who serve at Miuraya's, will never be drunk on only this much wine.

(Agemaki stumbles.)

Little Girl: Look out!

(Agemaki looks at her and laughs.)

Agemaki: Indeed, indeed! That is merely the opinion of a big little girl. On my oath, I am not drunk nor have I been recently.

Ukihashi: You say you are not drunk, but your face is as a cherry blossom flushed with drink.

Everyone: We can see!

Agemaki's Attendant: Child, give the courtesan the usual medicine to sober her.

Small Girl: Certainly. (She goes toward Agemaki.) Here, take this "Sleeve of the Plum Blossom"—the medicine to sober you.

Agemaki: What! "Sleeve of the Plum Blossom!" That's a lovely song.

Small Girl Attendant: No, no, it is a medicine that you always take.

Agemaki: Very well, thank you. (Agemaki drinks it.)

Servant: Will you go to the bench over there?

(Agemaki calls for small girl attendants and goes onto the stage.)

(Manko, wearing a large straw hat, usual when traveling in this period, enters and looks closely at the writing on the paper lanterns carried by the attendants.)

Manko: How fortunate—there it is.

Young Courtesan: Go away, Old One!

[257]

Manko: That's the crest!

Young Courtesan: Look here, Old One, I saw you a few minutes ago. Have you any business with the courtesans? Why are you looking at the lanterns?

Manko: I have business. This is the paper lantern with the peony crest and Agemaki's name. This is it.

Servant: What is this? Old Woman, I have never seen you before. What is this looking at the courtesan's crest and saying, "This is it—this is it."

Small Girl Servant: What a frightening old woman she is!

Agemaki: Child, don't be like that. (Turns to Manko) Oh, Aged One, I have never seen you before but I am, as you can see, Agemaki. Where have you come from?

Manko: I have nothing to conceal. I come from Sukeroku—

Agemaki: Oh!

Manko: Oh! Was it so thoughtless of me to say it openly?

Agemaki: I am the thoughtless one. That reminds me. (She looks around as if she wants to be rid of the others.) Kasuke, I am sorry to trouble you, but would you go to Matsuya's in Naka-no-cho?

Kasuke: Isn't that just like a courtesan! We've just passed Matsuya's.

Agemaki: That is why I said I was thoughtless! I am sorry to trouble you, but go to Matsuya's and see if Ikyu is there. Go quickly, but return at your leisure. Have a few drinks of wine while there.

Kasuke: What a strange task—to go quickly, to return at leisure, and to drink wine!

Agemaki: (To Kasuke.) You said you wanted a tobacco pouch, didn't you?

Kasuke: Yes, I did ask for one. (Agemaki glances significantly at a servant who takes some paper out of a box and gives it to Kasuke.)

Servant: From the courtesan.

Kasuke: Oh! Money.

Agemaki: Please go quickly.

Kasuke: Certainly.

Agemaki: I have still another request. Otatsu, may I trouble you to take everyone and go to my room and bring me the letter which is in the closet.

Servant: Children, come with me. (They leave the stage and go under the curtains covering the entrance to Miuraya's.)

Yaeginu: Everyone, look. Agemaki seems to want to say something to the Aged One. Shall we go to the reception room?

Aizome: Yes, we are in the way here.

Kocho: Let's be considerate.

Aizome: Yes, indeed. Agemaki——

Everyone: We are leaving.

　(Agemaki and Manko are left alone on the stage.)

Agemaki: Now we can talk. Please sit here.

Manko: May I? (She sits down.) Agemaki, I have come today to make a request which is most difficult for me to ask.

Agemaki: Please speak freely. You are not a stranger to me—am I not to be your son's bride?

Manko: It is precisely because of your devotion that it is so difficult for me to speak my plea.

Agemaki: What plea?

Manko: My plea is for Sukeroku.

Agemaki: Sukeroku?

Manko: Please don't call him to the pleasure district any more.

Agemaki: Eh?

Manko: Your surprise is only natural. Why should I conceal the truth? Sukeroku has upon his shoulders the grave responsibility of avenging his father's murder. And in spite of this important pledge, he comes daily to the pleasure district and brawls. When I hear these rumors I, as his mother, am uneasy and cannot sleep. I wonder why he frequents the pleasure district—why he has become so quarrelsome. Hear a mother's request—do not call him here. I understand your devotion, but this is why Sukeroku fights so much. For a little while, please stay away from him.

[259]

Agemaki: Of course you are right. Why has Sukeroku, who is so gentle, become such a quarrel-seeker? Who killed the man by the bank—it was Sukeroku! Who struck the man in Naka-no-cho—it was Sukeroku! The opponents change, but he remains. I have thought constantly of this. Look here. (Manko goes to Agemaki's bench.) Look at my heart and feel the depth of my devotion. (Manko places her hand over Agemaki's heart.) To this extent have I worried over Sukeroku. Love is such that not to meet him for a night or even for a single moment—my lot in life is——

Manko: To love him thus? Then I cannot keep him from you. I will send him to you. Call him.

Agemaki: Are you in earnest?

Manko: Not only that but as his mother, I sanction it. Without hesitation, call him freely.

Agemaki: How happy I am!

Manko: But advise him to give up his quarreling and fighting.

Agemaki: I shall advise him.

Manko: At least I can be at ease now, hearing that.

(Servant comes out from behind the entrance curtain.)

Servant: Courtesan, I have looked everywhere, but cannot find the letter.

Agemaki: Is that so?

(Kasuke comes down the *hanamichi*.)

Kasuke: Courtesan, Ikyu is coming.

Agemaki: Ikyu is coming? Take this person to the room and give her a feast.

Servant: Certainly.

Manko: Then—may I enter?

Servant: Please don't stand on ceremony.

Manko: Agemaki, this matter——

Agemaki: Please, have no fear.

Servant: This way, please. (Manko and servant enter under the entrance curtains.)

Agemaki: How pitiful is that mother. She suffers because of Sukeroku, her son. And I, because of Sukeroku—I suffer the sorrows ever encountered along love's path. Indeed, nothing is so miserable as woman's lot in this world!

(Courtesans return to the stage. Ikyu comes down the *hanamichi* with his retainers, and stops.)

Ikyu: Truly a jewel of Agemaki's likes can be matched nowhere, even if the pillows of a thousand persons are tried. Not even Hankai, the renowned retainer of Koso, with his power and skill could move her with money. Such is the courtesan's pride. Tonight I shall be rebuffed—buffeted by the flowers of Naka-no-cho—the buffer has his pleasure though. Come, men, let's drink to death. By the way, is the girl I heard about from the attendant in that assembly?

Follower: Yes, those girls are all those which have been kept in Agemaki's care until recently.

Another Follower: Master, she's not experienced yet.

Ikyu: Excellent. Bring her out.

Shiratama: Ikyu, Agemaki will be offended with you if you allow your heart to be so expansive.

Attendant: If you are so naughty, we'll smear your face with ink.

Another Attendant: Not only that, but we'll strip you and burn moxa all over you.

Small Girl Attendant: And we will help.

2nd Small Girl Attendant: We will burn moxa all over you.

Servant: Now, won't you apologize for being so rude?

Ikyu: Yes, I apologize. You are quite right to call me unfaithful. (To Shiratama) You faithful pig!

Shiratama: Faithful?

Ikyu: The famous Shiratama of Goju-Cho is always occupied, but there is no one who has ever seen her patron. Therefore, this hiding from all eyes to meet one's lover is what I term "Faithful."

Shiratama: Ikyu, I shan't trouble you further. If you go so far as to inquire about my patrons, I won't carry out your request. (Translator's

Note: To persuade Agemaki to receive Ikyu.)

Ikyu: I apologize. Please help me.

Ikyu's Followers: Master!

Ikyu: Let us proceed. (They advance to the stage.)

Courtesans: Ikyu has come.

Ikyu: (To the Courtesans) Thank you for knowing my name.

Yaeginu: Humble as we are, even we know Ikyu's name.

Ikyu: That is pleasant to hear. I would like to meet with you at leisure.

Ukihashi: Is your intimate engaged tonight?

Ikyu: My intimate?

Kocho: Don't you know whom we mean?

Ikyu: Oh, Agemaki?

Aizome: Of course!

Agemaki: Ah!—the grandiose Ikyu. I have waited for him.

Ikyu: Waited for me? Don't you mean for Sukeroku?

Agemaki: But you told me long ago I could see Sukeroku—of course, after reproaching me.

Ikyu: Yes, I said you could.

Agemaki: Then why do you reproach me again now?

Ikyu: I remember well saying you could meet him, but on thinking it over now, I regret it. What do you think Sukeroku is? He's a thief! Have you ever watched him fight? I use the word "fight," but is it fighting? He always puts his hand on the hip of his opponent. That is the mark of the pickpocket. Tell me, do you intend to see him forevermore? Do you find pleasure in seeing this thief? Tell me!

Agemaki: It is no pleasure to love Sukeroku, but he is——

Ikyu: Your lover!

Agemaki: Fate has made it so.

Ikyu: That is not fate. An evil spirit has entered your body. If you are kind to that sort of man you will lose everything. Is that not a pitiful fate to contemplate?

Agemaki: Call me what you like. Say that I am fickle or a fool to put aside

OPENING SCENE OF GAPPO GA TSUJI

Baigyoku as the daughter returning to her home after pretending to have fallen in love
with her stepson; Kichiemon as the angry father pretending not to hear her

wealthy patrons only in order to meet my secret lover. But to call Sukeroku a thief is too much, Ikyu.

Ikyu: Too much? What else is there for a poverty-stricken man like that than to steal? If you continue to be constantly intimate with that rogue, you will become a thief too. You will start by searching through your patron's pockets. Then finally the two of you will be only the two of you—without a roof even over your heads. When you have been reduced to that, will you still say you want to see Sukeroku forevermore?

Agemaki: Ikyu, how can you speak so stupidly! Do you think I would be capable of falling so deeply in love if I were a person to fear anything? Even your striking me in the middle of Nako-no-cho for secretly meeting Sukeroku? I am Agemaki, bold as it may be to proclaim it! The virile Sukeroku is my companion. If I am the wife of a devil, I have the devil's power. Now it is my turn to abuse—Listen! Hear me out! (Agamaki removes her outer garment.) Ikyu, if I were to compare you and Sukeroku like this—(Agemaki holds up the index finger of each hand)—on this side there is a magnificent man; on this side, we have a disagreeable, disgusting creature. The difference is that between snow and ink. We call the little space for water in the writing box "sea," and we call the deep straits of Naruto the "sea" too. The word is the same. But the deep is the lover; the shallow, the patron. And oh, the bitterness of the courtesan's life without a lover! Though it be the black of night I can see the difference between you and Sukeroku. Do you wish to kill me now? Strike me! Kill me! but the thought of Sukeroku cannot be cut from me. Strike! Ikyu!

Ikyu: Go away!
Agemaki: Where to?
Ikyu: To Sukeroku!
Agemaki: May I?
Ikyu: Get out!
   (Agemaki starts to leave.)

Shiratama: Agemaki! Wait! When you lose your temper in this way, you forget what hardship you might impose on the person you love. I don't mean to be rude, but I must stop you. I am only a young camelia bud

[263]

and I may be scolded for being so forward. You will think that I am no more than a young sparrow who has hardly lost her accent,* but for my sake, Agemaki, please come back.

Agemaki: I am happy to go to my lover's place, but how can I refuse the request of you, dear friend.

Shiratama: Then you will come back?

Agemaki: Yes. (To Ikyu) Ikyu, I will never see you again. Shiratama!

Shiratama: Agemaki!

Agemaki: Come, children.

Small Girl Attendants: Yes, yes.

(Agemaki, Shiratama and girl attendants pass through the entrance curtains. Off stage is heard the sound of a flute. Sukeroku comes down the *hanamichi* and dances. He is wearing a purple cloth band (*hachi-maki*) tied around his head and carrying an umbrella. He has a flute in his *obi*.)

Music:
> "Drawn by the sound of the samisen
> The dashing lover comes.
> His face reflects the rainy sky."

Courtesans: Sukeroku! That cloth around your head!

Sukeroku: Is it so strange?

Music:
> "A token of a lover's pledge
> Which never is to be forgotten.
> As the color of the pine remains,
> So will our minds not change.
> Along the Sumida river,
> The willows and the cherries have burgeoned
> Fuji and Tsukuba are seen through the flowers.
> Flowers, don't hurry to fall,
> Don't be impatient for the day of appointment.
> The night of rendezvous will come in time."

* Beautiful girls from all over the country were brought to Yoshiwara in order to eliminate coarse and country accents. Yoshiwara developed a special speech which all courtesans used.

Sukeroku: My beloved, my beloved.

Music:

> "From the bottom of my heart,
> My life is Agemaki's."

(The courtesans applaud his entry dance.)

Aizome: Sukeroku, we have waited for you.

*

Sukeroku: Now, now! What a beautiful array of faces. Could I squeeze in among you?

Courtesans: Please do. (All the courtesans offer Sukeroku their *kiseru* (a long, thin pipe filled with enough tobacco for two or three puffs.) He accepts all of them.)

Sukeroku: That I should receive such an abundance of lighted pipes from you should put the fire watchman on the alert.

Ikyu: I would like a smoke.

Yaeginu: Nothing could be easier, but there are no pipes.

Ikyu: But I see so many pipes there!

Ukihashi: But they are all in use.

Ikyu: And who is using them all?

Sukeroku: I am. Isn't it extraordinary—every time I come to Naka-no-cho, they simply ply me with pipes. Last night I had a basketful of them. This is the way it goes when one has such power of control over courtesans. I don't care how great the man or braggart may be, money cannot purchase power of this sort. Who is it who wants to smoke? I shall be pleased to give him one of my pipes. (Sukeroku puts the pipe between his toes and extends his leg towards Ikyu.) Ha! Aren't you going to take it? How about it? How about it?

Ikyu: This fellow looked like a splendid chap, but unfortunately his hands are paralyzed. His feet are as well-trained as a food-treader's might be. A chivalrous person is firstly honest, not immoral, is never impolite, never quibbles, and as a matter of pride, refines his spirit. That is a true

---

* At this point the play may be interrupted on the occasion of an actor succeeding to a new name, or of a child making his debut. All the actors bow, and Sukeroku and Ikyu kneel and announce the occasion and beg the audience's continued favor. Then the play resumes.

man. Any man who doesn't know right from wrong or who doesn't understand etiquette is a worthless poltroon. Pleasure districts are always plagued with these, like the mosquitoes that buzz around your ears. One can slap them between one's hands.* What's the use of talking to a man of this sort—it is wind by the ear of a horse. Light some aloes-wood and the fumes will drive the mosquito away.

Sukeroku: Methods change. The more the enemy is different, the more the strategy is different. The opponent determines the treatment. Only the man who knows can judge right or wrong. The braggart is to be kicked. The man who gives instructions as to propriety is to be hit with a wooden clog. There is neither training nor tradition other than to draw your sword when you are struck. The deepest aim of the chivalrous person is to kill when he draws his sword. That's what I am. (Sukeroku addresses the courtesans.) By the way, courtesans, recently a great snake has come into Yoshiwara.

Courtesans: How frightening!

Sukeroku: Oh no—there's nothing terrifying about this snake. His brazen face is covered with white hair. The strangest thing about him is that the courtesans shun him every night, but unconscious of this humiliation he still comes. What a persistent snake! And do you know why he often burns aloes-wood—because all his hair is infested with lice. Aloes-wood alone gives him relief. How he smells of aloes-wood! (From inside Miuraya's is heard the voice of Kanpera Monbei.)

Ikyu: What's the matter, Kanpera?

Kanpera Monbei: Master, listen. What an unpleasant attendant. She insulted me by trying to sell one girl twice.

Attendant: What are you saying, Monbei?

Kanpera Monbei: Don't try to make a fool of me. I had drunk too much wine; so I ordered a bath. My idea was to get into the bath with all the courtesans and have my back scrubbed. You said "Yes," so I got in first, alone. I waited and waited but no one came. I nearly melted away in the heat. Bring all those stubborn women here. I want them in the bath like tea poured over a bowl of rice.

* Here Ikyu gesticulates and "cuts" a *mie*.

[266]

Yaeginu: Look, Kanpera, you're not the only patron. Now stop calling us stubborn women.

Ukihashi: Don't go too far. Stop or I'll put a door on your mouth.

Kanpera Monbei: Shut up! Put a door on my mouth, and I'll talk through my nose.

Attendant: This is sickening.

Kanpera Monbei: Confound it! Bring the women here! I will rope them all together, one by one like a rosary and make a show of it in the middle of Naka-no-cho.

Aizome: You are going to make us all laugh at that sour face of yours.

(The courtesans laugh. At this juncture, Fukuyama, a seller of noodles, appears carrying his ware in square boxes tied to both ends of a long stick which is borne on his shoulder. Inadvertently one of the boxes of noodles brushes against Kampera Monbei, who cries out and grabs the stick.)

Fukuyama: I beg your pardon.

Kanpera Monbei: What's that! You strike a man with your box and say "I beg your pardon"? You noodle fool! You bean-paste ass! You used tea leaves idiot! Can't your eyeballs record?

Fukuyama: I was hurrying so. Please, I most humbly beg your pardon, sir. Courtesans, please apologize for me.

Yaeginu: Monbei, forgive him.

Courtesans: Please.

Kanpera Monbei: I won't.

Fukuyama: You mean this isn't enough?

Kanpera Monbei: You know it's not enough!

Fukuyama: There is nothing more to be done. Do as you please then! I am well known in the pleasure district and have a reputation for speaking sharply and pointedly like the boxes I carry my noodles in. I love a fight. My deliveries are as quick as my temper. Before my proud noodles spoil, you'll see the strength or faintness of my heart which has been washed in the gutter of water of Edo! Despite what you may think, I wear a loin cloth of crimson silk! (Translator's Note: An inordinate mark of elegance for a commoner.) Look!

Kanpera Monbei: You fool! Having no guard at the portals of your mouth, what wondrous things you say! (Kanpera Monbei starts to strike Fukuyama but Sukeroku takes hold of his arm and twists it. Kanpera Monbei cries out in pain.)

Sukeroku: Say you forgive him.

Kanpera Monbei: Wait a minute.

Sukeroku: (To Fukuyama) Go, quickly.

Kanpera Monbei: (To Fukuyama) If you move, I will kill you!

Sukeroku: Come, man, that's enough. Control yourself!

Kanpera Monbei: Control yourself?

Sukeroku: Yes, I said, "control yourself!"

Kanpera Monbei: From the very first you have been offensive. Do you know who I am?

Sukeroku: How can you ask that? In Yoshiwara there is no one who—why in this whole world——

Kanpera Monbei: Then you know me?

Sukeroku: Never heard of you!

Kanpera Monbei: So you like to pretend, do you?

Sukeroku: Who would know a cheap lout of your sort!

Kanpera Monbei: You speak boldly. You say you don't know who I am. Then I see you are quite a stranger to the area. If you've been brought to pray at the shrine at Yoshiwara, hearing this will protect you from smallpox. Clean out your ears and listen! Here is my lord and master (he points to Ikyu), the Bearded Ikyu, named in remembrance of the beard of Kanu, the Chinese General. I have taken the first character "Kan" from Kanu for the rich Kanpera, and Monbei comes from the precious temple gate. I am the wealthy Kanpera Monbei. Take off that purple cloth around your head, and bow three times!

Sukeroku: I see. I see. Thank you for your personal history, but I fear that during the length of your speech, the noodles have spoiled. (To Fukuyama) Go, quickly.

Kanpera Monbei: Do not go!

Sukeroku: That's peculiar. Here's a man who has apologized and still you persist. You must be very tired and hungry. How fortunate that the noodle seller came just at this time. I'll treat you to a dish of noodles. (Fukuyama puts some noodles in a dish.) I'll pay for it. Is this noodles and vegetables only?

Fukuyama: No, there is fish in them too.

Sukeroku: (To Kanpera Monbei) There may or may not be fish in this dish, but as I am serving it to you, eat it.

Kanpera Monbei: No.

Sukeroku: Well, then, don't get excited. I'll put some pepper in it. (He throws some pepper at Kanpera Monbei's nose. He sneezes.) Eat it, or do you want me to feed you by hand?

Kanpera Monbei: I've had enough.

Sukeroku: What? You've had enough when I've given so little?

Kanpera Monbei: Enough, enough!

Sukeroku: Very well, have it your own way. (Sukeroku dumps the dish of noodles on Kanpera Monbei's head.)

Kanpera Monbei: Help, I am wounded!

Fukuyama: Now are you satisfied?

Senbei: (Coming from within the curtains to Kanpera Monbei's side) Master, master, what's wrong?

Kanpera Monbei: I have been taken unawares. Look and see if the wound is deep.

Senbei: Wound? There is no wound, master.

Kanpera Monbei: What—no wound? I thought I was cut. This is only noodles! Kill that man! (Some young men waving sticks in the air cross the stage. Sukeroku stops them.)

Sukeroku: Touch me with one of your sticks and I will pile Gocho Machi* high with your corpses! (The men are frightened and withdraw.)**

* Gocho Machi is the area outside the great gate of Yoshiwara.

** This moment of action has no significance other than to give Sukeroku an opportunity to show his prowess and later to afford opportunity for Shinbei's entrance.

Senbei: I have never known a man to show his sword to my master Monbei, and this man dumps noodles on his head! Cheap noodles at that! (Sukeroku trips Senbei, who falls to the ground. Kanpera Monbei goes to Senbei.)

Kanpera Monbei: What happened?

Senbei: I tripped on a root of a tree. That's why I lost in the encounter.

Kanpera Monbei: I don't know who lost in the encounter, but surely you tripped on a root, and there it is. You with your acrobatics! What a fool you are!

Sukeroku: Now listen to this. Anyone who comes to Gocho Machi hears my name and never forgets it. This will cure your malaria. There is more to come! Now, when you come through the great gate of Yoshiwara, write my name three times on the palm of your hand, then lick it off. Then you will never be refused by a courtesan in all your life. My stature is small, but my deeds are great. News of my prowess has traveled far and wide—from the toothless charcoal seller of Hachioji to the pickled-plum-like attendant at Sanya all gossip over their tea of my exploits. I am first to lose money and last to lose a fight. My hair is always in a knot with a purple cloth around my head. Spread the hairs apart and peer at me! The more numerous the enemies, the greater my strength—like a dragon in water. In all of Edo, I am not unknown. My crest is leaves and peonies. My domicile is cherry-flower scented Naka-no-cho. I am known as the young man called Sukeroku, although I am also known as Agemaki's Sukeroku. Come close and worship at my face. You boards across a ditch! You bean-paste asses! You used tea leaves idiots! Go away!*

Kanpera Monbei: Let's kill him! (They fight. Sukeroku defeats them.)

Sukeroku: Draw near and I'll kill you!

Courtesans: Sukeroku has won!

Sukeroku: (To Ikyu) There are your followers for you and I'll do the same to all others. Surely you cannot endure this humiliation! Draw your sword and strike! (Ikyu remains silent.) Why don't you speak?

---

* This is Sukeroku's famous *nadai*, name-saying speech. Since Genroku times these lines have been written and illustrated with a drawing of Sukeroku, to be sold as a souvenir of the play.

Are you deaf, or are you dumb? Draw your sword! Draw! What an unspirited fool. You're like a speechless rat chased by a cat. You don't utter a sound. Perhaps you are dead. Well then, I'll perform last rites for you. (Sukeroku recites a Buddhist funeral prayer, then takes his wooden clog and puts it on Ikyu's head. Ikyu takes it off.) Now things are getting interesting. Draw your sword!

Ikyu: No. (He throws the clog away in anger.)

Kanpera Monbei: Master, if you are to act so cowardly, what are we, your followers, to do?

Senbei: What has become of your battle arts of which you have up to now been so proud?

Both Together: What a pitiful person you are!

Ikyu: Do you need the same knife for dressing a chicken that you would use for slaughtering an ox? This man is not worthy to be Ikyu's opponent. Kanpera, Senbei, watch out for your pockets! (Sukeroku, with his sword, slices in two the elbow rest upon which Ikyu is leaning.)

Sukeroku: So this is what a coward you are. (Sukeroku puts away his sword.)

Ikyu: You can strike me all you like. (Ikyu, Kanpera Monbei, Senbei and the courtesans enter under the curtains. A large group of youths waving sticks appear. Sukeroku drives them away. Shinbei, dressed as a wine seller, is among them. He hides on the *hanamichi*.)

Sukeroku: What a weakling Ikyu is—words, only words. Oh well, I'll have a cup of wine in Agemaki's bed.

Shinbei: Brother! Wait a moment.

Sukeroku: Brother? Are you one of those here a moment ago? What do you want? (Sukeroku looks around but sees no one.) What, no one here? Who called me? Show yourself. Who do you think I am? I am the bravest of the brave. I am Agemaki's Sukeroku.

Shinbei: Bravest of the brave, wait a moment.

Sukeroku: You call again. Where are you hiding? Draw near me and I throw you in the ditch. I'll ram a house boat up your nose!

Shinbei: Wait a moment.

Sukeroku: What a nuisance. Stay where you are. Who are you?

Shinbei: It is I.

Sukeroku: Who's I? Come near, show me your face. (Shinbei comes up to Sukeroku.) It's your brother, Sukenari!

Shinbei: Then you still have eyes to see me as your brother!

Sukeroku: Why have you come here?

Shinbei: Is there a sign up forbidding pleasure districts to Sukenari?

Sukeroku: Of course not.

Shinbei: Then toss me in the ditch. Ram a house boat up my nostril. Which one—the right or the left?

Sukeroku: Please—that's because I didn't know who you were.

Shinbei: You didn't know who I was?

Sukeroku: If I had known could I have spoken that way to you?

Shinbei: Tokimune, what has made you this way? Can't you wait until the end of May, after we have avenged ourselves on our father's enemy? Recently, you have been coming to the pleasure district, and every day you engage in some fight or other. Mother has taken this very much to heart and has asked me why I haven't counselled you. Who killed the man in Takemachi? Sukeroku! Who tossed the man in the gravel pit? Sukeroku! If there were a day in which crows did not fly in the sky, then on that day I would not hear news of some fight of yours. What devil, Tokimune, has entered your body to turn you into such a person? You know your fights better than I, but what if you meet an opponent stronger than you? What then would become of the promise you made me, your brother, eighteen years ago? I can't understand you, Sukeroku. More than this, you have sundered the bonds of our blood-brotherhood. Is that not contemptible? I don't know what punishment you will meet in hell for this!

Sukeroku: Listen, brother. The very counsel which you have given is my reason for fighting. It is from loyalty to my parents.

Shinbei: Loyalty? To make you fight so?

Sukeroku: Yes. My sword named Tomokirimaru was stolen. The sooner I recover it, the sooner I can kill our enemy Suketsune. My heart is fretted beyond all reason; I have no clue as to its whereabouts. Many people come to this pleasure district; so I come and unreasonably force them into a fight. I make them draw their swords. Always I say: Is that it? Is that it? It has been most cruel to hear your harsh words of reproof before you asked my reasons. But that is all right. I will fight no more. Furthermore as penance, I will become a priest. (He clasps his hands and pretends to pray.)

Shinbei: I knew it all along. I was sure that my clever brother was only looking for his sword. How could I have spoken so harshly to you just now? It was this mouth! Mouth—why did you speak thus? Have you apologized? My mouth apologizes! But since you feel like that——

Sukeroku: I will never fight again. (Sukeroku prays.)

Shinbei: Tokimune, but since you feel that way, how could I have spoken so harshly? If I hurt you, it is because I am your brother. Forgive me, I take it back.

Sukeroku: Then you mean it's all right for me to fight?

Shinbei: Yes, yes. To show your fights in the open even is all right!

Sukeroku: Do you really mean that?

Shinbei: Go ahead. Fighting becomes you well. If fighting were rice and tea, then help yourself to it.

Sukeroku: Very well then, I shall fight.

Shinbei: Good! Eat and drink as many cups of fighting as you can hold.

Sukeroku: You cannot know what peace those words bring to my soul.

Shinbei: I too am at peace now. Tell me, have you no clue as to who has Tomokirimaru?

Sukeroku: Not as yet. But a little while ago I tried to make the Bearded Ikyu draw his sword, but in vain. He may have it.

Shinbei: Yes, judging from his face he might easily have stolen the sword you seek. I have a plan! Tonight since I am here, let's search for the sword together. We will fight side by side.

Sukeroku: But look at your idiotic garb! (Translator's Note: Shinbei's costume, that of a wine seller, is unsuitable for brawling.)

Shinbei: I alone am helpless. But if I am behind you, I can give you breathing spells. Our spirits will be high and we will do our best.

Sukeroku: Very well, but first I must teach you how to fight. Place your elbows out like this. Place your right leg thus. Then say, "Hey there, Warrior! Why have you struck me! See here, what do you mean by it! I shall kick a house boat up your nose!" If you don't do it that way, you won't get your opponent angry.

Shinbei: I see. What an unusual thing, to do it that way. See how I do it. "Hey there, Warrior! Why have you struck me! See here, what do you mean by it! I shall kick a house boat up your nose." (He trips himself when he tries to kick.)

Sukeroku: No, no! That's not the way at all, you see. Do it this way. "Hey there, Warrior! Why have you struck me! See here, what do you mean by it! I shall kick a house boat up your nose!"

Shinbei: Good! Not as easy as I though. "Hey there, Warrior, why have you struck me! See here, what do you mean by it! I shall kick a house boat up your nose! (Shinbei staggers slightly.)

Sukeroku: That's it! Not bad! (Sukeroku looks off stage.) Look, brother, a fool comes! (Translator's Note: Some passersby appear on the stage. After Sukeroku determines that they have not his sword, he and Shinbei, symbolizing their combined prowess, make them crawl between their legs as an act of humiliation.)

(Agemaki's voice is heard behind the curtains.)

Sukeroku: That's Agemaki's voice. She told me to come tonight as she would be alone. Now hear, she is seeing some patron to the door. I'll speak to her about this.

Shinbei: Yes—you should.

(Manko, wearing a large straw hat which hides her face, comes out followed by Agemaki with her girl attendants.)

Agemaki: If you must leave, then go in safety.

Sukeroku: Hold on!

Shinbei: Wait!

Agemaki: Don't do that, Sukeroku!

Sukeroku: Shut up, slut!

Agemaki: Don't be so abusive!

Sukeroku: And what if I am?

Shinbei: If Sukeroku angers that warrior, then the pleasure of flaying him will be mine.

Sukeroku: (To Manko whom he does not recognize) Hey there, Warrior! In this wide road, why have you stepped on my foot? Take out your handkerchief and wipe the dirt off.

Shinbei: Yes, wipe it off!

Agemaki: You will regret saying that.

Sukeroku: This is not your affair! Hey, Warrior! Why don't you speak? Are you dumb or are you deaf?

Shinbei: Are you a spectre without a face? Speak! Speak!

Sukeroku: First take that hat from your face. If you don't I'll take it off for you. (Sukeroku starts to take the straw hat from Manko and sees her face. He is dumbfounded.)

Agemaki: Now, Sukeroku, take the straw hat and scar the face. How about it!

Shinbei: What stopped you in mid-stream! I'll take it off. (Shinbei starts toward Manko. Sukeroku stops him.) Leave me alone. I can manage him all right. (He brushes Sukeroku away.) Look at these feet of mine! One is lame, one is club, but my thoughts are on the banks of Sendai River. (He pretends to be tripped by Manko.) Ooooh. How expensive on the feet it is to be a chivalrous person! But I must endure the pain. See here! My stick when wielded like a sword can draw blood. I am Agemaki's Sukeroku's Master! I am Kasubei, the white wine seller! With this stick between your nose and eyes, I'll—(Manko reveals her face.) Oh, my God!

Manko: (To Sukeroku) What behavior for Agemaki's Sukeroku! (To Shinbei) That you would strike your mother! I am speechless.

Sukeroku: Uhhh—Is it you, Agemaki, who put my mother up to this?

Agemaki: Why should I have anything to do with it?

Sukeroku: Then whose idea is it?

Agemaki: Your mother, hearing rumors of your fights, has become so fretted and worried that she cannot sleep even at night. (Agemaki wipes the tears from her eyes.)

Manko: Agemaki, say no more. Stories of him reached my ears, but I did not expect it to be as bad as this. What can I say—to persons who bear the responsibility of a pledge and yet could start to take a stranger's straw hat as you just did. Kasubei, the white wine seller, association with bad companions has turned you. What bitter thanks to see my precious sons become like this. I ask the memory of your dead father to forgive me. It has been my fate to have failed in training my sons. I will go now to the grave of your father, and in penance for my failure, there will I take my life.

Shinbei: Wait, please. Why do you think I have become so? Tokimune, quickly explain to her.

Sukeroku: Mother, I know you hold me in contempt for being so quarrelsome, but please hear my reason. Since the theft of my sword, Tomokirimaru, I have had to put aside all thought of your distress or of avenging my father's murder. I have come to the pleasure district to look for the sword, and I fight only to make the opponent draw his sword in order to find Tomokirimaru. I do not fight for glory. You must believe me.

Shinbei: That is true, Mother.

Sukeroku: Please don't doubt me.

Manko: I understand now. I see how right you are, and I do not doubt you. Therefore, my only request is fight to win and be careful in your quest.

Shinbei & Sukeroku: We are grateful, Mother, for your understanding.

Manko: Agemaki, now we need not worry about Sukeroku. I will give him a charmed jacket to protect him in his fights. (She hands Sukeroku the jacket.) Take it. Take care of it, for if you don't it will tear. No matter how insufferable the situation, if you control yourself, it will not rip. If you lose your temper, it will split. And whatever happens to this jacket will happen within the heart of your mother.

Sukeroku: Thank you. I shall wear it immediately.

[276]

Shinbei: A charm of forbearance! (Sukeroku puts the jacket on.)

Agemaki: A wondrous charm!

Shinbei: It fits you well.

Manko: It is perhaps not becoming to one so young, but think of it as you would of your mother and take care of it. Sukenari, my heart is eased. Now I will go.

Shinbei: I will accompany you—Sukeroku, come!

Sukeroku: Not yet. I will return after I follow up one more clue.

Agemaki: (To Manko and Shinbei.) Go in safety. The wind is strong to-night. Be careful not to catch cold. (As they leave, Ikyo's voice is heard from within.)

Ikyu: Agemaki, Agemaki.

Sukeroku: That's Ikyu.

Agemaki: Don't forget the charmed jacket!

Ikyu: Agemaki, Agemaki! (Ikyu enters with Shiratama and an attendant carrying an incense burner. Sukeroku hides behind Agemaki.) There you are! I've been looking for you. Do you forget the past and will you obey my heart as you said a few minutes ago?

Agemaki: Well, I said so, but—that is——

Ikyu: Eh?

Agemaki: Not a lie.

Ikyu: Then come inside.

Agemaki: I will not.

Ikyu: Why not?

Agemaki: I drank too much. I'll come in after I have enough fresh air. Go to bed ahead of me.

Ikyu: No. If you cool off in the wind, I will stay here with you. But here, if Sukeroku were to see us together, he would be disturbed, wouldn't he, Agemaki? (Sukeroku pinches Ikyu's leg.)
Who pinches me?

Agemaki: Is something the matter? Must be some child who pinched your leg.

[277]

Small Girl Attendants: Not we!

Agemaki: Now, now, don't try to cover up. Go inside.

(The small girl attendants withdraw.)

Agemaki: Look, Ikyu, the sky is filled with stars.

Ikyu: Is it so strange? What star comes out every night and is called "Night Crawler" as I call a man whom I have engaged. No matter how that star wishes to squeeze in, I am the Milky Way, and will not budge from here tonight.

(Sukeroku pinches Ikyu's leg again.)

Ikyu: Who is it! Who pinched me?

Agemaki: Oh, the children again.

Ikyu: There are no children here.

Agemaki: If not children, then it must be a rat.

Ikyu: Indeed, it is a rat. A ditch rat who roams the country as a thief. A house rat who hides in ditches. (Sukeroku appears in the open.) There it is!

Sukeroku: Ikyu!

Ikyu: Sukeroku!

Agemaki: Don't forget the charmed jacket.

Ikyu: Ikyu, the wise cat, sees Sukeroku, the ditch rat, hiding behind the skirts of Agemaki, the slut. Do you expect to accomplish your great pledge by acting like a thief? Tokimune, you are a coward.

Sukeroku: Hold on, Ikyu. Since you know my true name, then how can you say I am a coward?

Ikyu: Aren't you? Despite the lamentable death of your father, you have no heart for vengeance. Your foolish brain is for the courtesans only. Your enemy Suketsune is now a renowned lord, firmly entrenched in the hills of Kamakura. That's why you think vengeance impossible. Therefore, you dissipate your energy in wine and lust. Out of pity I'll beat some warrior's spirit into you with this fan. You coward, Tokimune. (Ikyu strikes Sukeroku with his fan.)

Sukeroku: How fortunate you are. My brother and I have waited eighteen years and even now have not been able to strike at our enemy. But you, on the contrary, with merely a fan, can strike at your enemy-in-love who stands here before your eyes. How envious this makes me! Let that fan train me. I am wearing my mother's charmed jacket and cannot strike in return! Hit, Bearded Ikyu, to your heart's content!

Ikyu: The care you take of your mother's charmed jacket shows that you are not devoid of some filial piety. (Ikyu looks around and sees the incense burner.) Here's the example! Tokimune, the three legs of this burner are the three Soga brothers: Suketoshi, Sukenari, Tokimune. If, like this incense burner, their hearts were as one and their energies pooled, then it would be easy to strike not only against Suketsune, but even against your uncle's enemy, Yoritomo. (Translator's Note: The Shogun). If you harbor ill-will toward Yoritomo, I, Ikyu, though I am old, would add my assistance if the occasion required me. If your brothers were as this incense burner, whose tripod can carry a weight of a hundred pounds, you would be invincible, incorruptible. But separated—(Ikyu draws out his sword and slices the incense burner and stand in two. Sukeroku stares at the sword.)

Sukeroku: That is it.

(Ikyu quickly hides the sword and goes inside through the curtains.)

Agemaki: Sukeroku, the jacket is torn.

Sukeroku: What, it's torn? I endured all that only in order to keep from tearing it. If it's already rent, then there is no longer need for forebearance!

Agemaki: Do not lose your temper.

Sukeroku: Agemaki, the sword Ikyu just now drew is the one I have so long sought.

Agemaki: Tomokirimaru?

Sukeroku: Quiet!

(Sukeroku whispers to Agemaki.)

Agemaki: Then, you——

Sukeroku: I will await Ikyu's departure tonight!

Agemaki: Hide, quickly!

Sukeroku: Yes, that's it!

[279]

(Sukeroku goes to the *hanamichi*. The curtain is drawn as the bell strikes the hour.)

Translator's Note: There is a final scene known as *Mizuiri* (Immersion). When Ikyu leaves Miuraya's with Senbei, Sukeroku attacks them both and demands the return of his sword. He kills them, takes his sword and as soon as he draws it in order to examine it, people arrive and cry out, "Murder, murder." Sukeroku jumps into a barrel of rain water saved for use in case of fire. Agemaki assures the passersby that the murderer has fled and the people leave the stage in hot pursuit. Sukeroku emerges and escapes from the scene by climbing a ladder which enables him to flee over the roof-tops to safety. The final curtain falls as Agemaki calls out "Sukeroku."

INDEX

Index

6, 182; music, 218; musical instruments, 21, number still in existence, 15; Okina, 171; permeation by Buddhist teachings, 25; plays, 7, 15, 16, 25; rank of players in, 23; reason for present grace, 23; style of, 21; subject matter of, 25, 26; theatre, 16; theatre type of, 20; treatment of subject matter, 62; type of role, 25

Noh Plays of Japan, The, 1913, 13

Nohgaki Kai, xx

Nohgaku, "skill-music," 15

Nomori, demon play, 15

Nuregoto, "tear-jerkers," 74

Nyo, "Woman," *Noh* play, 15

Obi, long belt, 156

Obi-hiki, pulling of the obi, 156

Ochi, Fukuchi, author of *Omori Hikoshichi*, 166

Occupation, 225, 226, 227, 230; Army, 202; attitude toward plays, 108; ban on Kabuki, xv; forces, rescript of, 62

Oda, Nobunaga, warrior, 161

Odyssey, 28

Ogata, Korin, painter, 28

Ogi no sabaki, fan tricks, 174

Ogiya Kumagai, play, 147

Ogyu, Sorai, scholar of Chinese learning, 58

Okina, dances, 16, 17; symbol of long life, 16

Okinawa, 205

O-Kuni, a dancing girl, 41, 144, 195, 208; activities of, 41; command performance for ruling Shogun, 45; death a mystery, 43; fame of, 42; growth of dance dialogues, 51; performances of, 42; popularity of, 40; use of her creation, 44

Okura, a theatre in Osaka, 32

Omi Genji Senjin Yakata, play by Hariji, 123, 124, 125, 126, 127, 128, 129

Omori Hikoschichi, dance, 168; last Kabuki play written, 166, 167

Onnagata, players of female roles, xii, 49

Onoe, Baiko, xx

Onoe, Shoroku, xx

Onoe family, 138, 141

Ono-no-Tofu, dynasty piece, written by Takeda Izumo, 162, 163

Osaka, 32, 46, 56, 58, 59, 60, 61, 63, 65, 73, 74, 96, 108, 122, 123, 152, 161, 174, 218, 219, 222; castle, 123; economic rise in, 122; establishment of theatre in, 33; Kabuki in, 123; puppets, 92; theatres in, 58

O-satsuma, music for bold or weird effects, 166

Oshimo Doshi, one of the "18 Favorites," 92

Otani, Hiroji, puppeteer, 146

Otojrio, Kawakami, playwright, 209, 210, 211

Otokodate or kyokaku, "chivalrous commoner," 76

Otsu-e, Genroku type of drawing, 168

Outcast's Revenge (Hinin no Adauchi), play, 50

Oyabun, district bosses, 77, 226

Pacific War, xviii, xix

Peri, Noel, author, 18

Pine, play adapted by John Masefield, 97

"Plays of divided loyalty," popularity of, 133

Plays, historical, 161; revision of, 148

"Plays of Living History" (*katsureki geki*), 206, 207

Playwrights, duties of, 148

"Political Drama" (*soshi geki*), 208, 209, 210, 211

Pound-Fenellosa adaptations, 14

Prostitution in Japan, 225

Puppet Theatre, 20, 54, 92; importance of, 34; number of, 32; position of, 34

Puppets, manipulations of, 33, 34; in "Narrations," 190; when introduced, 32

Rama Rau, Santha, xx

Reinhardt, Max, 144

Resurrection, play by Tolstoi, 232

"Revenge Plays," 72, 73

River of Life (Seikatsu no Kawa), play, 224

Role-types, actors in, 138; children (*koyaku*), 132; comedians (*doke-yaku*), 132; handsome young men (*wakashu-kata*), 132; old men (*oyaji-kata*), 132; old women (*kyasha-gata*), 132